Snapshots

Matthew Lightfoot

ISBN: 9798716814035

Amazon Print edition

Copyright 2021 Matthew Lightfoot

Whilst all the stories in this book are as factually accurate as the author's memory allows, names of people, places and businesses have been changed in some cases.

Any requests, comments or queries can be emailed to TwoWeekTraveller@Outlook.com.

For everyone who had their travelling wings clipped in 2020.

Contents

Introduction

"These photos are important?" The middle-aged Thai's nose wrinkled as he squinted through wire rimmed spectacles at a USB memory stick held between a tobacco-stained thumb and forefinger. A greying moustache of wiry, two-inch-long hairs twitched like a mouse's whiskers as he contemplated the device in the dim light of his Bangkok workshop.

It was a good question. Were the photos important? There were thousands of them stored on the device, covering over thirty years of travel, but the truth was that I hadn't looked at most of them since the day they'd been taken. In the days before camera phones, most of my photos had been taken on holiday. The resulting images would then be reviewed as I eagerly opened an orange Supasnaps envelope, or, in more recent times, when I downloaded them from digital camera to computer. A small selection might be shared with family and friends to add some visual spice to my travel tales. They would then be relegated to a box at the back of a cupboard, bulging with hundreds of similar photo packets. Those stored digitally would be automatically sorted by date or location and would remain similarly untouched, hidden in the depths of Windows file manager.

So the answer to the Thai man's question was complicated. The photos can't have been that important, as I hadn't bothered to look at them for years. Most were technically poor. Blurred, over-exposed, grainy, low resolution images. And the reason for the poor quality was the same reason I hadn't thrown them away. Because these weren't carefully planned, posed and executed photographs. They were snapshots. Moments in time that I probably didn't even remember, and I'd certainly never get back. To throw them away would be to discard all those memories, to make a conscious choice to forget the past.

Standing in the Bangkok computer repair shop however, my answer was more straightforward, as the photos had become important to me beyond the usual nostalgic reminisces.

It was the first day of eight months of travel. A career break for myself and my partner Kirsty, visiting New Zealand, Fiji, South East Asia and South America. Whilst travelling, I planned to write a book to tell the tales of my travels over the last three decades. I had a title, The Two Week Traveller, which reflected the fact that all my trips to date had been undertaken using my work leave allowance. I was pretty sure I had enough stories to fill a book. I was unsure though, whether I could recall individual details of people I'd met, places I'd visited, cars I'd wrecked and animals which had tried to kill me. I hoped to use my repository of photos to fill in those gaps. I had thousands of images on my computer, some taken in digital format, others scanned from 'old school' 35mm film, all stored in date and country order. My plan was to call upon those snapshot memories as required, to add colour and authenticity to my anecdotes.

Unfortunately, the process to transfer my photo image files to a USB memory stick had taken longer than anticipated and I'd had to curtail the process when it was only around 80% completed. This had resulted in a screenful of blank photo files and a potential blackhole in my storytelling capabilities.

Thankfully, my new Thai friend proved more proficient at digital file recovery than he was at growing facial hair, and I was presented with a new USB stick containing about two thirds of my photo collection, which was better than nothing. Unfortunately, my previous, careful filing system had been lost, and my well-ordered photo files ended up as a random, scattergun collection of travel memories appearing on my laptop screen in absolutely no order whatsoever.

Although initially frustrating, as our trip progressed I began to savour the unexpected delights of a long-forgotten image appearing suddenly before me, as I settled down to write my book in some strange and faraway location – bouncing along a Bolivian mountain road, or rattling around in a bunk on an Asian night train; in a Kiwi campervan during a thunderstorm, or loafing in an eccentrically furnished Air B&B apartment in Pukaki or Puno, La Paz or Paraguay.

Snapshots tells two stories in parallel - My adventures during 250 days of travel, spanning four Continents, twelve countries and multiple modes of transport; also, the memories prompted by a collection of long forgotten snapshots, appearing randomly on my laptop screen to rekindle memories, good and bad, from a lifetime of travel.

It's a book for anyone who loves a traveller's tale, and everyone with a box full of photos they never look at, but couldn't ever imagine throwing away.

One Night in Bangkok

Day 1- Bangkok, Thailand

Y ou can visit a city too many times. That initial enjoyment prompted by the unfamiliar, culture-shock overload of a chaotic metropolis on the other side of the world, can begin to fade on a fourth or fifth repeat visit. The exotic, steamy, vibrant streets, alive with noise and colour can suddenly become claustrophobic, sweaty and irritating. The once amusing interaction with local fixers, drivers and hawkers can quickly lose its novelty value once your rebuttal of a repeated hard-sell pitch stretches into treble figures. As our Thai Airways flight descended through a thick, late afternoon blanket of soupy smog towards Suvarnabhumi International airport, it's fair to say that any affection I once had for Thailand's sprawling capital had been replaced by a feeling of ambivalence. Our three day stay was one of necessity – a break in what would have been a tortuously long direct flight to Auckland in New Zealand, or one which entailed a three hour connection in one of the Middle East's uninspiring airport transit terminals.

As we jumped into a taxi for the forty five minute journey into town, I recalled our last visit to Bangkok, which I had decided would be my last, if I could help it. Amidst a clammy deluge of warm tropical rain, a rogue tuk-tuk driver had taken us on an unwarranted detour to a commission-paying gem shop, and I'd angrily refused to get out of his vehicle until he returned us to the place where he'd picked us up thirty minutes earlier. Then I refused to pay, which prompted a display of histrionics, accompanied by squeaky voiced threats, and a roadside display of Kung Fu moves from the now enraged driver.

That night, while trawling the neon-lit streets of Silom for somewhere to eat, we attracted the attention of a girly-bar fixer. Clearly resembling a couple seeking ping-pong perversion rather than Pad Thai, the little pock-faced pimp wasn't taking no for an answer. With his floppy-fringed head bobbing irritatingly at my shoulder, he bounced alongside me with a gait that suggested he had drawing pins in the heels of his shiny black shoes, whilst whispering his seedy sales pitch into my ear.

"Wha'you wann mister? I got everything in my club. Everything you wann see."

"No thanks. We just want something to eat."

"Awww, mister. I got nice girls and boys. They do everything for you."

"Do they cook noodles?"

"No noodle. Sexy girl mister, for you and lady. I got everything full sexy."

After ten minutes of the little vice-pusher not taking the hint, I finally lost patience and called his bluff the next time he told me there were no limits to his club's range of perversions.

"So you've got everything?" I stopped and turned to face him, and he looked taken aback by my sudden interest.

"Everything mister. Wha'you wann see?"

"Do you have a nun?"

The fixer's eyes narrowed, and he rubbed his chin.

"What is nun?"

"Nun. Black dress." I mimed a veil and habit, as he tilted his head to one side as if considering the possibility of Mother Superior hanging upside down from a pole next to the bar.

"And an ostrich."

"Oss-rich? What is oss-rich?"

"Big bird." I leaned towards him, fashioning my hand into a beak and pecking at his forehead as he took a step back. "I want to see a nun performing sex with an ostrich. Do you have that?"

"Oh. No have." He dipped his head, and a crestfallen expression clouded his perspiring face.

"Well you haven't got everything then have you?!" I concluded triumphantly and pecked the top of his head with my imaginary ostrich beak. "Now piss off!"

It was therefore fair to say that I felt I'd seen everything Bangkok had to offer, as we crawled along the traffic-choked four-lane highway into town, and it occurred to me that I'd done very little research when booking our guest house. It seemed fairly central, and more importantly on a long trip where neither Kirsty nor I had any source of income, the price was reasonable. I was therefore pleasantly surprised when our taxi turned off Soi Samsen, and began negotiating a labyrinth of narrow lanes, which seemed to largely comprise of local homes, small shops and streetfood stalls, with an occasional guest house and traveller laundry. Our hotel was situated opposite a small Buddhist temple where old ladies manned stalls outside the gates, selling incense sticks, candles and flowers for use as offerings by worshippers.

The sun had set by the time we dumped our bags, and with our body clocks still registering a European mid-morning, we set off to explore. Google maps told us that Khao San road was a fifteen minute walk away, and having not experienced the self-proclaimed 'centre of the backpacking universe' for a few years, we decided to head in that direction.

Our Lonely Planet guide described the kilometre long, pedestrianised street as having an infectious atmosphere, and within five minutes of arriving, we decided that was probably referring to something akin to genital herpes. It felt like 5am at an illegal rave being held in a secure mental hospital. A teenage Australian girl slumped over an overflowing litter bin, while her friend picked vomited food debris from her hair. Hawkers touted friendship bracelets bearing personalised embroidered messages, which the purchaser had obviously chosen not to collect. We soon realised why with 'I screw midgets' and 'I love horse cock' being two of the tamer slogans available. Streetfood stalls sizzled and smoked outside every bar, boasting fresh produce seemingly sourced from behind the establishment's fridge rather than in it, with cockroaches, spiders and multiple species of beetle deep fried and available as an alternative drinking accompaniment to a bag of nuts. Every inch of the street was filled with a slow-moving wave of sweating, inebriated humanity of every age, shape, size and nationality. Each was clutching a plastic cup of brightly coloured alcohol or 500ml bottle of Singha beer in one hand, and a helium balloon in the other, from which they sucked nitrous oxide gas, the so called 'hippy crack' which delivered a brief moment of euphoria, before a middle-aged Russian puked on their flip flops.

It seemed that Bangkok was predictably living down to our low expectations, and after a quick beer, which we drank on a balcony overlooking the Khao San carnage, we headed back towards our guest house. We'd just crossed the Klong Banglumphu canal, when I glanced right down a sidestreet and spotted a small bar with streetside tables. We headed down the narrow lane and found ourselves in a different Bangkok, a world away from Khao San Road's hissing helium canisters and riotous Eastern European package tourists. It was undoubtably a traveller enclave, spread across two blocks of largely traffic free lanes, but a different type of traveller to the ones we'd left a mile down the road. Screeching teens and staggering sex tourists were replaced by a quieter crowd, who gave the impression of being seasoned travellers, with a smattering of older package tourists from a nearby chain hotel.

The narrow lanes comprised of crumbling three and four storey buildings with street level family businesses operating as small bars, simple restaurants, single-sewing-machine tailors, and laundries offering a kilo wash of travel-soiled garments for thirty Bhat. Small children played by the kerbside as their mothers dished up plates of rice and noodles; cats skulked between tables looking for scraps, and ancient Thai ladies sat on plastic chairs, critically surveying the Buddha-head tattoo on the shoulder of a dreadlocked bohemian from Sweden. It felt to us like less-visited areas of South East Asia, or perhaps how Bangkok had been in the late 60's or early 70's. We liked it immediately and pulled up two stools at a streetside table and ate two spicy Thai curries, washed down with a litre of Chang beer for less than a fiver. I decided that maybe I'd written Bangkok off prematurely, and began to look forward to the next couple of days in the city.

I was up early the following day, manoeuvring my laptop into a shaded area of our guest house's small courtyard. The thermometer was nudging above 80° though it wasn't yet 9am, and I relished the warmth after half a winter in chilly Northern England. I switched on the computer, eager to begin tapping out my idea for the book's opening chapter, and retrieved a USB SD card reader from the laptop case. This was to be my aide memoire. Although I had countless recollections and ideas stored in my memory bank, I hoped that my collection of photos, taken on trips over the last thirty years would be a vital tool to fill in any gaps, and help me to recall the finer detail of long forgotten people and places.

Unfortunately, I'd only considered this a few days earlier, while we were spending the New Year in our campervan in the Yorkshire Dales, and had therefore only got round to uploading the thousands of photo files, including hundreds of scanned images from the pre-digital era, on the day before our departure. The length of time taken to transfer multiple gigabytes of data had meant I'd had to leave my PC whirring away through the night, as a continuous flow of photographic memories were magically duplicated onto the centimetre long plastic card. I was hopeful that the night-shift transfer would have successfully picked up all my images, but predictably, on the morning of our departure, Windows photo file icons were still slowly floating across my computer screen, indicating that the job was far from complete. They say a watched kettle never boils and the theory was proved correct, as I stood impatiently and vainly willing the little floating squares to get a bloody move on, until a car horn outside my window told me that I'd lost the race against time. My final Leeds Uber for a long time was waiting to transport us to the railway station. I yanked the USB stick from the computer, dropped it in my bag, did a final check around the house, and set off to the other side of the world.

A day later, Kirsty could tell that all had not gone according to plan as she emerged, blinking into the sunlight of the courtyard, clutching a cup of coffee. The sun had shifted, so I was now sweating in its glare, but I was too preoccupied to change position. Scowling and muttering, I held my head in my hands and flicked at my wireless mouse in irritation.

"The bloody SD Card is corrupted. I can see the files but can't open them," I snarled, before she'd asked. "It must have been the X-Ray scanner at the airport," I added, convincing myself that I wasn't to blame.

Kirsty pulled up a chair and joined me in staring at a screen filled with hundreds of tiny file icons, each bearing the blue and white double-peaked Windows Photos logo. The yellow folder icons which had arranged the images into trips, sorted by country and date, were nowhere to be seen.

"At least the files are there," Kirsty observed. I clicked one and grimaced as a message appeared on the screen saying 'unable to open file.' I clicked at a couple of others and received the same message.

"Can you write the book without the photos?" I was more hopeful on this point, though I knew there were gaps in my memory that would require a photographic memory jog. There was only one thing for it. We'd need to seek out the Bangkok equivalent of PC World.

After a sweaty, hour long, Google map inspired search, we arrived at a signless shop unit on a busy main road. A middle aged man with round, wire framed glasses and a mop of greying hair sat on a stool, fiddling with a circuit board. He had the dusty, dishevelled air of a down-at-heel genius, like the creator of Bitcoin living in a shed. I brandished my faulty USB stick and he screwed up his nose and deftly flicked out the SD Card with a paper clip. His initial high-tech approach of spitting on a grubby tissue then wiping the card resulted in him receiving the same error message upon plugging the stick into his computer.

Scowling and shaking his head, he twitched his droopy rodent whiskers in frustration. "Two o'clock!" He tapped his retro, 1970s style digital watch, which showed us it was approaching midday. I took this to mean he needed a couple of hours to try and resolve the problem, so Kirsty and I left the shop and strolled along a nearby khlong, one of the filthy canals whose semi-stagnant flow criss-cross central Bangkok. We noticed a group of locals pointing at the water beneath the windows of their tenement block and were surprised to see a crocodile trailing a sizeable wake along the scum-coated surface. The reptile revealed itself to be a metre long monitor lizard, which hauled itself from the water and disappeared along a sewage pipe leading into the building. The concerned looks on the faces of the residents left us thinking they'd be leaving their toilet seats down for the foreseeable future!

Back at the computer repair shop, we were greeted with a smile which I took to be a positive sign. The USB stick was back in the computer and our friend turned the monitor to display a screen still liberally sprinkled with blue and white icons, but which were now punctuated by small coloured images. A double click of the mouse revealed a sunset beach scene which I immediately recognised as Tunco in El Salvador, where a feral dog had terrorised Kirsty during an early evening stroll. Another click revealed me scrambling up a mountainside in Austria, but the next resulted only in a depressingly familiar 'File not found' message. Clicking again revealed a smiling child monk in a saffron robe; next, a dhow being hauled onto a beach by a group of dark skinned, bare chested men; another click produced a Lesothan shepherd in a balaclava helmet; next click, 'File not found'.

It seemed our computer genius had achieved a photo recovery rate of around 70%. Ominously though, I realised as I perused the screen that there were still no yellow file icons, which had previously grouped the photos into countries, and dates. Re-ordering the files to see their details revealed another problem – all the dates were reset to January 4, 2019. It was obvious that the recovery of the photos had required our man to recreate all the files in a new format, which left me with thousands of digital images, in no order whatsoever. I clicked the cursor and was transported back through Nicaragua, Taiwan, Australia, Norway, and Brazil to an onion domed building somewhere in Eastern

Europe that I couldn't remember. I paid the man for the repair, dropped the USB stick into my pocket, and wondered how the hell it was going to help me write a book.

The Wolfman of Brasov

 "**R**emember her?" I turned my laptop screen towards Kirsty as she joined me to sit at a table in the courtyard of the Bangkok Guest House.

The photo on the screen showed two women standing in a cavernous, non-descript building. Behind them is a currency exchange and what may be a travel agency. One lady is six inches taller and maybe ten years younger than the other subject. Both are smiling but the one on the left, who is a younger Kirsty, seems particularly excited and is grinning almost manically.

"Maria?" Kirsty smiled. "Brasov in Romania. God! look at my hair..."

"She was one of the Brasov Maria's anyway," I raised my eyebrows as I recalled our encounter with a real-life travel urban myth of the early 2000's.

The Romania and Moldova Lonely Planet, 2004 edition, had delivered the tourism equivalent of a lottery win for Maria Bolea and her husband Grig, by naming them as the 'go-to' people for arranging accommodation in the Transylvanian town of Brasov. Maria's fame had been earned through her uncanny ability to locate a room of some description for travellers, even when her little town was bursting at the seams. Her 'office' was the main railway station, and it was here that Maria would apprehend travellers as they disembarked from the overnight sleeper from Bucharest. The Lonely Planet article wholeheartedly recommended Maria's services, and as her fame spread, so did the number of 'Marias' working the streets around the station, all claiming to be the Lonely Planet's fabled room fixer. A bedraggled traveller stepping from the overnight train brandishing a Lonely Planet and seeking a room, could expect to be greeted by a scene straight out of Spartacus, with a scrum of plump, middle-aged women in headscarves stepping forward shouting "I'm Maria!", "No I am!", "No, it's me, I'm Maria!"

Which Maria was the genuine article was hard to determine, but the friendly, dark haired woman who accosted Kirsty and I on the platform within seconds of our stumbling from the train, assured us she was indeed the one and only Maria Bolea. Before we could argue, she'd demonstrated her prowess by securing us a 'basic room in a family house' via a single call on a battered Nokia, and we were soon lugging our backpacks through the cobbled streets as our Maria raced ahead, her constant chatter keeping pace with her quick steps.

To say our room was off the well-trodden tourist track was something of an understatement, and we were soon following the Maria through narrow streets of single storey, wood and concrete dwellings. Compared to the uniformity of urban housing developments in most of Europe, the only thing the streets of Brasov had in common was that every single house was different. A mismatch of architectural styles, colours and states of disrepair told us that here, people obviously bought a patch of land and did whatever the hell they liked with it.

We eventually arrived at a bungalow with an overgrown garden surrounded by a rusty wire fence. Maria pushed open the creaking gate, and we were greeted by two large, snarling mongrels who appeared at speed from the rear of the property. A hasty retreat was called for, and Maria slammed the gate closed, before ripping a three-foot wooden post from a neighbour's fence. Obviously feeling better equipped, she now felt more confident in showing us to our room and pushed open the gate, before raising the stick above her head and striding towards the barking hounds. Not surprisingly, the sight of the stocky little woman brandishing a large piece of wood, replete with rusty nails, had the desired effect and the canine welcoming party skulked back to the rear of the house, while growling their disapproval.

As we reached the door, Maria thrust the piece of wood into my hands and smiled.

"Take this. For later." She winked, and I tried not to think about getting back into our room after dark with two Transylvanian hell hounds keeping watch. After locating a door key under a plant pot, Maria showed us into the room. We would actually be staying in the cellar of a family home which Maria informed us was owned by 'very old people.' It certainly looked that way, with décor and appliances which seemed to pre-date Nicolae Ceaușescu's mid 1960's presidency. A rusting fridge hummed and rattled in the corner and Maria opened its door, then flinched and closed it very quickly. I resolved not to investigate further. The small bathroom enjoyed a feature I've experienced all too often in 'budget' accommodation, in that the temperature was around ten degrees lower than it was outside the house. This was potentially pleasant in the heat of high summer, but not so much in early May, when the thermometer had been struggling to achieve double figures. Also, the shower comprised of a section of foot long hosepipe taped onto each tap, which dripped into a suspiciously stained bathtub.

"It's certainly authentic." I tried to stay positive as we heard the gate rattle, followed by the muffled sounds of a postman being mauled by dogs.

It was still relatively early, so we decided to set off to explore the picturesque medieval town at the same time as Maria departed, having been impressed by her dog marshalling skills and still able to hear the dogs feasting on the contents of the postman's sack in the back garden. We parted company with her in the impressive town square, which is said to be the spot to which the fabled Pied Piper led the children of Hamlin. Above Brasov's red tiled rooftops, the tree covered Carpathian Mountains formed an impressive backdrop to the town, and the peak of Mount Tampa, which can be reached by cable car or via an hour long hike uphill through the woods, was an obvious focal point.

In the 1950's Brasov was named Orasul Stalin, and the hillside was cleared of trees in order to etch the name of the Soviet dictator into the mountain. The area is now a nature reserve with a number of walking trails affording panoramic views of the town below, and Kirsty and I took our time on the ascent, while trying unsuccessfully to pick out our homestay in the jumble of small streets on the outskirts of the town centre.

An early Summer sun was peeping through the clouds as we reached the top of the mountain, then continued along a wooded trail to arrive at a grassed clearing, surrounded by towering Mountain Elm trees. The steeples of Brasov's old town were just visible in the distance through the foliage, and we sank down onto the grass and enjoyed the warmth provided by an extended break in the cloud cover. I love travelling on sleeper trains in Eastern Europe, but a late night of drinking cans of Ursus beer, a hard bunk in a rattling carriage and a dawn arrival in Brasov had left us both feeling drowsy. It wasn't long before we were both asleep.

I awoke with a shiver and squinted upwards into the clouds which had brought an end to the brief spell of sunshine, while trying to work out where I was. I slowly lifted my head from the grass and looked at my watch. Just after 11.30. We'd been dozing for around forty minutes. As I sat up with a groan, I became aware of movement to my right and turned to see an elderly man approaching, clutching two supermarket bags. His lined face bore a nervous, pained expression, which suggested a man whose grandkids often popped balloons next to his head as he dozed in a favourite chair. He was talking loudly and quickly and seemed highly agitated. Kirsty blinked her eyes open and sat upright with a start, as he drew closer and placed his bags on the ground in front of us. We could now see that they contained a variety of berries and other fruit, which he'd clearly foraged from the woodland around us.

The old man removed his blue flat cap and used it to mop his brow. He then embarked on an unintelligible tirade of shouted Romanian abuse, accompanied by a frenzy of gesticulation which led me to guess we'd inadvertently strayed onto private land. I raised my hands in apology, but this just caused him to shake his head and curse under his breath, as the realisation dawned that we were foreigners and couldn't understand a word he'd said.

I helped Kirsty to her feet and we picked up our rucksack. I embarked on my usual tactic of smiling and nodding to demonstrate my contrition at having trespassed on the old farmer's land, in the hope that this would calm him down. If I was unsure of the response this would elicit, I certainly hadn't expected his reaction.

He looked deep into my eyes, took a breath, and raised his hands to shoulder height, fashioning his gnarled fingers into makeshift claws. He then stepped towards us while emitting a low, resonant growl from deep within his chest. Not surprisingly we backed away as he tossed his head back and bared what remained of his teeth while spitting, snarling and tearing at imaginary flesh with his extended clawed hands. If we hadn't been in Transylvania, the display may have been amusing. As it was, it seemed we'd found ourselves in a remote mountain clearing with a madman harbouring werewolf tendencies. The only saving grace was that he appeared to be about eighty years old and was a foot shorter than me. I reckoned I could repel him easily enough if he maintained his human form, but the potential for shape-shifting was obvious and I nervously scanned the palms of his hands for signs of increased hairiness, as he pawed the air in front of my face while growling and snarling.

Retreat seemed the most sensible course of action and we backed away down the track with the old chap staggering after us, baring his teeth and clawing at the air with his thankfully still hairless hands. Upon arrival back in the main square in Brasov, we sat and looked up towards the forested hills, wondering about the strange old wolfman and his supermarket bag of berries.

The mystery remained until the day we departed Brasov. At the station, we pushed through a crowd of skulking Maria's, and spotted our own fixer in prime position on the platform. She greeted us like old friends, and I produced my camera and snapped the photo of her with Kirsty, which was destined to appear on my laptop again, some fifteen years later. We chatted while awaiting the arrival of our train and mentioned the elderly werewolf we'd encountered on the mountain. As I described us dozing in the mountain clearing, Maria's smile was replaced by wide eyes.

"You must never fall asleep on the mountain," she gulped and shook her head. I laughed and anticipated some far-fetched Transylvanian legend about vampires or werewolves stalking the hills. The next word Maria uttered stopped me in my tracks.

"Bears!"

Kirsty and I looked at each other. "Here?" We responded in unison.

"Yes, many bears in the hills around town. In October a brown bear killed two mushroom collectors and attacked six others. Very dangerous. Never fall asleep in the hills, you may wake up with a bear eating you!"

Suddenly, our encounter with the strange old mountain-man made frightening sense. Not knowing the English word for a bear, he'd resorted to mimicry, though I guessed it was unlikely he won any games of Christmas charades based on his animal impressions.

In Bangkok, I clicked my mouse with a growl and the image disappeared from my laptop screen.

"We got lucky that day." Kirsty took a sip of her coffee.

"Not the only time." I smiled and clicked onto the next image.

Meeting John Andrew

Day 7- Rotorua, New Zealand

"Bonjour Monsieur!" The elderly French woman greeted me with a cheery wave, as I peeped round the corner of an eight-foot privet hedge. Her heavily mascara'd eyes blinked beneath a mask of gloopy grey mud, which dripped from matted hair that appeared to have been styled in a cement mixer. Her eighteen-stone husband sat facing her in the foot-deep puddle, and attempted unsuccessfully to swivel his balding, mud spattered head to greet me.

"You will join us?"

I smiled and shook my head. They resembled two dejected hippos trying in vain to wallow in a drought-dried waterhole. Wispy clouds of steam rose from the mud, which belched and bubbled sulphurous gas from the earth's molten core. I don't even like hot baths, so rolling around in boiling slime with two French pensioners held little appeal.

We'd just arrived in Rotorua, the geothermal hotspot of New Zealand's North Island, after a 150-mile drive from Auckland, where we'd spent a few days before collecting our campervan at the start of a month long roadtrip. Having rented campervans previously, we were well aware of the potential for initial glitches with electrics, gas bottles and appliances, so had opted for an initial two night stay at a campsite, where we thought it more likely we could get assistance in the event of any problems. While Kirsty had begun unpacking, I went for a wander around the site, which described itself as a 'Geothermal Park' with hot pools, thermal showers and a traditional Maori 'hangi' steam oven. Our fellow campers were largely, like us, Europeans fleeing winter to spend Summer in the southern hemisphere in either a rented motorhome or campervan.

The cost of the trip placed us firmly in the latter category. A fully equipped motorhome with shower, toilet and fixed bed started at around a thousand pounds per week. That was well beyond our budget, so I shopped around and located a company which rented out older campervans for around half that cost.

Reviews were favourable, and an added bonus was that the paint-jobs were understated in comparison to some of the larger companies, who seemed to be trying to outdo each other in terms of outlandishly embarrassing colour schemes involving lurid greens and pinks and scantily clad cartoon beach bunnies.

Our allotted vehicle was a fifteen year old, converted Mazda minibus. With three hundred thousand miles on the clock, it was likely to have covered virtually every road on New Zealand's two islands. Everyone gives their campervan a name, and ours was immediately obvious when we spotted the dealership logo displayed on its licence plate. John Andrew suited him perfectly. If a vehicle had a personality, John Andrew's was that of a middle-aged accountant, working for a small firm in a country town manufacturing pencil sharpeners. Sensible and diligent, eager to avoid any conflict or drama, John Andrew would wear a tweed jacket with leather patches on the elbows. He'd sit at the same desk for twenty years without the bosses knowing his name. He'd live with his mother in a neat bungalow, and would bring the same sandwiches in his briefcase every day. Plain ham and cheese, definitely no mustard.

John Andrew had no bathroom. He boasted a small cooker and fridge and a sink with a tap which detached to become a shower. Unfortunately, the hose only extended a foot in length, so it was fine if you wanted to wash your hair while sitting in the passenger seat. He also came equipped with a 'Porta-Potty'. A small plastic lavatory, which would enable us to wild-camp or freedom camp, as the Kiwis called it. Kirsty and I regarded the sealed square box with suspicion and immediately agreed a 'liquids only' rule. With space at a premium, the logistics of unpacking our rucksacks and repacking in John Andrew's tiny cupboards was an important task. As was stashing our cash.

We'd been planning our extended trip since the middle of 2018, against the backdrop of the UK's 'Brexit' departure from the European Union, which had seen a painful reduction in the value of sterling on currency exchange markets. Brexit day was originally scheduled for 29 March 2019, right in the middle of our trip. I was concerned that a dramatic fall in the value of the pound could have a catastrophic impact on our finances. In basic terms, a halving in the value of the pound would double our costs if we were using credit cards and withdrawing cash from our UK accounts via ATM'S while abroad. That would probably be manageable in the second half of our journey in South America, but in an already expensive country such as New Zealand, it could result in us running out of funds and having to return home early.

I'd therefore looked into ways of fixing our costs before travelling, to protect us against any future UK currency crash. The only bank which appeared to offer accounts which allowed customers to hold funds in a foreign currency was HSBC, and upon enquiring, I was assured that I could purchase New Zealand, and United States dollars, hold them in designated currency accounts, and access the funds via ATM machines around the world. This seemed the perfect solution, and I purchased enough dollars to cover our expected costs in both New Zealand and South America.

A couple of weeks before we left the UK, I decided to check how many branches 'the world's bank' actually had in New Zealand. I was puzzled to find only two, in Auckland and Wellington, so decided to clarify which cashpoints I'd be able to withdraw cash from while in the country. The answer provided by the HSBC call centre was as straightforward as it was disappointing. The answer was none. It wasn't, in fact, possible to withdraw funds from a currency account via an ATM at all. I would have to go into one of the two branches and do it there.

As our New Zealand trip had started in Auckland, there would be little point accessing cash there, so we were forced to withdraw the majority of our NZ dollars before leaving the UK, with a plan to 'top up' in Wellington before catching the ferry to South Island. Carrying several thousand pounds worth of cash was a concern, particularly as we'd have to leave it in an unattended campervan, without any alarm system, while potentially parked well off the beaten track. The solution was obvious – stash cans. Favoured by drug dealers to hide wads of bank notes and bags of illegal produce, an Ebay search revealed a host of ingenious fake containers, designed to conceal illicit valuables. Tins of Heinz beans and ravioli, torches and anti-perspirant sprays, jars of coffee and cans of Strongbow cider, all hollowed out, and redesigned with screw-on bottoms to provide security for people with something to hide.

We opted for a hairbrush with a thick handle that could easily accommodate a thousand dollars, and an Avon factor 30 suncream (two grand, if rolled tight). I also improvised and bought a large tub of Lidl curry powder, which I emptied, but obviously failed to wash thoroughly, so any notes retrieved from there always carried an unmistakable aroma of Bhuna, and prompted a pang of homesickness for a traditional British curry. Kirsty and I also each purchased a belt with a concealed zip running along its length, which was able to conceal another couple of thousand dollars between us. I was quite happy with our security arrangements in the run up to departure, until a friend raised the inconvenient question of 'what happens if the campervan catches fire?'

In addition to our hidden cash, both Kirsty and I had a laptop and an e-Reader tablet, so any opportunist smash and grab artist would have struck gold had they popped open John Andrew's low-tech sliding door. We therefore went to elaborate lengths to hide our valuables in the most obscure and hard to reach corners of the van's interior, before setting off to explore Rotorua.

The town is situated on a lake which shares its name, but strangely it seemed almost embarrassed by the eighty-kilometre expanse of water on its doorstep. We'd expected to find bars and restaurants lining the water's edge, but Rotorua's small, low-rise centre sat a few hundred yards back from the lapping waves, and seemed to be trying to ignore the obvious charms of the lake. We found a restaurant with a small roof terrace, from where it was possible to see the water across a stretch of grassy parkland, but we were the only customers who seemed interested in a lake-view seat, and we sat alone and watched the sun set, while sipping ten dollar 'craft' beers.

The town centre reminded me of smalltown America. It was Saturday night but there was a disappointing absence of rowdiness. Even the indoor mall, which seemed to be the epicentre of Rotorua nightlife, had a family-friendly air, with parents and kids chomping fries and burgers, beside gangs of young bucks in chinos, enjoying their big night out of the week. After a couple more beers in busy but sedate bars, we headed back to the campsite, where we were greeted by the sizzle and smoke of dozens of barbecues, most of which played up to predictable stereotypes of their owners. The elderly German parked next to us risked singeing his walrus moustache as he bent to turn a grill full of frankfurters; the French family opposite were barely visible through a garlic-tinged smokescreen; and the young Korean couple were flash-frying some unidentifiable aquatic cuisine which looked like it was still flapping and gulping, having been plucked from the lake only minutes earlier.

After eating the first of many barbecues of the trip, we disassembled John Andrew's dining table to transform it into a bed, which proved surprisingly comfy. We hardly stirred until we were woken at 8am the next morning by a French swingball tournament taking place by our back window. Our plan for the day was to walk three miles to the other side of Rotorua to visit Whakarewarew Maori village, which is built around an active geothermal area with hot pools, boiling mud and erupting geysers and is situated along a seismic fault line. As we entered the village across a wooden bridge and were encouraged to toss coins for diving kids to retrieve in the river below, I couldn't help wondering whether our donations were to help pay for their house insurance premiums!

We had a wander round the timber-housed village before heading to the Pohuto Geyser which sends a jet of boiling water thirty metres into the air about fifteen times a day. Given our usual level of luck in witnessing natural phenomenon (Northern Lights, Iceland, covered by cloud; Arenal volcano, Costa Rica, covered by cloud etc etc) we expected a couple of puffs of steam at best. We were therefore pleasantly surprised to see the geyser erupt twice while we were present, and a little perturbed that it did so while a gang of local kids were diving into the steaming waters of an adjacent pond. Knowing the safe spots to swim here obviously made the difference between a refreshing dip and bobbing to the surface broiled like a lobster in a pot.

After visiting Whakarewarew we walked back into town on a long, straight road, past rows of motels with neat gardens and names like Geyser Lookout and Thermal Stay B+B. Traffic was light, the sun was shining and again it felt like rural America or a British market town of the 1960's. The walk was pleasant enough and Rotorua was without doubt the sort of town most people would love to be able to retire to, but this wasn't what I'd come to New Zealand for. I dreamt of camping beneath soaring snow-capped peaks or beside brilliant blue glacial lakes, cooking over campfires and drinking beer at midnight on deserted moonlit beaches. It was time for us to move on.

Santa Town Saturday

The persistent rain dripped off my hood, trickled down my nose and splashed onto my laptop screen. Smoke from our barbecue grill drifted across the fast-flowing river to our left, and a blanket of mist shrouded the tops of the steepled pines on the hills surrounding our camp. For the first time since we'd arrived in New Zealand, it felt like we were in the wild. We'd travelled south from Rotoruwa, via Lake Taupo and Tongariro National Park, navigating via two mobile phone apps - Campermate and Rankers NZ, which provided directions to all manner of camping possibilities, from family friendly resorts with every facility imaginable, to wooded clearings in the middle of nowhere, with an exposed 'drop' toilet if you were lucky. The location we'd found near the tiny settlement of Ruatiti fell firmly into the latter category.

John Andrew had bumped and scraped his way down a rough dirt track, through thick cloud forest, after a 17KM detour from the main road. It would have been a painfully long diversion had we needed to turn back with dusk fast approaching, but thankfully the forested clearing we arrived at was perfect. We parked alongside the river, with a rough-sleeping couple in a battered estate car a few hundred metres away destined to be our only neighbours for the night. The river splashed and gurgled, birds twittered in the canopy above us and the rain pattered on the campervan roof. I cracked open a beer, brushed raindrops from the laptop screen and inserted the USB memory stick from the Bangkok repair shop. I clicked on the file icon and launched the Windows photo app to be transported back to a far less peaceful evening.

The first photo to appear on the screen showed Kirsty standing by a wooden tree-trunk sign proclaiming 'Arctic Circle'. Rather than the extreme cold-weather polar exploration equipment which such a sign may suggest, Kirsty is wearing light trousers and a summer top. In the centre of the sign, the location is stated - Rovaniemi airport, Northern Finland.

Rovaniemi is a town which thousands of tourists have visited, though few would recognise its name. That's because most flights landing there are day-trip tours to a destination which conjures up magical images for children of all ages – Lapland, home of Santa Claus. Situated on the main road, five miles out of town, Santa Claus village welcomes half a million visitors a year to enjoy dog and reindeer sled rides through spectacular snowscapes, drinks in ice bars and beds in real igloos. And obviously they also get to meet the main man himself- the genuine Father Christmas.

Peak season in Rovaniemi is the winter months leading up to Christmas, but that held little appeal for us. We'd chosen to visit in the height of Summer, to experience 24-hour daylight and the phenomenon known as the midnight sun. We'd rented a motorhome and taken advantage of 'Everyman's Law' which allows wild camping, fishing, fire-lighting and foraging in all rural areas. We'd devised a route as we travelled, with no set agenda, hiking in pine forests, swimming in deserted lakes and drinking supermarket beer by a crackling fire, which was vital to keep the voracious midges at bay. At midnight we watched as the sun dipped towards the horizon, and birdsong ceased for a brief moment as it hung in the sky like a milky orb, before beginning its slow ascent to mark the start of another new day.

It was the first time I'd driven a motorhome and the rental company had surprised us by upgrading our rental to a nine metre, double-axled monster. Adapting to that sized vehicle could have been a daunting prospect on narrow city roads but thankfully the depot was situated close to Rovaniemi airport on a quiet street a few miles out of town. The roads as we headed north were straight, well maintained and we saw only light traffic and the occasional wandering moose or reindeer. Apart from a minor incident where we became trapped between two trees in a pine forest, I thought I was doing pretty well with the driving, until we found ourselves on a narrow forest track, seeking a place to camp for the night. Nowadays, motorhome wild camping is made easy via apps such as Park4Night, where users add locations, photos and reviews of places you can spend the night for free. Back then, there was no such technology, and we tended to use Google Earth to identify likely pitches.

On this occasion, using Google's aerial viewpoint, I'd spotted a lakeside beach a few miles off a quiet country road, and we turned off and bumped along a dirt track to investigate. The main drawback with Google Earth was that it was impossible to gauge the width of a road, and it quickly became apparent that this one wasn't suitable for a car, let alone a three metre wide motorhome. Branches scratched and scraped the side of the vehicle as we crawled along at snail's pace, and I cringed, knowing there was a 500 Euro excess on the van's insurance policy. When we began to hear ominous thuds and clumps as branches bounced off our roof, I knew we had to turn back, but a three-point-turn was definitely not an option, and reversing would have been a tortuously slow exercise. After fifteen minutes of driving, which had started to feel like jungle exploration, we spotted a gateway on the right. Two large wooden gates were open, and I decided that it represented our best opportunity to turn around.

We proceeded cautiously, as I was half expecting to be greeted by a Finnish 'prepper' hermit in a fortified shack brandishing an automatic weapon, or an Alt-right cult militia, training covertly in the dense forest. Instead, we arrived at a circle of log cabins in a wooded clearing. The structures were similar to those found in Santa's theme park with ornately decorated roofs and low eaves, and the whole place seemed deserted. I managed to turn the motorhome round in the circle and had just set off back towards the gates when there was a loud bang which caused Kirsty and I to duck involuntarily, then turn slowly to look at each other with 'Oh shit' expressions. I looked in my side mirror and spotted a section of roof lying on the pine covered drive. Clearly, I'd underestimated the height and width of our vehicle in relation to the nearest log cabin.

I considered getting out to see if I could find anyone to inform about the collision, but it looked like the place had been deserted for a while. We therefore drove on, not daring to assess the damage to the motorhome.

Back in Rovaniemi, the rental depot clerk sucked his teeth as he examined a large black scrape on the side of the van.

"It might rub out?" I offered hopefully, but he shook his head. No such luck.

Ten minutes later and with my wallet 500 Euros lighter, I ruefully snapped the photo of Kirsty as we waited for a taxi back into town. Our flight was the following day, a Sunday, which meant we'd get to experience a Saturday night in one of the most northerly towns in the world, located at 66° North. A night's drinking with Santa's little helpers on their summer break might help me forget the unwelcome penalty which had nearly doubled the cost of the rental.

The inhabitants of Rovaniemi don't fare as badly as some Arctic Circle settlements in terms of winter daylight. They at least get a couple of hours of murky twilight during December and January, while more northerly towns such as Tromso experience total darkness, with the sun not rising at all between November and January. All of the Arctic circle settlements have to contend with the insomniac nightmare of endless daylight during the summer months though. With such seasonal extremes of light and dark, and temperature, it's no surprise Finland has one of Europe's highest suicide rates.

Our taxi dropped us at our hotel, a two-storey concrete complex with echoing, disinfectant scented corridors, which had the definite air of a young offenders' institution. We dropped off our bags and set off to explore. From the taxi, I'd spotted an interesting looking little bar on the road into town so headed in that direction. Located between two large outlets selling an ambiguous selection of industrial products, was a single storey wooden shack with pine decking and picnic tables, shaded by two large parasols branded with the emblem of the local Lapin Kulta beer.

I could hear some 70's 'prog rock' playing as we approached, and quickened my pace in anticipation of a welcome cold pint. I thought I heard glass smashing as we ambled across the quiet road, and by the time we'd reached the far kerb, could hear the unmistakeable clamour of raised voices from inside the bar, which was now about a hundred yards away. The first barstool to emerge from the dark interior in a shower of shattered window-pane, almost cleared the wooden fence bordering the beer garden. The bottle which closely followed, bounced off a picnic table and smashed onto the pavement. Kirsty and I stopped to observe a balding man of around thirty, in a checkered lumberjack shirt burst through the single wooden door backwards at speed, and tumble down three small steps onto the pavement. He was closely followed by a bearded youth in a red t-shirt who was aided in his swift exit by a muscular, red faced and angry looking man brandishing a table leg. The sounds from the interior of the bar hinted at continuing multi-participant violence, and this was borne out by a scrummage of flailing men, and a single woman with badly bleached hair, who all somehow squeezed through the narrow doorframe as a single punching, kicking, shouting scrummage. Another barstool flew through the shattered window as the protagonists wrestled and brawled around the picnic tables, while being eagerly encouraged by other drinkers who had exited the bar to watch the show.

"Maybe give this one a miss?" I suggested, as Kirsty stepped back to avoid the man in the lumberjack shirt who was sprinting up the path towards us, with his table-leg wielding opponent in hot pursuit.

It was a fifteen minute walk to town, and en-route to the main street we passed a group of semi-conscious, bottle-toting teenagers sprawled on a grass verge; a middle aged man slurred an undecipherable song as he pushed his sleeping friend home in a supermarket trolley; a pensioner slumped asleep on a bus stop seat, a drool of saliva glinting in the early evening sunlight as it pooled on the collar of his anorak. As we approached the main street, a police patrol car slowed to observe Kirsty and I, the officers seemingly suspicious and disbelieving that we were walking in a straight line and with unsoiled trousers.

We found a crowded and predictably rowdy bar and retreated to a small beer garden to the rear. It was quieter there, with just ourselves and a few other scattered couples present. We selected a bench style table and a smartly dressed, late-fifties couple on our right smiled a glassy eyed greeting. By the time I'd taken the froth off my pint, my attention had been drawn to our neighbours. The woman had joined her partner on his side of the bench and was playfully ruffling his thinning hair, while exploring his inner ear with her tongue.

"Stop looking," Kirsty hissed, so I faced the other direction. Within seconds though, I could see her furtively glancing sidewards.

The woman was now attempting to straddle her partner while slurping at his sweaty forehead like an over-affectionate spaniel. Initially, an overtight skirt prevented her legs from splaying wide enough to position her on his lap, so she hitched it up to mid-thigh level, then began to grind her pelvis into his, while clutching his ears and pushing his now saliva-soaked head into her heaving cleavage.

"You stop looking!" I countered as Kirsty grimaced.

We both faced in the opposite direction and tried to think of something to say, but the moans, groans, giggles and slurps from our right made it hard to concentrate. A sudden prolonged silence caused us both to glance over to see the middle-aged lovers

24

engaged in a grotesque, tongue filled, open mouthed snog. The man's right hand seemed to be engaged in some nefarious activity around the lower reaches of his partner's skirt, but none of the other occupants of the beer garden gave the would-be porn stars a second glance. Unwilling to witness what the public foreplay would lead to next, we swiftly finished our drinks and headed onto the busy main street.

Here, throngs of staggering locals lurched and swayed between bars, observed by a vanload of riot squad police officers and muscular, black clad bouncers with blond buzzcuts and full sleeve tattoos. Although still early evening, the atmosphere in the bars was akin to a seaside bank holiday at closing time. It had clearly been a long day of boozing for most of Rovaniemi's inhabitants, as they eagerly embraced the never-ending daylight of midsummer.

At around 10pm, the town was approaching peak lairiness, and Kirsty and I took up position at a table outside a bar which afforded us a prime view of an establishment across the street. With booming music, flashing lights and a door team who looked like special forces operatives, this was clearly the go-to pub for the town's youngsters. We watched a non-stop stream of altercations as intoxicated punters were refused entry by steely-expressioned, arms folded bouncers, culminating in a spike-haired youth in skinny jeans and a Metallica t-shirt being pulled away from the scene by his friends and girlfriend. He looked as game as an angry badger as he jabbed a finger towards the impassive doormen, and slurred a shouted warning of the damage he'd inflict on them if released from his pals' clutches.

He'd been gone for less than five minutes when I noticed one of the steroid enhanced bouncers nudge his colleagues and nod down the road. I glanced right and saw the teenage protagonist striding purposefully down the pedestrian street towards the bar. His friends and now tearful girlfriend were trailing in his wake, trying to persuade him that his suicide mission wasn't a good idea. Undeterred, he ripped off his t-shirt to reveal a scrawny, badly tattooed torso, clenched his fists and broke into a sprint. He was about a hundred metres from the bar, and loudly broadcast his intentions to the assembled doorstaff as he approached. They seemed to have a brief team meeting to decide who would deal with the imminent threat, and nominated a look-a-like for Dolph Lundgren in Rocky IV. A 6'4, sixteen-stone frame explained his nonchalant demeanour as he uncrossed his arms and stepped forward to meet the youth, whose run-up now morphed into a hop, skip and jump, fists clenched, bouncing stance.

The sound of the lad hitting the floor was reminiscent of a body falling from a skyscraper in a bad gangster movie. He'd barely raised his arm in a futile attempt to throw a punch, before he was hit by a body slam which sent him reeling back into the road. Dolph then enveloped him within two meaty arms, flipped him over and drove him headlong into the concrete, as his watching girlfriend let out an ear-piercing scream. An impressive cross-departmental clean-up operation was then implemented as a police van drew up, the rear doors were opened, and two bouncers retrieved the prone body of the youth and slung him in. The doors closed, the van drove on and the only evidence of the action was a sobbing girl and group of swaying young men lamenting their friend's apparent death wish.

We'd seen signs for a midnight outdoor disco by the river, so decided to end our night in Santa's hometown there. The sun was dipping towards the rooftops on the hill behind us, as we crossed a bridge spanning the Kemijoki river and headed towards flashing lights and a screech of guitars, in an area of parkland adjacent to the river. Having witnessed the early evening carnage of a Summer Saturday in Rovaniemi, we wondered whether we ought to be packing body armour or rape alarms as we made our way to an open terrace with a bar and small stage, upon which a grizzled bunch of pot-bellied long-haireds were murdering a Status Quo classic. Any concerns over drink-fuelled teenage violence were soon dispelled as we purchased a couple of bottles of beer and reviewed our follow ravers.

Elderly ladies in multi-coloured puffa-anoraks, too-tight jeans and high heels, hobbled and lurched around the packed dance floor. Their husbands shuffled along in their wake, slopping more beer onto an already treacherous surface, as they tried in vain to revisit the golden age of 70's Finnish disco. A golden bear of a man, bearded and sporting a ginger pony tail, seemed eager to dislocate his tiny Sami wife's shoulder blades, as he rag-dolled her through the melee. The undisputed highlight of the floorshow though was Charlie Manson. Although apparently incarcerated in a high security penitentiary in California at the time, it seemed the notorious cult leader had somehow secured a weekend pass-out, and was now displaying his dancefloor prowess in small-town Northern Finland. Wearing an olive-green combat jacket and brown corduroy flares, the slight, bearded figure had taken up pole position in front of the stage and was treating us to an unforgettable display of morris-dancing inspired moves. Legs flailing and arms aloft, he seemed to be ringing a pair of imaginary handbells as the band swung effortlessly into a woeful rendition of Brown-Eyed Girl. Charlie clearly took his role as the Rovaniemi disco king seriously, and not a flicker of emotion could be detected on his deadpan face as he kicked and span around his own personal mosh-pit.

Kirsty and I resisted the urge to join the locals on the dancefloor and were content to watch from the sidelines, until the sun began to rise above the buildings of the town on the hill above us at 2am. It was at that point that a rotund reveller with a bubble perm and tight 80's style football shorts appeared on stage, seemingly to request a favourite song. Unfortunately, he seemed to lose his footing in a tangle of cables, and careered headlong into the drum kit, to the accompaniment of a pleasing, final drum roll and crash. That seemed an appropriate time to call it a night.

Kirsty and I crossed the bridge and headed back through town. The streets were still busy with locals staggering home, sleeping on benches and throwing glasses at bouncers. The sun was shining, the birds were singing, and 3am felt like a Summer Saturday afternoon in a rough seaside town. It would have been all too easy to stay out, but we'd had enough. We'd seen what Santa's helpers got up to in their Summer holidays and weren't sure the old man would approve!

Down and Out in Wellington

Day 16- Wellington, New Zealand

It was over a week since we'd left Auckland, and we'd travelled around 400 miles down the West Coast of New Zealand's North Island. With no set agenda, we decided on our daily route while eating breakfast, either sat in the warm, early summer sunshine, or on a couple of occasions, sheltering inside the campervan as torrential rain bounced off its roof. The names on our map meant nothing to us, as we idled through smalltown New Zealand, a world away from the skyscrapers and commuter bustle we'd left behind in urban Auckland. Finally, this was the New Zealand I'd envisaged, as we camped beside rivers, lakes and beaches, sometimes alone, and sometimes in the company of other campervans and motorhomes. Often it felt like we were the only people on earth, but sometimes we were all too aware of our neighbours. In the inky midnight blackness of an unlit shower block, on a tiny rural campsite in a hamlet called Scotts Ferry, a huge Maori with wild hair and mad staring eyes leapt at me from the darkness, with a blood curdling 'Haka' style roar. If his assault was typically Kiwi, my reaction was probably stereotypically 'Yorkshire.'

"Fuck off you big idiot!" was my instinctively blunt response as I defensively flailed at him with my wet towel.

"Sorry mate, I thought you were my missus," was his sheepish explanation for nearly giving me a heart attack.

We meandered through Waitotara, Whanganui, and Waitarere, enjoying the laidback atmosphere in small towns which felt like they belonged to a bygone era. Smiling old ladies on bikes with handlebar shopping baskets waved as they passed, and tanned, blonde kids in school uniform slurped on ice creams outside neighbourhood 'dairies'. I'd already forgotten about work and the UK Winter we'd left behind.

We were heading south towards, predictably, yet another town beginning with 'W'. Wellington was our only pre-scheduled destination, as we'd booked the ferry to South Island from there early on a Saturday morning. Forty miles along State Highway 1 was the town of Waikanae, and Thursday night was spent beside the Waikanae River estuary, where we walked on a deserted white sand beach and watched the sun setting behind the hills of Kapiti Island, while being buffeted by a chill wind blowing off the Tasman Sea.

We'd only stayed on one campsite since Rotorua and had grown accustomed to performing our morning ablutions in the great outdoors. Our riverside pitch was perfect for a freshen-up, and I ensured I fully immersed myself in the fast flowing, icy waters, as I had an important business transaction to attend to upon arrival in Wellington. The bundles of cash secreted in John Andrew's unlikeliest nooks and crannies were rapidly depleting, and Wellington's HSBC branch represented our only opportunity to replenish our funds via the $2000 remaining in my foreign currency account.

I felt Kirsty's critical gaze as we sat drinking our breakfast coffee on the riverbank, and returned it with interest. Her shoulder length hair was looking increasingly unruly after several days without shampoo and conditioner, and I obviously exuded a road-weary air myself - unshaven, grubby from campervan maintenance duties and sporting my usual roadtrip wardrobe of sandals, stained cargo shorts and T-shirt.

"We're only withdrawing cash," I reflected "not meeting the manager to ask for a loan."

An hour's drive along North Island's West Coast Highway despatched us into the fast flowing three lane carriageways of the world's most southerly capital city. As we pulled off the highway towards the city centre, we ploughed into a swarm of huge hornets which exploded on John Andrew's windscreen in a crescendo of sickening splats, and left me negotiating bumper to bumper lunchtime traffic peering through what looked like a liberal spread of peanut butter. We stopped at a gas station and the puzzled attendant helped me scrape away the debris of the wasp holocaust as he gave me directions to our destination for the night.

You have to take the rough with the smooth on a campervan trip, and if the 'smooth' was the idyllic campfire on a beach scenario, the rough was definitely to be found in Wellington. Our overnight pitch would be a city centre carpark - a small square of concrete, packed with commuter cars and surrounded on four sides by ugly high rises. There were five designated spaces for campervans, with electric hook-up leads, but annoyingly all were occupied by small hatchbacks. Luckily, there was a single car space free, so I squeezed John Andrew in and managed to drag an electrical lead far enough to plug him in, therefore electrifying his tiny fridge and saving our precious gas bottle reserves.

We'd located HSBC on Google maps, so after hiding our remaining stash of cash a bit more carefully than usual, we set off to withdraw our remaining New Zealand dollars. Wellington felt more like a large provincial town than a capital city, with an eclectic mix of independent stores and bars, alongside the usual city centre chain outlets. Located in the 'roaring forties' and exposed to icy winds whistling along the Cook Strait, Wellington is known as the world's windiest city, but there was nothing more than a welcome cooling breeze as we set off in bright summer sunshine to find the HSBC branch. We paused at the harbour front, and watching local teenagers bombing and diving from a wooden plank into the choppy waters thirty feet below, reminded us that school was now out for Summer.

Heading into the central business district, we could clearly see the HSBC building on the map displayed on our phones, but seemed to be circling the building without spotting anything resembling a bank branch. We walked round the block twice and asked a smart-suited secretary and a Chinese hot-dog vendor if they knew where the bank was, but were rewarded only with shaken heads and puzzled expressions. I looked up at the 25-storey, glass fronted block looming above us, and confidently predicted that the HSBC branch must be somewhere within the towering edifice.

"Come on," I encouraged Kirsty, and removed my sun hat to appear more business-like as I joined a throng of suits heading through a revolving glass door.

"I don't think...." was all I heard from Kirsty before I span through the doors, instantly replacing the heat of the street with the air-conditioned sterility of the reception area of the building, which clearly housed a plethora of New Zealand's blue-chip wealth. Silver foxes in suits rubbed shoulders with neatly bearded thirty-somethings wearing Thom Browne, and tech start-up whizz-kids in jeans and t-shirts. Tango-tanned blondes clutched take-out coffee and air-kissed potential clients, and I shuddered at being suddenly re-immersed in a world I'd been so eager to escape just a few weeks earlier.

I couldn't fail to notice the critical gaze I was attracting from a jowly old security guard, so urged Kirsty towards the lift before he could apprehend us.

"Keep walking. Don't look at him!" I hissed.

I cast a nervous glance over my shoulder as we waited with a dozen employees for one of three lifts to arrive at the ground floor. My first inclination of how out-of-place Kirsty and I were in this polished corporate environment, was when my nose started to twitch. I had my nose broken playing football years ago, and generally have a non-existent sense of smell. Waiting for that lift though, I experienced an olfactory epiphany. My previously useless nose began to detect sweet top-notes of jasmine and cinnamon; my nostrils flared and I leant forward and inhaled deeply on a heady mix of lemongrass and cedarwood emanating from a plump legal secretary standing in front of me, before a dig in the ribs from Kirsty brought me back to earth. As the lift pinged to announce its arrival and the doors slid open, it dawned on me that the likely reason everyone else seemed so fragrant, was that Kirsty and I must have become accustomed to our own more 'natural' aroma.

I surveyed the company names on the buttons representing 25 storeys, and caused some uncomfortable shuffling as I reached across to select the top floor for the HSBC branch. I was positioned between two slick-haired suits who were discussing 'ballpark figures' and 'headwinds approaching quarter two' as the lift accelerated upwards briefly, before stopping at each floor to disgorge a couple of post-lunch employees. Eventually, there were only four of us left, and the stainless steel lift doors provided an embossed, semi-reflective surface which allowed us to take stock of our fellow passengers, while pretending not to. To the left was a dark suited, early forties woman, cropped and dyed black hair perfectly matching her outfit and demeanour. Bright red lipstick on an alabaster face only heightened her bunny boiler potential. To the right was a tall, slender man in his late twenties sporting a suit of the same powder blue hue that Don Johnson just about got away with in Miami Vice. He caught me glancing down to see if he was wearing socks, and tossed his floppy fringe and frowned. Kirsty and I had stood at the back of the lift to try and appear inconspicuous, but that was impossible now, and Cruella de Ville and Sonny Crockett both stared at our reflections with ill-disguised disgust.

Eventually, a final ping heralded our arrival at the skyscraper HSBC branch, and the lift doors slid open. Our fellow occupants hastily made their exit, as if to distance themselves from the two apparently homeless visitors they'd been forced to share the elevator with, and Kirsty and I shuffled our grimy sandalled feet out behind them. I glanced to the left, looking for a service counter but saw only an open plan office. The lift doors closed behind us as I scanned the rows of desks and computer terminals, searching in vain for some ATM machines, or racks of promotional leaflets on cheap loans and cybercrime prevention. As heads began to appear, meerkat style, from behind desk partitions, it quickly became apparent that this wasn't a bank branch at all. Branded decor indicated that this was the bank's wealth management and corporate investment arm.

With the lift departed, Kirsty and I shifted uneasily as we felt the eyes of every employee on the 25th floor settle upon us. I saw multiple furrowed brows and caught snippets of numerous whispered conversations. The words 'Big Issue' and 'drug addicts' were clearly audible. We pressed the lift button and grimaced as we saw that the nearest elevator was still fifteen floors below us.

"Excuse me guys, can I help you?" An employee in his early thirties had clearly drawn the short straw, and had been nominated to eject the homeless folk who'd blagged their way into this air conditioned eyrie in search of loose change, crack and a free coffee machine. He had a nervous, twitchy demeanour, giving the impression of a man who would squeal and recoil from a swooping pigeon.

"I'm trying to get some money," was perhaps not the best opening sentence I could have chosen, and caused the smartly dressed employee to retreat slightly, coincidently as he came within sniffing range of us.

Brandishing my useless ATM card seemed to convince him at least that we weren't murderous street junkies, and bought us enough time to explain our predicament.

"Sounds like those guys in the UK need better training." Our new friend, now introduced as Patrick, shook his head, and explained that HSBC's only remaining retail banking branch was situated over 600KM to the north in Auckland, and that would be the only place we could access my currency account.

"But you have $2000 of mine, and I need it." Dressing like a vagrant clearly increased the pathos level and Patrick took the bait.

"Okay, I can give you an office with a computer for half an hour, so you can get online and transfer the funds to your current account. You should be able to use any ATM then?"

Although this would mean a financial hit due to HSBC's punitive currency exchange rates, it seemed our only option. Twenty minutes later, I'd managed to convert the NZ Dollars into sterling and transfer the funds to my current account, which I could access from a cash machine at ground level. Patrick escorted us to the lift, and we chatted about our trip to date and he recommended some must-sees on South Island. He also seemed quite taken by the notion that we'd washed in a river that morning.

"A river huh? Wow, I must try that someday," he smiled unconvincingly while straightening his tie.

Back at street level, I accessed the maximum daily withdrawal from my current account, and we set off to find lunch. I'd spotted a couple of passers-by munching on tasty looking sausage rolls, and had a sudden pang of homesickness with the 'Greggs' logo featuring prominently. I soon located the source of the obviously home-baked snacks in the form of a stall in a small square, which had attracted a large queue of customers.

Kirsty was sauntering ahead of me and failed to hear my call to alert her to this pop-up artisan bakery, which seemed quite at home in the funky, eclectic streets of Wellington's compact centre. I joined the queue behind a middle-aged man sporting a red bandana and carrying a drooling pug, which grunted and snuffled as it observed me from its perch on his shoulder.

A lady of pensionable age with wild, snow-white hair and black teeth joined the fast-moving queue behind me, and I spotted Kirsty a couple of hundred yards down the road, looking annoyed as she realised that, as often happens, I'd been distracted by something and gone off-piste alone.

It didn't take long to reach a trestle table where a Chinese lady and a boy with Downs Syndrome were dishing out sausage rolls from a large Tupperware crate.

"Two please," I smiled, salivating slightly.

The Chinese lady retrieved two golden pastry rolls, wrapped them in kitchen towel and handed me them.

"How much?" I asked, brandishing a handful of coins.

"Oh, you're new aren't you? I thought I didn't recognise you! Have you just landed in town?"

"Yes, we arrived this morning." I persisted in proffering my coins which seemed to confuse the lady.

"There's no charge sir. It's all free. Michael will fix you a coffee."

Michael smiled shyly and thrust a polystyrene cup in my direction.

"Here take this, you'll need it if you're new in town." Seeing my hands filled with coffee and sausage rolls, the woman folded a leaflet and inserted it in the side pocket of my shorts.

Kirsty was as confused as I was when I told her that the Farmers' Market was dishing out free homemade food and coffee.

"No wonder it's so popular. Nice sausage roll too!" She wiped the crumbs from her lips as we sat on a bench in the shade of a ribbonwood tree in a pedestrianised street.

It was only when we'd finished eating that I remembered the leaflet and retrieved it from my pocket.

"What?" Kirsty could tell by my expression that something was amiss.

"Erm...it wasn't actually an artisan bakery," I began, and Kirsty snatched the leaflet from my hand.

"Wellington City Mission - helping the homeless for one hundred years...." We both grimaced as the realisation dawned that I'd blagged our lunch from a soup kitchen.

We headed back to John Andrew, and reflected that our camping spot for the night somehow now seemed quite fitting. After a day spent resembling hobos, sleeping in a city centre car park suddenly felt totally appropriate.

City of Miracles

Cowshed Bay, Marlborough Sounds. The location sounded typically Kiwi to my ears and the view before me was as stunning as any we'd seen on the trip so far. The Marlborough Sounds are a collection of Pacific Ocean inlets on the northern coast of New Zealand's South Island, with forested islets and sandy bays lapped by aquamarine waters. On a sunny Summer's day, it felt like paradise.

I tutted and shifted my camping chair forward as a shadow fell on my face and temporarily blocked my view of the small beach twenty feet ahead of me. Kirsty was busying herself with domestic chores, which today entailed laundry, and constructing a makeshift washing line, extending from the campervan mirror to a nearby tree, which unfortunately ran directly in front of me.

Our anticipated leisurely ten minute drive to the ferry port at Wellington that morning had turned into a somewhat panicked journey, as we'd been unable to locate the correct highway exit, even though we could see our boat moored in the distance. Having chosen the wrong junction, we'd found ourselves frantically trying to decipher various map apps on our phones, with the 8am check-in deadline drawing every nearer. Luckily, we were joined in the scrubby layby we'd stopped at by a white-van-man answering his phone. I tapped on the window and explained our predicament to a young Bruce Forsyth lookalike with a tight man-bun. He scratched his ski-slope chin and considered how to direct us. It seemed we weren't being totally daft in our direction finding, as he shook his head.

"Nah, it's not easy. Think it's best if you follow me."

I jumped back in the campervan and he sped off, with John Andrew's ancient engine struggling to keep pace. Five minutes, and a number of high speed moving violations later, he bade us farewell with a wave and a horn blast, on the roundabout at the entrance to the ferry port.

Our boat seemed way too small to accommodate the six hundred or so cars and campervans queuing on the quayside, but onboarding was carried out with typical Kiwi efficiency and we departed on time at 9am for the three hour, sixty mile crossing of the Cook Strait. We had no planned destination in mind on South Island but the explosion of islands and inlets lying just off the northern coast looked intriguing, so upon driving off the ferry, as usual, we decided to just follow the road.

Cowshed Bay was a small site with a sandy beach and a rustic, flyblown drop-toilet, set amidst native bush on Kenepuru Sound. Situated close to the 70km Queen Charlotte 'tramping' track, the site was more popular with overnight camping hikers than campervanners. Luckily, we'd turned up before most of the day's lead-legged arrivals, so secured a prime waterfront pitch.

Once escaped from the shade of Kirsty's makeshift clothes-line, I inserted the Thai USB stick into the port on my laptop and pressed the 'power' button. Accessing the 'Photos' app, I selected the first icon on the list, then screwed up my eyes as I tried to work out what I was actually looking at.

A livid red porcine face, sporting a post-mortem smirk and a fetching Mohican hairstyle. The pig's severed head was resting on a streetside table, accompanied by a selection of meat cuts, all being liberally seasoned by a mix of street dust, fly saliva and diesel fumes. The strange image before me conjured up memories of an equally strange city. Kathmandu, capital of Nepal. Like Timbuktoo, and Shangri-la, Kathmandu is a name which conjures up alluring images of exotica and adventure. A word which has appealed to me since I first span a globe as a small child, and promised myself that one day I would visit the city.

It didn't disappoint in terms of culture shock and strangeness, even though we'd flown in from Varanasi in India, which has to be one of the most 'foreign' cities in the world to Western eyes. Kathmandu was an assault on the senses from the moment we stepped out of the door of our hotel on a main road in Thamel, the town's main traveller enclave. A five minute stroll transported us from a crowded, exhaust choked thoroughfare, filled with honking cars and auto-rickshaws, to a somnolent, cobbled backstreet, with tethered livestock and living conditions akin to the middle ages. It was here that I snapped the image of the unfortunate porker's head, outside a butcher's stall, dyed tikka red and smiling its sinister greeting.

The streets of Kathmandu were filled with wandering sadhu holy men, aging seventies hippies who never went home, and saffron robed child monks, blowing washing-up-liquid bubbles into the prayer flags fluttering above the narrow lanes of the old town. Wandering tiger-balm salesmen in sandals made from old tyres rubbed shoulders with Gore-tex clad Westerners, recovering from an assault on the distant Himalaya, as they perused the selection of rip-off North Face gear on offer in every Thamel store.

The influence of religion is everywhere in Nepal and after a day spent exploring the backstreets and markets around Durbar Square, we headed 5Km out of town to the Pashupatinath Temple, which is one of the holiest sites in the world dedicated to the Hindu God Shiva. The temple's burning ghats are situated on the Bagmati River, the waters of which flow into the holy Ganges, and it's widely believed that being cremated at Pashupatinath guarantees reincarnation in human form, irrespective of the earthly sins of the deceased. Like Varanasi, it therefore attracts terminally ill and elderly Hindus, eager to die in such an auspicious location in order to enjoy a favourable rebirth.

Unlike the burning Ghats at Varanasi, the production line of open-air cremations seemed much more laidback here. At Varanasi, photography was frowned upon, and my attempts at capturing some furtive shots from a derelict building resulted in my being enveloped in pyre smoke, and inhaling the potentially diseased remains being incinerated below me. In Kathmandu, a smattering of tourists wandered freely, and some took photos from what seemed an inappropriately close range. We observed the proceedings from the far bank of the Bagmati, around fifty metres from the funeral ceremonies, along with a large congregation of macaque monkeys who were grazing on assorted debris they'd fished from the murky waters.

Five stone platforms lined the river, onto which a pyre of logs and fast-burning chaff was piled. The corpse arrived on a bamboo stretcher, covered by a saffron shroud and garlanded with marigolds. It was borne by family members who generally seemed unemotional and stoical, though we were told that the wealthiest families often employ professional mourners, paid for their ability to howl with grief at appropriate moments.

The chief male mourner, usually a son or husband, clad in white robes and his head shaved by an attendant priest, turned back the shroud to expose the face of the corpse, onto which was sprinkled rice and flowers. A flaming torch was then applied to the pyre, sending the dear departed relative on their journey towards rebirth.

Watching from the far bank, the public cremation seemed less shocking to us than the general atmosphere around the burning ghats. Mourners mixed with an ensemble of general moochers, and vendors of balloons, bags of toxic coloured drinking water and hunks of roasted chicken on sticks. All were clad in non-typical funeral attire of oversized anoraks, baggy arsed tight-legged suruwal pants, baseball caps and plastic sandals. Small boys chased and play-fought round the legs of the mourners. Old ladies carrying wicker baskets wafted pyre smoke from their faces as they chatted with temple cleaners wielding homemade sweeping brushes. Dogs and pigs snuffled and snorted in the shallows of the river, lapping up the filthy water, rich with the protein of melted human flesh. And everywhere were monkeys. Screeching, wrestling, rifling through rubbish bins, bag snatching or occasionally just watching a group of humans creating their magical fire to reduce one of their number to ash. Eventually two Sadhus ambled over, each toking on a huge spliff, and asked if we wanted to see a miracle.

"Why not?" I responded and the smallest of the dreadlocked holy men led us over to a wooded clearing opposite the main temple complex. His friend, who was the only obese Sadhu I'd ever seen, closed his bright red eyes and slumped on the steps, his beehive of matted dreads bobbing in time with his laboured breathing.

A Canadian couple were already in attendance, having been drawn to witness the miracle by the elderly ascetic, who stood around five feet in height from toe to turban, and weighed about the same as an average American toddler.

Clearly the miracle was a regular occurrence, as the props for the performance were already in place on the scrubby grass, in the form of a small, gnarled stick and a large round boulder. We had no idea what to expect, but it certainly wasn't for the bearded pensioner to remove his dhoti robe to expose a pair of shrivelled testes and a surprisingly elongated penis.

"Oh dear, Keith, I don't think..." the Canadian lady blushed and turned towards her ashen faced husband.

"Please. Lady. Watching please!" With an eye on his fee, the mini miracle worker was keen for no one to miss the show.

I had a small Canon camera at the time, with a video function which allowed you to capture thirty seconds of footage at the expense of about half the total memory card capacity, and I whipped it out and pressed the record button. I revisited that poor quality film on numerous occasions in the following years but never really understood what actually occurred next.

The little holy man rested his loosely rolled joint beside the boulder and picked up the stick, which was around 10cm in length and 1cm wide. He placed it beneath his leathery scrotum and began to twist...and twist...and twist. On the video footage I can clearly be heard groaning and Canadian Keith says 'Oh my God.' With his testicles now wrapped in a knot around the stick, and with Keith and I involuntarily clutching our own undercarriages, the little sadist sadhu took hold of each end of the wood and snapped it with a sickening crack. He then withdrew the two separate, broken segments...and had somehow managed to conceal his scrotal sack within his skeletal body.

"See! Balls gone!" He proclaimed proudly as he lifted his penis to reveal the genitalia of an action man.

"That's great man, really great..." Keith was fumbling in his fanny pouch for some coins and seemed eager to depart.

"No, No. Miracle still awaiting!" It seemed that testicular concealment was merely a warm-up for the main act, and we got an idea of what that might entail as the newly created eunuch relit his spliff and fashioned his loin cloth into a sling, which he began to attach to the large boulder at his feet. The rock probably weighed about 20KG and it seemed unlikely that the little man could raise it with his spindly arms. That was no problem though, as he didn't intend to. On my video, the sound of the old man shouting 'LIFT!' is obscured by Keith and I shouting 'NO!' as we suddenly deduced what the miracle would entail, and presumably why the sadhu's penis was such an impressive length. How a six stone pensioner managed to lift a boulder weighing half his body weight, using only his wrinkled manhood and a loin cloth, and then swing it between his legs is something I still struggle to comprehend. A miracle indeed!

We departed the temple complex down a stone staircase, and halfway along were overtaken by a chattering, hooting troop of two hundred monkeys, on their way to terrorise the inhabitants of a nearby village. Kirsty and I shrank into a rocky recess to allow them to pass, then hurried to the road where we flagged down a tuk-tuk. Our next destination was an appointment with a living Goddess.

The Kumari Ghar in the centre of Kathmandu is the palace home of the Kumari Devi, a child Goddess who is the earthly incarnation of the Goddess Taleju. Selected from the Newari Buddhist community as a toddler, the unfortunate little girl is worshipped by Nepal's Buddhists and Hindus alike, until she reaches puberty. Upon the day of her first menstrual flow, her time as a goddess ends, and the search for a new Kumari Devi begins.

Five senior Buddhist priests then scour the countryside for a young female child displaying certain physical criteria which include – a neck like a conch shell; a body like a banyan tree; eyelashes like a cow; thighs like a deer; chest like a lion and a voice as clear as a duck's. In the UK, five elderly men door-knocking and asking to examine toddlers for such attributes would no doubt quickly attract the attention of social services, but in Nepal, selection as the new Kumari is the greatest of honours.

Once a suitable child has been identified, she must be tested for signs of serenity and fearlessness, which are not normally qualities we'd associate with a three year old. The test takes place during the Hindu festival of Dashain, and the child is subjected to 'Kalrati' or the Black Night ritual, where 108 buffaloes and goats are sacrificed and decapitated. Their severed heads are impaled on poles and illuminated by flickering candlelight in a courtyard containing an ensemble of drummers and masked dancing men. The little girl is pushed into the melee to gauge her reaction. If she remains calm, she then has to spend a night alone in a room filled with the severed beast heads. If she shows any fear, the spirit of Taleju is clearly not present, and the toddler is sent back to her village, most likely deeply traumatised and made redundant before she's even started school. If, however, the child shrugs and asks when she can watch Peppa Pig, she has one final test to pass. She must be able to identify the belongings of the previous Kumari from an assortment of objects laid out before her. As the previous incumbent was a thirteen year old girl, that's probably easy enough, if there are some Korean boyband CD's, cheap make-up and rip-off Adidas trainers scattered amongst a pile of dusty religious artefacts.

Final test passed, the little girl undergoes a tantric purification ceremony, says goodbye to her family and walks along a length of white cloth into the Kumari Ghar palace to begin her new life. The next time her feet touch the ground will be when she begins puberty and the spirit of Taleju leaves her body. For the next ten years or so, she will only dress in elaborate red and gold costumes and have her face made-up like a 1970's barmaid. She'll wear thick mascara, bright lipstick and have a large Agni Chasku or 'fire eye' painted on her forehead, as a symbol of her powers of perception and wisdom.

Unfortunately for Kirsty and I, the Kumari Devi's schedule isn't as predictable as, say, the Pope's regular Wednesday audience. Crowds gather below the Goddess's window in Kumari Chowk, the courtyard of the palace, in the hope of catching a fleeting glimpse of her. The child's actions are closely monitored, and can be accurately interpreted for onlookers by resident Kumari pundits. If she cries or laughs out loud, serious illness or death is imminent for the beholders. If she rubs her eyes, again, it means imminent death. If she trembles in your presence, it means you're going to be imprisoned. If she picks unenthusiastically at offerings, you're destined to suffer catastrophic financial losses. If, however, the small child sits still, impassive and silent, as small children never do, it means your wishes will be granted.

We were therefore somewhat nervous as we gathered in the small, cobbled courtyard with a handful of locals and a smattering of Western tourists. Signs told us that on no account should we attempt to take photos of the Kumari, should she appear. I was beginning to think that our general bad luck in witnessing unpredictable natural phenomenon was going to be replicated with sacred beings, when the red velvet curtain in a small window above us twitched. A ripple of excitement and anticipation amongst the Nepalese onlookers was palpable, and there was an audible gasp as a little face appeared in the open window frame. Eight or nine years old, face beautifully painted and wearing an ornate traditional outfit, she regarded us as a child might observe an amusing monkey in a cage. The locals bowed, and we shifted uneasily, unsure how to greet a child Goddess. She seemed to be distracted by something in the room behind her and kept ducking back behind the curtain. Maybe she was receiving Facebook notifications, or an attendant was asking if she wanted Turkey Twizzlers for lunch, but it was clear we were but a minor diversion in her schedule. I looked for signs of tears or laughter but thankfully found neither, as she maintained an enigmatic 'Mona Lisa' style smirk.

She looked at us, and we looked at her, unsure what the correct protocol was, but the locals seemed delighted that she hadn't shown any sort of emotion which would surely condemn them to a terrible fate. Eager to break the impasse, I stealthily sidled to the back of the small crowd, which caught the Kumari's attention. Our eyes met, and I did what I usually do to small children who stare at me in public places. I went cross-eyed and stuck my tongue out. The goddess seemed taken aback. It was highly unlikely anyone had ever reacted in this way to her before, and I wondered if she was about to cry. I was forgetting though, that this was a kid who'd spent a night alone in a room full of severed beast's heads, so a bit of face pulling was unlikely to faze her. She ducked momentarily behind the curtain, then reappeared, looked me in the eye and poked out her own tongue for a second, then disappeared.

There was a momentary silence from the Nepalese worshippers, then an explosion of chattered debate, accompanied by shaking of heads and waving of arms. The Kumari had displayed her tongue. This was clearly a sign, but of what? Brows were furrowed and heads scratched, and it was clear that advice would need to be sought from a senior Kumari expert. Kirsty cast me a suspicious glance and I shrugged. Kids eh?

On our last night in town, we conducted our usual tour of the many lively bars in the Thamel area, and returned to a small restaurant where, on our first night, I'd enjoyed the best burger I'd ever eaten – a four-inch thick patty of hand reared yak beef, char grilled to pink, juicy perfection. Kirsty had opted for chicken on our first visit and had watched, salivating, as I'd gorged myself on neighbouring Tibet's national beast, and she insisted we return so she could indulge in her own carnivorous frenzy.

Having had our fill of yak meat, we chanced upon a sidestreet bar with logs burning in a courtyard brazier and settled down, wrapped in blankets against the chill November evening air, to enjoy a few bottles of the local Gorkha beer. Last stop of the night was the legendary Rum Doodle bar, one of the most famous bars in Asia. Named after a 1956 novel, the Ascent of Rum Doodle, the bar is an important staging post for those en-route to, and from, the Himalayas. Dinner used to be free for anyone who had climbed Everest, but with almost a thousand people a year now summiting the world's highest peak, I'm guessing this impressive offer may have been replaced with half a lager!

The bar was crowded, cozy and warm and the walls were filled with climbing memorabilia and photos of bearded mountaineers hoisting flags on distant snowy peaks. Kirsty and I tried to blend in at the bar, but felt like frauds amongst the trekking-tale-swapping, gore-tex-clad climbing crowd. I was dreading some rugged explorer asking me what my highest peak was, and having to admit to the towering 736 metre hill of Whernside in the Yorkshire Dales!

A rumbling, overfull stomach didn't make for a restful sleep that night and may have contributed to dreams of chanting monkeys in top hats carrying a burning coffin, and the Kumari Devi crying because I wouldn't buy her an ice cream.

I awoke at dawn with a start. Kirsty was still sleeping soundly beside me, so obviously I woke her up.

"Did you hear that?"

"Hear what?" She grumbled, then turned over when I admitted I didn't even know what it was that had woken me.

I dozed, fitfully, until I was roused by what sounded like a football crowd celebrating a goal. A sudden, loud eruption of roaring, then silence. I sat upright.

"You must have heard that!"

"I was fast asleep until you woke me again." Kirsty groaned. "What was it?"

"People cheering maybe. Like a crowd roaring."

I checked the bedside clock. It was 8am on a Sunday morning. Our hotel was on a quiet road leading to the university, with our room facing peaceful gardens to the rear. I looked out but saw no signs of life, except for an ancient gardener sweeping leaves. I sniffed the air and detected the faint scent of smoke from his fire.

I returned to bed and lay awake for a few minutes before drifting back to sleep. Ten minutes later I was awake again, and this time so was Kirsty, as another disembodied roar shattered the peace and sent birds clattering skywards from the trees outside our window.

"There must be a sports ground nearby," Kirsty reasoned as we got up to begin packing our bags for a flight to Delhi, but agreed it was a strange time to be playing football. We showered, then headed downstairs for breakfast. As we reached the hotel lobby, an old concierge with a tattered army cap gave us a bright smile and a 'Namaste' greeting. His grinning, ever cheerful appearance suggested a man who, in times past, might have trimmed his neat moustache during an artillery bombardment. He was clutching a broom and sweeping broken glass into a dustpan held by a crouching teenage girl. It was only when I looked beyond him that

I realised there was no longer any glass in the hotel's double doors, and diesel-tinged black smoke was drifting across reception. The old man saluted and stood aside as I crunched through the broken glass to thrust my head through the doors to look into the street.

My attention was first drawn to the charred skeleton of an upturned yellow auto-rickshaw which was smouldering, thirty feet along the road. Two ancient police wagons were parked alongside a platoon of sweating officers, who were drinking from bottles of water and peeling off layers of armoured equipment. As is always the case on the Indian sub-continent, crowds of moustachioed men skulked and stared, and skinny dogs scratched and sniffed. The most shocking element of the post-disorder scene was to be found on the road itself. Hundreds and hundreds of half bricks were scattered along the street, as far as the eye could see. We use the phrase 'half-brick' loosely to describe any large stone, but these objects were literally house bricks, carefully broken in half, in order to fashion the perfect projectile for lobbing at the police. It had clearly been a missile barrage of frightening intensity.

I turned to the old doorman, with a perplexed expression which removed the need for my obvious question.

"Riot sir!" He smiled proudly.

"But...Who? Why? It's Sunday morning." I stammered.

"Stooodents sir. From university, you see." He waggled his head happily, as if that explained everything. It didn't.

"But why would they get up at eight on a Sunday morning to have a riot?" I could only imagine this happening in Britain if the rioters were on their way home from the night before.

"Because stooodents is studying in week sir. Sunday is day off. So is good for rioting today." The little girl wielding the dustpan nodded her confirmation.

"You will be having breakfast sir?" The old man waved us towards the dining room, and we wandered in for our chai and banana pancakes, still none the wiser.

I asked our waiter and the lady on reception what the riot was about, and whether it was a weekly occurrence, but they just smiled and shrugged. Obviously one of those stupid questions that tourists ask, and you just need to humour them.

So we never found out what had happened, or why, and in a way that felt quite appropriate for Kathmandu. It's one of those places which is shrouded in an air of eternal mystery, and finding out the answers would only spoil it.

Van Life

Day 27 -Queenstown, New Zealand

I 've spent significant periods of my life being wet. I'm from Yorkshire and I do a lot of walking. I also followed my football team around decaying stadiums with open terraces in the 1980's, so being damp and cold comes with the territory. But this was a different kind of wet. The kind which soaks through every layer of clothing, with chilled rivulets of liquid trickling into hidden bodily recesses you weren't even aware of. Feet squelching in soaked socks, T-shirt sticking to your back, even though it's beneath a fleece and a supposedly waterproof coat. Droplets of water tickling their way through your hair, before coming to rest in your ear, or tracing a route down your forehead, to make you blink as they drip into your eye.

To my left, a 300-foot-drop waterfall cascaded down a sheer cliff face, its spray merging with the unrelenting rain to make us feel that we were hiking through a car wash. Not surprisingly, Kirsty and I were the only people walking along the Waiho Valley floor leading to the Franz Josef Glacier on New Zealand's South Island. The region had been battered by unseasonal summer storms for the previous 24 hours, which saw roads closed, landslides, trees felled and homes left without power. We'd managed to locate a campsite with welcome hot showers and the first hair dryer Kirsty had seen in almost a month! Franz Josef village may have been rustically appealing in the sunshine, but with grey skies and rain lashed streets, it didn't warrant a stay of more than two nights, so after arriving the previous afternoon, it was now or never to hike to the glacier.

When formed in the last Ice Age, the glacial mass extended all the way to the Tasman sea, but after many millenia of slow retreat, it was now located 19km inland, at the head of a rocky canyon in Tai Poutini National Park. Three quarters of a million people visited the glacier each year, with many paying $600NZ for a helicopter ride and hike on the glacier. We decided that a two hour walk to within 500 metres of the ice flow would be more appropriate for our budget, which was just as well, as there was no way any choppers would be getting airborne in the terrible conditions.

We saw one other couple during our soggy march - a pair of bedraggled Koreans trudging glumly back towards the car park. The mountaintops were shrouded in thick grey cloud and after witnessing the expressions on the faces of the rain soaked couple, we wondered if our reward for a two hour hosing down would be limited to a view of a blanket of swirling mist.

We ploughed on with heads down, and just as my skin seemed to be losing its water repellent quality and adopting a sponge-like texture, we rounded a large boulder on the rocky path, and the cloud cleared to reveal the glacier spilling through a gap in the rockface ahead. Soaked by the deluge and under a glowering black sky, the ice flow glowed a strange aquatic blue, like a giant cup of spilled slush-drink dripping down the mountain.

In all the promotional photos I'd seen of grinning tourists stood before the glacier, there was always a large crowd in the background as Pablo flashed a 'V' for victory, or Viktoria and Natasha leapt in unison as the camera clicked. But today, there was only me and Kirsty. And a life-sized cardboard park ranger informing us of how unstable the ice sheet was, especially after heavy rain. Also, that tourists had been killed here by falling rocks and drowning in the river during flash floods. On another day, with no one there but us, I may have been tempted to cover the final half kilometre, to say I'd actually walked on the ice. Today though, with the rain falling in sheets, the river a raging torrent, and distant thunder and a howling wind echoing along the valley, the threat posed in such an isolated environment was easy to appreciate. We grabbed some rare, crowd-free photos, wrung out our socks, and set off for a two-hour hike back to the village.

One of the downsides of 'Van Life' is that if the sun isn't shining, with limited space in your vehicle there's little to no chance of drying out wet clothes. And ours were literally dripping. While Kirsty headed to the shower to reacquaint herself with electricity and a hair dryer, I heaved the sopping mass of anoraks and clothing layers into a bin liner, and headed to the village laundrette to make use of their tumble dryer. Upon arrival it was clear that we weren't the only campervan travellers in town who'd experienced a good soaking, and most of the dryer drums were spinning, as bedraggled foreigners made use of the strong Wifi signal extending from the bar next door.

As I slopped our clothes into a vacant machine, I caught sight of the laptop screen of a mid-twenties girl with blonde pigtails. She was uploading a Facebook photo of herself in front of a lake of such ridiculous blue luminosity that I assumed she must have photo-shopped it. Mesmerised by the image, I kept staring over her shoulder, as she flicked onto the next photo, showing the same lake, then the next – a different angle, but the same extreme swimming pool blue, backed by a soaring mountain range. She obviously sensed me looming behind her and turned to catch me Peeping-Tomming her photo stream.

"That looks amazing. Is it here?" I asked sheepishly.

"Maybe five hours from here, it's in the centre of South Island," she smiled, "but I can't remember its name. Begins with a 'P'. My friend will remember."

I'd correctly guessed by her accented, but perfect English, that she was Dutch. Lieke and her friend Eva were heading in the opposite direction to us, so when Eva returned from the supermarket, we spent a useful half-hour exchanging campervan tales and recommendations of where to go and what to see. The brilliant blue lake was called Pukaki, and once Lieke had convinced me there was no photoshopping involved, I tapped the name into my phone and added it to our itinerary for the coming week.

Our next intended stop was the self-proclaimed world capital of adventure sports, Queenstown, but as often happens on an unplanned roadtrip, we chanced upon a deserted freedom-camping site on the shores of another picture-postcard lake, backed by more snow-capped mountain peaks. This was Lake Wanaka, with wind-whipped whitecaps lashing a stony beach, carpeted with a layer of dry driftwood which caused my pyromaniac eyes to light up. A perfect spot for a beach bonfire drove our decision on where we'd be spending the night.

For me, this was the kind of place I'd dreamt of when planning our New Zealand adventure. Wild and remote, early evening sun still shining but with a chill breeze requiring three layers until the fire was lit, and foaming waves rolling in from a shade-shifting lake backed by soaring, cloud shrouded peaks. Previous overnighters had constructed a pebble and driftwood bivouac on the beach, which sheltered our barbecue from the wind and the predatory weka birds, from which constant vigilance was needed to protect our food. The size of a chicken, these flightless scavengers haunt New Zealand's campsites and will steal anything not nailed down. We heard tales of sunglasses, shoes, watches and underwear being pilfered from unwary campers. The birds we encountered seemed more food focused though, with one, seemingly unaware that it was supposedly omnivorous, tugging a string of sausages from the flaming barbecue.

I'd already carried out the important task of stick foraging and fire pit construction while Kirsty fended off avian invaders around the campervan, so as the sun set over the Buchanan Peaks on the far side of the lake, and the temperature dipped, I sparked up the fire.

Sleeping on a makeshift bed in a ten-year-old Mazda campervan, eating a daily meal consisting of a rotation of different barbecued meats, and not knowing where you're going each day until you arrive there, isn't for everyone. Emptying toilet cartridges and filling water tanks from dribbling taps in the pouring rain would feel like a holiday from hell to many. But for me, the privations you experience when camping are far outweighed by opportunities to experience nature at its most majestic, and in the absence of any other humans. As had happened many times previously, particularly on Scandinavian campervan adventures, our night around the campfire at Lake Wanaka became a long one. An inexhaustible supply of dry driftwood, a full fridge of beer and an effective shelter against the wind was a perfect combination, leading to a memorable late night.

The next morning dawned bright and we swapped our usual leisurely breakfast for a fast-track coffee and a banana each. We only had a 60km drive to Queenstown, but I'd already decided we'd be going the scenic way - via the Crown Range Road. This steep, winding route climbs from the village of Arrowton to the 1076 metre Crown Saddle, the highest paved road point in New Zealand, before descending to the town which bills itself the country's adrenaline sports capital. There was an alternative route along Highway 6, down the west coast of Lake Dunstan which would undoubtably be quicker, but the Crown Range Road is widely viewed as one of New Zealand's most scenic drives. We were aware that it regularly closed in winter due to snow and ice, but with the sun shining on an early summers day it seemed the obvious route to take.

A deserted, straight road through coniferous woodland led us out of the small town of Wanaka, and for twenty kilometres or so, John Andrew was cruising. With the windows down and the sun shining, local radio segued from Tom Petty's Freefalling to the Wichita Lineman, before Glen Campbell's Mid-Western drawl was replaced by Steve Nicks, sounding like a chain smoking angel on Dreams, and van life couldn't get much better. Slowly we began to ascend and the upward bends in the road became more pronounced. The campervan had five gears, but it wasn't long before fifth was a distant memory. We maintained a steady speed in fourth for less than five minutes, before more severe switchbacks and a sudden increase in gradient dropped us to third, then second in the space of a few minutes. We'd now arrived at the steepest section of road, with spectacular views of the Crown Range stretching to infinity beyond a steep drop to our right, and John Andrew began to feel the effects of the sudden increase in altitude. Like an aging marathon runner hitting the 'wall', the old Mazda suddenly seemed to be experiencing the delayed impact of every one of the 300,000 miles it had clocked up over the years. The drop from chugging third to screaming second hadn't increased our speed much beyond 15MPH and I winced at a growing tail of cars building behind us. Rounding every bend, I prayed for a levelling out of the route ahead, but instead all I saw was a serpentine strip of asphalt heading ever upwards.

I was dreading the drop to first gear as I knew there was nowhere to go from there, but when John Andrew had a diesel-fuelled coughing fit at 10MPH and threatened to chug to a standstill, I knew we were at the point of no return and rammed the gear stick forward. A strange calm descended as we struggled onwards in first, with the speedometer stuck at its minimum recordable speed, and to a soundtrack of John Andrew's engine screaming in protest at being forced to climb a mountain. An occasional driver was confident enough to leave the traffic jam behind us, to fly past on a blind bend, horn sounding, and hand raised through the driver's window, gesticulating to indicate how he thought I spent my spare time.

Blowing up the engine of a rental vehicle may seem like a relatively minor issue when you have full insurance, but the concern for us was the knowledge that the company we'd used had a limited supply of vehicles, and it was the busiest time of year. If we killed John Andrew, it was highly unlikely they'd provide us with a replacement to similarly abuse, and our trip would become one of rental cars and expensive last-ditch motel rooms. Therefore, every second we spent listening to John Andrew's engine screeching in protest as we crawled up that mountain, felt to us like hearing a sackful of puppies being tortured. We resorted to turning the radio volume up to mask the noise, and tried to focus on the breathtaking mountain scenery as we struggled to keep ahead of two cyclists who were rapidly gaining ground on us as we approached the Crown Saddle.

A much-needed reduction in incline allowed us to pull away from the bikes and we began to gain speed to the point that I was almost contemplating the heady heights of second gear, when I saw a car indicating left at a sharp turn ahead, and spotted the most welcome oasis imaginable - a pull-in off the road which was the Crown Saddle Lookout point. Never has a scrubby mountain car park looked so inviting, and John Andrew bunny-hopped his way in, to a fanfare of car-horns from the dozen or so vehicles which had trailed in our wake for the last twenty minutes. The view from here, across the Crown Range and distant Lake Wakatipu to Queenstown's high rises glistening in the sun, was something to behold. As, unfortunately, was John Andrew's temperature gauge, now sitting dangerously in the red zone, as indicated by a fan whirring like chopper blades and the unmistakable smell of electrical burning. We felt it best to let the campervan recover while we had a short hike on the saddle. It was all downhill from then on, though throughout our free-wheeling descent, all I could think of was that there was no way we could put John Andrew through that ordeal again. It would be Highway 6 for the old timer on the return leg!

Driving in a city again was a shock to the system after a period in the wild, though Queenstown had more of a feel of a large, upmarket lakeside holiday resort than a metropolis. Our guidebook described the town as 'one of the most beautiful and dramatic natural scenes in the country, with a cosmopolitan dining and arts scene, fine vineyards, a diverse range of bars and enough outdoor pursuits to keep the adrenaline pumping from dawn to dusk. It's unique, and it knows it.' Further research suggested that the town's self-confidence in its ability to pull in the tourists could often manifest itself as arrogance and a take-it-or-leave-it attitude. With that in mind, plus a lack of campsites within the city boundaries, we'd reserved a pitch at the only viable option which would allow us to walk into town and back. Unfortunately for us, it came at a cost of $70 NZD, which was significantly more than the $5-$10 we'd been paying when wild camping. We were assured though that this site offered spacious shared kitchen and bathroom facilities for campers, coin operated barbecues, a kids playground, free Wifi, TV Lounge and lake views from large campervan pitches. Thinking it would be nice to again acquaint ourselves with the delights of a hot shower, though not a TV lounge, we decided to treat ourselves.

The site also boasted holiday cabins and 'tourist studios', and the reception exuded the air of a recently refurbished Travel Lodge, as I passed a family of untypically overweight, baseball cap clad Kiwis, who'd just received the keys to their lakeview cabin. Hoping I'd be around to see fat Dad attempt a bungee jump in the town where it was invented, I strolled to the front desk and provided my details to a no-nonsense, middle-aged woman with a tobacco-tinged, brutalist blonde bob. She thrust a sheaf of glossy promo leaflets towards me and made me sign a copy of the comprehensive site rules. I was also given two coloured wrist bands to identify Kirsty and I as 'powered campers'. (That related to the electrical status of our pitch, rather than our level of social influence). I was also given an allocated pitch number, which is never welcome. It's always preferable to be able to have a drive around and pick your own spot – A little shade, but also some late afternoon sun; avoiding the family with four screaming kids and the single bloke with a mullet and too-short shorts parked next to them; well away from the toilet dump point.

On this occasion though we'd been told we were on pitch 37, so we crawled a jerky John Andrew around the site, with the incumbent campers all indulging in the well-established ritual of sussing out the newcomers. The even numbered pitches were clearly marked, and we passed 36 and 38 without seeing anything in between, then drew a blank on the row behind, which comprised of numbers in the 80's. The site was already almost full, and we were unable to see any spare pitches as we circled for a second time. I got out between two large motorhomes which were occupying the gravel spaces signposted as numbers 36 and 38. In between was a thin slither of scrubby grass, measuring about three metres across, upon which the occupants of pitch 36 were drying wetsuits on a rack. An elderly woman with cropped purple hair and spindle legs was sat in a camping chair beside a motorhome in the opposite row, and, spotting me scratching my head in puzzlement, she limped over to assist.

"What number?" she asked, with a knowing semi-smirk.

"Thirty Seven. I can't find it."

"Yeah. Well, there it is." She nodded to the small grassy gap with ill-disguised disdain. "They must be full. It's what they do."

"What? They want us to park here?" I looked at the space and calculated that if we opened our door at the same time as our neighbours, we could visit them without going outside.

"Yep. That's what they do. Squeeze small campervans in between the pitches when it's busy." She shrugged. "There's nowhere else in town. Take it or leave it I guess..."

At that point, my mindset was to leave it, and Kirsty rolled her eyes as I shook my head and strode purposefully back towards reception, while letting everyone know that "I'm not paying thirty five quid for this."

"It's all we've got. The site's full. Take it or leave it." The lady with the cig-stained hair chewed gum noisily and gave me a critical once-over while shaking her head.

The potential for hacking off my nose to spite my face is ever present in situations like this, and Kirsty was no doubt expecting me to reappear and say we were leaving town immediately. However, two factors curtailed my normal dummy-spitting performance. First, I was informed that leaving would constitute a late cancellation, and I would forfeit half the cost of the pitch anyway. Then, just as I was whipping myself into a frenzy of injustice about that, a pretty girl in her mid-twenties with a tanned, smiling face appeared from a doorway behind reception.

"Hey, where you from?" Her accent was unmistakably northern English.

"Leeds." I grunted, immediately hostile to her campsite logoed polo shirt.

"Oh wow, I thought so, I'm from Halifax!" She grinned, and bounded up to the desk beside her scowling colleague. "I can take over if you want to go for lunch Diane?"

Diane curled her lip and her piggy eyes flicked around my facial features, with an expression which suggested I'd suffered a sudden smallpox infection. She then slowly slid the bookings folder over to her colleague, who introduced herself as Emily. The fact that I lived less than twenty miles from the hometown she'd been away from for nearly a year, seemed to suddenly elevate me several levels from the gutter Diane had relegated me to.

"How big's your van?" Emily enquired while perusing the site plan before her, and grimaced slightly when I said 5 metres.

"Hmmm, small van you see. When it's busy we have to put them on the grass." She glanced over her shoulder then leant forward conspiratorially.

"Are you sure it's not nearly 6 metres?" She nodded very slightly as she said this, and I took the hint.

"Actually yes, now you mention it, I think the exact length is 5.9 metres."

"Ok, that's more or less 6 metres so we can't put you on the grass...let's have a look." She ran her finger across the laminated page and stopped on a single unshaded square within a sea of colour coding which clearly denoted 'occupied'.

"Here's one we keep spare for emergencies. It's out of the way, and a bit of a view over the lake." She smiled and gave me a wink as she changed the pitch number on our booking. "Enjoy Queenstown!"

We did enjoy the town, which was undeniably picturesque, sitting on the lake at the foot of the dramatic Southern Alps. The closest we got to extreme sports however, was watching backpackers hurl themselves off the Kawarau bridge into a 150 foot river gorge, while attached to a piece of elasticated rope. This was the original bungee jump – the first commercial site for the activity in the world, set up in 1988 by Kiwi entrepreneur AJ Hackett. Using a long zoom lens on my Nikon, I was able to capture the faces of the kids who'd paid $200NZD for the privilege of free-falling into the abyss, and, with the correct cord length, plunging their head into the icy waters of the Kawarau River. The bungee cord's eighty foot recoil then sent them soaring skywards, before a continuous repeat sequence saw them bobbing around beneath the bridge like a human yoyo.

The jumpers' demeanour ranged from cocksure youths who leapt from the bridge backwards or with arm extended and fist clenched, Superman style; to an oriental girl who seemed to pass out as she jumped, then to bounce around beneath the bridge, seemingly lifeless for a worrying length of time. My photographic highlight though, was a bare-chested youth in camouflage board shorts who may have had a couple of bottles of Speight's Pilsner for Dutch courage, and whose recoil ascent was accompanied by twin 'vapour trails' of liquid. One was river water from his freshly dipped head. The second appeared as a faint golden arc from the leg of his shorts and seemed to prove the importance of the old adage -Don't drink and dive.

The next morning as were pulling away from our spacious pitch, we passed Diane, who was ticking off another camper for not adhering to the over-complex recycling system rules. Kirsty cringed as I predictably sounded the horn as we passed, and gave her a cheery wave. Diane flicked her smoke-stained bob and stared and scowled but didn't respond, clearly having learned the lesson that Queenstown may be unique, and it knows it, but it's no match for the clan loyalties of the Yorkshire mafia!

Poltergeist

 I see dead people. It's a 'gift' I inherited from my mother. "Do you ever see the faces?" she once asked me, knowing that, like her, I had an interest in the paranormal. At that point, I was in my twenties and had no idea what she meant.

"They come when you're in bed. I wake up and they're floating above me." She shuddered as she told me this. "I pull the covers over my head. They scare me."

My mother always fully believed in some form of after-life, that there's something more after we depart this world. As teenagers, she and her sisters used to view 'going to the spirits' in the same vein as a trip to the cinema, as they took a bus to a spiritualist church on a Sunday night. There they watched resident mediums become the earthbound channel of the dead, to pass on messages to loved ones in the congregation. If they were lucky, someone would speak in tongues, or adopt the persona of a visiting spirit, perhaps causing a well-dressed clairvoyant lady to utter expletives in the gruff tones of a belligerent navvy. Later my mum visited a succession of clairvoyants for one-to-one sittings. Always alert to charlatans, she only visited mediums who took no details from callers, and was careful to give nothing away as they probed with their hopefully ambiguous suggestions...'Do you know anyone called Jim?' 'What about an old man with a bald head?'

Nevertheless, my mother had experiences which couldn't be explained. A couple of clairvoyants in particular told her things that they could only have known via use of phone taps, 24 hours surveillance and a large team of genealogists. All were unlikely given that these sessions were paid for with a couple of quid from her housekeeping allowance.

A few years before she died, a medium told my mother something she'd already guessed. That she had 'the gift,' and was herself clairvoyant. She urged my mum to go the spiritualist church to develop her talent in a safe and controlled way. The offer was declined. My mum had taken comfort from some of the messages she'd received, but had no desire to become a receiver of spirit chatter herself. And those night time faces hinted at a dark element of the afterlife she had no wish to explore.

I was probably in my mid-thirties when my own nocturnal experiences began. Occasionally it was the faces my mother mentioned, but for me, they were ill defined. She could see facial features, but my visitors manifested only as a shape hanging above me. More often, it was a dark figure, standing at the end of the bed watching me, or occasionally, crouching in the corner of the room like a malevolent dwarf.

If my mother's fight or flight response was to hide under the bed clothes, mine was, and remains the exact opposite. I instinctively attack the dark shape which has appeared before me as I awake. I propel myself towards the entity, punching out and emitting a blood curdling cry. This has the obvious effect of terrifying Kirsty, especially on one occasion when we were in a tent in an otherwise silent Malawian safari camp. On that night, I awoke in the night to see the silhouette of a tall, slender man standing at the end of the bed, observing us as we slept. As usual, I told myself that the figure wasn't real beyond my imagination. I closed my eyes and opened them again, but he was still there, standing and watching us. Instinctively, I flew forward, throwing punches at thin air and roaring expletives. As is also usual, and unsurprising, Kirsty was violently jolted from her sleep by the disturbance in the room and her screams of terror added to my roars of aggression. After she'd convinced me that the figure wasn't real, I collapsed into bed, panting and with my heart beating like a tribal drum. It didn't take long for the impact of my visitation to filter through the silent camp. Our tent was illuminated by the beams of multiple flashlights and we heard the hushed, urgent tones of guards and safari guides and the snuffling of dogs, as they nervously tried to trace the source of the noise, which they unsurprisingly interpreted as a wild animal attack on a guest.

It's therefore likely that I've inherited an element of my mother's 'gift', and I was reminded of that fact as I looked at the image on my laptop screen of a twenty-something blonde woman in a fetching maritime-style outfit of navy shorts and stripy top. The fashions and slightly bouffant hair-do, plus a low-resolution, scanned image, hint at the late 1980's, and the sign on the wooden structure behind her reads 'Hog's Breath Inn.' The young woman is my ex-partner Karen, and she's standing outside the bar in Carmel, Northern California, owned by the then mayor of the small town, Clint Eastwood. It wasn't Dirty Harry who sprang to mind upon seeing the photo again after around thirty years though. Nor was it the quaint village of wooden cottages, art galleries, crashing surf and white sands. My immediate memory was of a night's sleep ruined by that mischievous, childish prankster of the spirit world, the poltergeist.

The word is derived from the German 'Poltern', meaning to rumble or make noise and 'Geist' or ghost, so the literal meaning is a noisy ghost, and the one I encountered in Carmel certainly lived up to its name.

It was 1990 and we'd arrived in the coastal village by rental car, having driven up the legendary Pacific Coast Highway from Los Angeles, heading to Santa Cruz and San Francisco. We checked into a clapboard guest house in the village centre, and were allocated a green painted wooden cottage in the cypress-fir shaded grounds. It was late afternoon when we arrived, so we dropped our bags and headed out to explore. There was a chill in the late September air, and by 7pm, we'd retreated indoors to a cosy bar filled with chattering locals and a smattering of tourists, and the first log fire of the Fall. 'Craft Beer' is ubiquitous throughout the world now, but thirty years ago, you struggled to get anything more interesting than Budweiser or Michelob in most American bars. Northern California was different, even back then. The Anchor Brewing company had produced their famous Steam Beer since 1896 and this deep, amber ale with a foaming head was a welcome respite from tasteless, gassy lager. Noting my choice at the bar, the locals proceeded to tell me that Steam Beer was actually crap, and recommended a succession of microbrewery ales which the bar sold on tap. It seemed that producing anything under 5% alcohol content was forbidden in Northern California, and I was soon swilling lethally potent pints while Karen wisely stuck to Michelob.

After a few hours of sampling the local brews, we headed to the Hog's Breath for a burger, where we were told we'd missed Clint, who'd called earlier but had gone home, presumably to feed his monkey. I was feeling the effects of my evening's exploration of the local brews, so we decided to head back to the Guest House at around 10pm. That's when the paranormal fun and games began. I awoke about an hour after retiring, to find Karen sleeping soundly beside me and all the room lights turned on. Assuming Karen had got up to use the bathroom, as the American's say, and left them on, I got up, turned everything off and got back into bed, giving Karen a poke in reprisal as I did so. I turned over, and, feeling the sedative effects of the alcohol, quickly fell back to sleep. Half an hour later, I was awake again, roused from my slumber by the light from a bedside lamp shining in my face. It seemed Karen had got up again, and left the bathroom light on, and apparently felt it necessary to also turn on the lamp.

"What are you doing?" I huffed and puffed as I dragged myself up again to turn off the bathroom light.

"Who doing what?" Karen mumbled and turned over.

An hour later, I awoke again and sat upright in bed. Again, the room lights were on, as was the bathroom light. Now I could hear running water. I poked my head round the bathroom door to see both of the sink taps open and water flowing freely into the basin.

"Karen... Karen.... Karen!!" I raised my voice in response to her continued snoozing.

"What?! What are you doing?" She sat up, bleary eyed and disorientated.

"Did you turn the taps on?"

"What taps? What's the matter with you? Stop waking me up!" She snarled and pulled the pillow over her head, leaving me in no doubt that she was denying any involvement in the disturbances.

I screwed the taps closed as tightly as I could, checked that the outside door was locked, then turned off the bathroom and room lights and got back into bed. I surveyed the room, and resisted the urge to look under the bed before I turned off the bedside lamp.

I lay in the darkness, waiting for something to happen, but all I could hear were the footsteps of the occupants of the room above us. It seemed they'd had a long night in Carmel's bars and were stomping around without having removed their shoes. Just what I need, I thought. I'll never get to sleep now.

It seemed like minutes later but checking my watch told me I'd been asleep for another hour. Now I was awake again, and I was able to check my watch as all the lights were on again. Water was again splashing in the sink and the doors of the large double wardrobe opposite the bed were wide open. Right on cue, one of our upstairs neighbours rode a pogo stick to the bathroom. I sat in bed, blinking. Karen was snoring next to me, and it was clear she hadn't stirred since the last episode. I now knew what I was dealing with, and my mind was flooded with cinematic images of a strange dwarf woman screeching 'stay away from the light Carol-

Anne' as a blonde toddler was tempted towards a flickering TV set by a malevolent spirit. A poltergeist.

Strangely, having read about poltergeists propelling people from their beds and levitating others to float around the ceiling, I wasn't scared. I was bloody annoyed, and tired. I climbed out of bed, turned off the taps, closed the wardrobe doors, and flicked the light switches while muttering 'You aren't frightening me, you're wasting your time. Piss off, you annoying little bastard.' Poltergeists are assumed to be the playful spirits of children, taken too soon, and although I have nothing against kids, (I was even friends with some about forty years ago) dead ones tend to really try my patience in the middle of the night.

Unfortunately, my ticking off obviously didn't work and the cycle of spectral pranks continued throughout the night. Lights on. Taps on. Wardrobe doors open. Drawers open. Curtains open. The most impressive display was the bath taps turned on to a trickle, and the plug inserted in the tub so that 6 inches of water had accumulated by the time my half hourly awakening occurred. Every time I got up, I admonished the playful ghost, to the point that I was goading it to carry out evermore impressive tricks. At 5.30, with the half-light of dawn starting to peep through the spook-opened drapes, Karen sat up in bed and stared in confusion at the scene before her.

All the room lights were on, and water was flowing from all the taps in the bathroom. The wardrobe doors were open and wire coat hangers were strewn across the floor. I was stood, naked and wild eyed, grinning and wagging my finger towards the ceiling.

"You think you're clever don't you? Thought your little tricks would scare me didn't you? Well they haven't. You're an annoying little shit. And you're dead!"

"What the hell are you doing?"

I was brought back to the earthly plane by Karen's raised voice.

"Poltergeist." I tried to appear nonchalant, not wanting to give it the satisfaction of knowing it had rattled me.

"What??"

"There's a poltergeist. Little bastard kept me up all night." I lowered my voice, hoping it wouldn't hear me.

Karen gave me a look which suggested I'd said Big Foot had popped in and stolen our complimentary toiletries.

"For God's sake, it's five o'clock in the morning, come back to bed." Karen's head was back beneath the pillow, from where I could still hear her grumbling about my ghost busting antics.

I got back into bed just as the occupants of the room upstairs got up and began assembling some flatpack furniture.

Daylight brought an end to the worst of the disturbances and I slept fitfully till 9am, when I awoke to find a pillow resting on my chest. My spectral playmate had obviously decided to have the last word with a response to my insults, which I interpreted as 'I should have put it on your face.'

Check-out was 10am and we'd decided to skip breakfast and get on the road to Monterey. Karen checked the room and emerged with her bag to find me standing on the gravel path in front of our cottage, looking upwards.

"What now?" She rolled her eyes.

"You heard the people above banging about at 5am didn't you?"

"Mmmm." She followed my gaze upwards to the gabled roof above the door.

"Look. There are no windows. There is no room above ours." I grinned smugly.

"Maybe it's an attic. Perhaps there are racoons or something in the roof void." Karen had dismissed my poltergeist tale and wasn't about to concede any ground to a supernatural theory.

In reception, I left Karen to settle the bill with a twenty-five dollar Thomas Cook travellers cheque, as I perused the visitors' book, which in the early 90's was as close as you got to a Trip Advisor review.

As soon as she turned from the counter Karen could see me waving excitedly.

"Listen to this!" I was brandishing the open visitor's book and began to loudly read out hand-written comments, as I flicked through the pages...'A haunting experience!' said the Anderson family of Lincoln, Nebraska. 'We met your ghost!' was the italic lettered message from Sofie and Roger from Strasbourg.

Karen took the book from me and began turning the pages herself...'A spooky weekend', she read, eyes widening as I smirked triumphantly. 'We never believed in ghosts before we stayed here...' her voice trailed off and she shuddered at the realisation that she'd slept soundly through a poltergeist visitation.

"Let's get out of here!" Bag in hand, Karen was already out of the door and heading to the car, as I followed and glanced back to our room, half expecting to see a small ghostly handed flipping me the finger as a parting gesture.

That was my only experience of a poltergeist, but not my only brush with 'the other side', and on a later occasion, my ghostly visitor made their presence felt more forcefully than their Stateside counterpart. I was visiting the Scottish border town of Dumfries on business, and had spent the night in a large Victorian hotel. My room was on the top floor, and was suitably decorated in period style, with high, wooden, vaulted ceiling and an old fireplace, which now housed an ornamental, brass coal scuttle. The floorboards were of polished mahogany, and the furnishings were all suitably faux antique, in keeping with the 19th century ambience of the building.

It was late May, with the approach of summer meaning fifteen hours of daylight, and I awoke around 5am as a chink of light from the newly risen sun partly illuminated the room. I squinted at my watch and realised it was far too early to get up, so closed my eyes and drifted back towards sleep.

From that ambiguous semi-conscious condition, I slipped further into a somnolent state. I began to dream. I was in bed, and was woken by the door opening. A young girl of around fifteen entered the room, wearing a long nightdress with a ruffle collar. She smiled at me, and had long, wavy, corn coloured hair which tumbled over her shoulders and reached almost to her waist. Surprised at her presence, I sat up. As I did so, she began to giggle, and crouched down at the end of my bed, so I was no longer able to see her, though I could still hear her laughing.

I awoke. The sun's rays were stronger now and I could sense the light in the room increasing through my still-closed eyes. I was laying on my back with my knees bent upwards in a 'V' shape. I thought about the dream I'd just had, and could clearly remember the girl's face and her mischievous smile. It suddenly occurred to me that the room in the dream was the room I was now in. The door the girl had entered through, was the door a few metres in front of me, and the bed I was occupying in the dream was this same bed. Before I could open my eyes to check I was correct, I was slapped, hard on my legs from the right. The blow knocked my upturned knees sideways and instantly electrified my entire body. I'd seen people's hair stand on end in Scooby-Doo, but now I was experiencing it myself. I can only liken the split-second experience to a combination of a mild electric shock and being plunged into an ice bath. Panting and terrified, I leapt out of bed and pulled open the curtains. The daylight streaming into the room was an immediate antidote to the panic which had momentarily consumed me.

It had taken me a while to realise what was happening in my earlier poltergeist experience, but I was now immediately aware of what had happened. I'd been slapped by a ghostly teenager! I had a quick wash without daring to look in the mirror, for fear of who or what may be behind me, threw my clothes into a bag and dashed down the stairs to reception. Unsurprisingly, at 5.30am, it was unmanned, so I avoided potentially embarrassing questions on why I was hurriedly checking out at such an ungodly hour, unshaven and without contemplating the complimentary Scottish breakfast.

✳✳✳

More than twenty years on I shivered again as I clearly recalled the girl's face, and wondered who she was and why she'd decided to give me such a rude awakening. It was early evening, and the light was fast fading, causing moths and other nocturnal flutterers to begin to bounce off my laptop screen. We were in a perfect location for ghost stories, camping beside an old abandoned hotel in the remote centre of New Zealand's South Island. Described as 'challenging' to reach in a campervan, the remoteness and history of the Lindis Pass Hotel site had appealed as soon as Kirsty and I spotted it on our camping app. Located in the central Otago region and 6km along a rutted dirt track off Highway 8, the hotel was built at the height of New Zealand's gold rush of the 1860's, and served as a base for prospectors, hikers and cross-country travellers, before falling into disrepair in the 1950's.

The stone building now stood as a roofless, single-storey, multi-roomed structure in a lush green meadow by a mountain stream. I love old buildings and entering through the main doorway it was easy to imagine being greeted by a friendly innkeeper, then shown through to the bar where a roaring log fire burned bright, and the evening meal was being prepared on a cooking range. The old fireplace and metal range were still there, but there was little else to provide clues as to what the hotel was like in its heyday. Lighting our barbecue grill in the shadow of the ruins, I couldn't help but wonder who else had taken in the view from this same spot over the last 150 years. I could easily imagine a wild night in the bar, with a bewhiskered old miner ordering drinks all round after a lucky day panning for gold, then sleeping it off under the stars, right where our campervan was now parked. One thing was for sure, with my track record, and unfortunate psychic skills, if there were any ghosts at large here, there was no need to guess who would be the first person they'd decide to rattle their gold pans and shovels at!

E noho rā Aotearoa

Day 41 – Auckland, New Zealand

"Are you sure this is it?" I enquired dubiously of our taxi driver, which is never the best question to find yourself asking as you arrive at an Air B&B rental. We'd just flown back into Auckland from Christchurch at the end of our New Zealand adventure, and were peering through the passenger window of an airport taxi at a scruffy tower block which loomed high above us.

"It's definitely the right address," confirmed our driver. "Looks like a university residence," he observed, viewing the crowds of young people loafing on the steps outside, and coming and going through a set of glass doors decorated with Chinese writing.

"Looks a bit like Grenfell Tower," I muttered as we hauled our bags from the back of the car, fully expecting to have to dodge a TV lobbed from a top floor balcony, then enjoy a ride in a urine soaked lift, in keeping with the stereotypical 1960's UK tower block which our accommodation resembled.

Upon entering the foyer, any thoughts of a high-rise British ghetto were quickly dispelled. This was nothing like England, but was also a totally different demographic to anywhere we'd seen in New Zealand thus far. Two youths of East Asian appearance manned a chaotic reception desk, at which a melee of late teens and early twenties queued in a haphazard scrum, while chattering loudly in the dialects of Hong Kong, Hanoi and Hangzhou. Glancing around, it quickly became apparent that not only were we the only Europeans, we were also the only non-Orientals. We were also older than everyone present by a margin of around 30 years, taller than them by around six inches and we were the only ones carrying large backpacks. Unsurprisingly, one of the reception lads, with pre-pinback Lineker ears and an expression of permanent dread, noticed us hovering at the back of the queue, and beckoned me forward. I brandished my Air B&B booking confirmation, and after a quick glance he disappeared below the desk momentarily, then re-appeared holding a key.

"14th Floor," he stammered, "So sorry for the chaos, it's fresher's week!"

We squeezed into the lift with six kids brandishing newly purchased domestic products and pots of steaming noodles, and selected floor 14. Exiting the lift and entering the corridor was like walking through an East Asian street food market. A fusion of spicy aromas and the sounds of sizzling woks came from behind every door, reminding us that our room was advertised as having its own kitchen, as, clearly, did everyone else's.

The room itself was fine. Small, clean, sparsely furnished and functional, and providing a fantastic view of the identical high-rise block situated fifteen feet away through the only window. A quick glance revealed a bespectacled girl engrossed in some homework on her laptop; two lads sat in bed like Morecambe and Wise, playing an Xbox basketball game; a vaguely sinister scene of a girl ironing while her boyfriend watched from an armchair, and a youth weeping tears of frustration at his failure to assemble some flat-pack furniture. It was like an all-inclusive resort for Peeping Toms.

We had a couple of days in Auckland before flying to Fiji, and while Kirsty unpacked and had a shower, I fired up the laptop in order to sort some of the photos I'd taken on the trip to date. The room began to vibrate as I climbed onto the bed, which made me worry about earthquakes, until I realised the person above was either moving some heavy furniture or dismantling the laminate floor with a pneumatic drill.

I flicked through the photos I'd taken on our trip, and realised I only had a handful from our time in Christchurch. The sad fact was that the earthquakes of 2011 and 2012 had literally ripped the heart out of the city, destroying most of its historic buildings and business district. Forty billion NZ dollars had been spent on a decade of rebuilding, but it still felt like a work in progress, with no defined focal point. There was little in the way of visual stimulation in the city centre, apart from the iconic cathedral with its quake destroyed frontage, and the huge murals painted on the gable ends of buildings adjoining the multitude of vacant lots.

If Christchurch had been something of a photographic let-down, the rest of New Zealand had more than compensated, and some of the images in my photo gallery looked like Microsoft wallpaper rather than snaps taken with my humble Nikon D40, as I flicked through them and relived our adventures of the last few weeks.

From Lindis Pass, we'd acted on the tip-off received from the Dutch girls in the Laundrette at Franz Josef and headed to Lake

Pukaki to satisfy ourselves that their photos really hadn't been due to Photoshop trickery. Reviewing my own photos, it was hard to believe they weren't employing any filters or software magic. The colour of the lake was hard to describe – a perfect aquatic blue, looking like a vast swimming pool backed by soaring mountain peaks. We'd arrived in the early afternoon and secured a prime pitch facing the lake in a quiet gravel car park. However, returning from a walk and swim, we found that John Andrew had already been hemmed in by an invasion of other campervans and motorhomes, and by early evening the parking lot was full to bursting. I'd already undertaken some furtive stick collecting and had identified a secluded lakeside cove which was perfect for constructing a fire pit, so when darkness fell, we'd slipped away from the crowds and enjoyed a secluded evening of beer and bonfire.

From Pukaki, we'd then made our way slowly via a succession of lakes and rivers of pure white glacial water, towards Mount Cook, the highest peak in New Zealand at 3700 metres, and known as Aoraki in Maori. Here, a picturesque gravel parking area, framed by craggy peaks became our home for a couple of nights as we hiked through the Hooker Valley, crossing what looked like fast flowing rivers of milk, via rickety wooden swing bridges, to reach Lake Hooker. Backed by the snow-capped summit of Mount Cook, the lake appeared a shimmering white in the afternoon sunlight, due to the presence of a glacial silt known as rock flour. The surreal colour, plus the presence of several sizeable icebergs, resulted in some stunning photos. The distant rumble of avalanches from Mount Sefton crashing into the Mueller Glacier, and a rocky outcrop adorned with brass memorial plaques to those who had lost their lives on the mountain, had served as a reminder to how untamed this part of New Zealand is.

Eventually, it had been time to bid farewell to our trusty campervan, John Andrew. Before the trip, we had wondered how we'd manage living in a five metre space with no proper washing and toilet facilities, but we both felt a pang of sadness at leaving him at the rental depot to head back to civilisation. We could have easily done a few more weeks, if not months!

I'd enjoyed my time in New Zealand though it wasn't my typical travel destination. The towns felt like a time warp compared to England, without the urban 'edge' I was used to abroad. Affluent, white, safe and photogenic, they seemed like English market towns in the fifties or sixties, where old couples sat on benches eating ice creams and gangs of pin-neat children pedalled to school on quiet, tree-lined avenues. Even the cities left me with the feeling that it would be pretty hard to get into trouble in them. We walked for miles through Auckland, Christchurch and Wellington, well away from tourist enclaves and I never even saw an area that felt remotely run down or dangerous. Even supposedly 'shady' parts of Auckland such as Karangahape Road, known as K Road, were more Goth-grungy than street crime scary.

The thing that struck me most about the country though, was a sense of space. New Zealand's land mass of 104,000 square miles is roughly the same as the UK, but the population of 5 million is less than 7% of that in Britain. It's therefore not surprising that New Zealand felt a lot less crowded than home. In the countryside you can drive for long periods without seeing another vehicle, something that's rare even in remote corners of Britain. We'd spent nearly two months in the country, but didn't feel we'd seen everything there was to see. I had a feeling I'd return someday, but until then, it was time to say 'e noho rā' or farewell to the land of Aotearoa.

I closed the laptop as Kirsty emerged from the shower while grimacing and casting a wary eye on the room's ceiling. The light fitting swayed gently as it seemed someone was landing a chinook on the roof above us, and we weren't hopeful of a sound night's sleep before our flight to Fiji.

"Come on, let's go get something to eat."

"What do you fancy?"

"Anything but Chinese." My nose twitched disapprovingly at the smells coming from a dozen neighbouring kitchens.

"Maybe we can find another free sausage roll?"

Rod Stewart and the Filipino Dwarves

"Wake up Maggie I think I've got summin' to say to you!" A crimson faced Australian teenager in a luminous tie-dye vest wobbled precariously on the table in front of us, as he blasted out the Rod Stewart classic into a beer-bottle microphone, to a backing vocal provided by his equally inebriated mates.

I re-positioned my laptop to avoid a persistent drip from the parasol shielding our table from an early evening tropical storm rolling in off the South Pacific. We'd landed in the Fijian resort town of Nadi on the main island of Viti Levu that afternoon, for a fortnight's exploration of the island, and checked into our $20 a night 'resort', which had seemed a bargain when we'd spotted it the previous day on a web booking engine. To be fair, it was excellent value. Overlooking the pool and bar area, our room was comfortable enough, and even had a balcony with a view of the white sands and aqua-marine waters of Nadi Bay. The raised eyebrows of the staff at reception, and the dozens of teenagers strewn around the foyer, greedily feasting on the weak Wifi signal explained why – The place was young backpacker central and Kirsty and I stood out like an Amish family at a swingers' resort.

Our initial investigation of the main room-booking sites had revealed that most visitors to Fiji seemed to fall into one of two target audiences. One was the 'once-in-a-lifetime' honeymoon market. Island idylls with exclusive, boutique resorts boasting stilt cottages, infinity pools and Michelin starred restaurants. Decadent body scrubs using crushed fruits and local honey foraged from virgin rainforests sounded great, but may have been a lifestyle shift too far after weeks of washing in rivers and sleeping on John Andrew's makeshift bed. Also, the £300 rack rate would have been acceptable had it covered our whole time on the island rather than a single night. Fiji's second target market was backpackers. European gap year kids who'd 'done' Australia or New Zealand, often stopped off in Fiji for a final blow-out before heading home, and for antipodean teens, Fiji was the equivalent of Magaluf or Benidorm for young Brits. It was clear which of Fiji's visitor demographics our resort was aimed at.

We didn't mind though. The February evening temperature rarely dipped below 28°, the Fiji Gold beer was ice cold, and the waves lapping on the shoreline helped to drown out the drunken sing-a-long on the neighbouring table. I'd finished sorting out our New Zealand photos, and it was too late and noisy to write my book. I couldn't resist a photographic trip down memory lane though, so reached for the USB stick containing the photos recovered in Bangkok.

The page filled with hundreds of thumbnail icons and I clicked one at random. A typical snapshot photo. Technically poor with a washed out sky and no adherence to the rule of thirds, but it still managed to make me smile. Four open sided jeeps idle at a red traffic light. They display painted names such as 'Father Joseph' and 'In God we Trust', and boast a surfeit of chrome and battered bumpers which hint at a Wacky-Races style existence. You can almost hear the throaty growl and smell the diesel fumes as their drivers gun the engines. The picture was taken in Manila and the vehicles in the photo, known as Jeepneys, are icons of that city. Originally customised from US army Jeeps left in the country after World War 2, they are the main source of public transport in the Philippines, numbering around a quarter of a million.

A swaying girl in denim shorts and with sand encrusted hair had joined the Aussie lad on the table for a Rod Stewart duet and I turned the laptop screen towards Kirsty.

"Appropriate soundtrack eh?" In our minds, Rod Stewart will always be associated with Manila, Jeepneys and one evening in particular.

We'd had a couple of nights in the Filipino capital, whose population tops 14 million and is said to be the most densely populated city in the world, before moving on to explore the islands of Panay and Negros. A night out in Manila was typical of a South East Asian megalopolis with steamy, neon-lit streets packed with hipster joints and international restaurants, local beer halls, karaoke clubs and girly bars. One online guide said 'when it comes to crazy, Manila makes Bangkok look like a rest home', and the Lonely Planet identified the city as the home of the world's most bizarre bar – The Hobbit House.

Always eager to sample a unique boozer, I read up on the pub, which, since being established in 1973, had famously only employed 'little people'. The Filipino hospitality industry was almost obsessively looks-focused, with any physical defect frowned upon and many job adverts specified a minimum height for front-of-house staff. That meant that bar or restaurant employment was closed to anyone born with dwarfism, until American Jim Turner opened his pub, and made a point of only employing 'height-challenged' staff. Word spread quickly, helped by publicity derived from some legendary drunken Hobbit House nights enjoyed by Marlon Brando and the cast of Apocalypse Now, filmed in the Philippines in 1978. The bar was soon well established on Manila's list of 'must-sees.' For me it was anyway!

My Lonely Planet map located the bar in Ermita, which was around five miles from our hotel in the Makati district, and the obvious mode of transport was a taxi. However, a Jeepney journey seemed to be a rite-of-passage for travellers to Manila, so I asked at our hotel's reception and, after some head scratching and biro-sucking contemplation from the helpful desk clerk, I was handed some instructions painstakingly scrawled on a napkin.

'Walk Kakarong Avenue to JP Rizal Street. Look at Bicycle Chop. Take Jeep R4, Green. Get off Jeep, Butcher shop Pedro Gil Street. Walk round corner. Small Hobbit bar, here we are.'

He thrust the note towards me, while nodding enthusiastically.

"Do you know the way then?" Kirsty enquired as she stepped out of the lift and saw me trying to decipher the already smudged writing.

"Yeah, sounds easy enough," I replied confidently.

Predictably, half an hour later we still hadn't found the elusive bike 'chop', and I'd resorted to thrusting the napkin at anyone who I felt looked likely to understand English.

Eventually, we deduced that we were on JP Rizal Street. All that we needed to do now was identify the correct Jeepney amongst the tide of honking vehicles bearing down on us, as we stood at the roadside, squinting into a fog of drizzle and exhaust smoke. Apparently, each Jeepney had its number and destination painted on a narrow strip beneath the windscreen, but as they pushed and weaved their way through the dense traffic with headlights on full beam, we had no chance of deciphering any of the locations.

We spotted a distant melee of locals hovering by the kerbside, and a swarm of jeepneys slowing beside them to allow passengers to leap on and off through the open rear hatch. Deciding this was the closest we'd get to a jeepney stop, we joined the jostling throng.

How the locals identified the correct jeep for their destination was a mystery to us, as each vehicle slowed momentarily to allow a slack jawed youth to shout unintelligible phrases towards the kerb, which prompted either a dismissive hand wave or a panicked charge for the back doors by our fellow commuters. I was left wondering whether all the jeepneys were actually going the same way, and the passengers were choosing their ride based on the driver's musical choice. Aside from the horn, it was clear that the most important component of a jeepney was its sound system and disco lighting arrangement. Rock ballads by 80's stalwarts such as Queen and Bon Jovi competed with Pinoy pop classics such as Anak by Freddie Aguilar.

An over-chromed jeep with a rasping exhaust and flashing strobe lights sailed alongside us, blasting out the Titanic theme, while jockeying for position with a rival who signalled his alpha-jeep status with an ear splitting rendition of 'Eye of the Tiger'. I was brandishing my napkin towards anyone who glanced in my direction, and eventually a rake-thin pensioner in a beige sports jacket nodded his understanding, grabbed hold of my arm and guided me through the commuter crowd towards the roadside, where a blue jeepney bearing the name 'Sunny Boy' was lurching to a halt.

"Come, come, quick, quick." The wiry little man had hold of my arm and attempted to drag me aboard, whilst alighting passengers were still trying to drag a large hessian sack of onions through the rear doorway. Kirsty scrambled aboard just in time, as the engine roared and our driver began to nudge his way into the traffic flow.

We'd bagged the last free places on the wooden bench seats which ran the vehicle's six metre length, so were seated precariously next to the open rear doors. Without the hand-rail above our heads, its likely our journey could have been cut spectacularly short, as we broke free of the traffic and accelerated along the rain soaked streets. It seemed that the old man had called out our destination and he nudged me to cough up a handful of peso coins, which were passed down the line of passengers to the driver's mate. Confusingly almost the same value was returned back along the line to me, leaving me to wonder whether the fare was extremely cheap, or if I was pocketing someone else's change.

Our increase in speed encouraged the driver to crank up the stereo and employ what he obviously felt was a suitable cruising soundtrack. I was momentarily thrown by our mobile 'name that tune' challenge, but soon identified the track as Rod Stewart's homage to the late 70's disco scene, and before long twenty commuters, including our aging, skeletal friend were nodding along, and joining in with a spirited chorus of 'Do ya think I'm Sexy'.

Green and yellow flashing lights lent a sickly pallor to the scene, as, in the style of commuters the world over, our fellow passengers did their very best to avoid eye contact, which was not easy with the passenger opposite you seated a foot away from your nose. No one spoke, and expressions were devoid of any emotion, but to a man, and woman, the whole Jeepney jigged, nodded and joined in with the best known lines of Rod's greatest hits. The lack of a defined chorus in Maggie May caused some confusion, but Baby Jane's singalong rhythm soon got the audience participation back on track. There was no do doubt about the highlight though. As soon as the first notes of 'Sailing' were identified, contented nods and half-smiles confirmed it as a Jeepney crowd pleaser. I can't think of anything which would prompt me to stay on a bus in England beyond my destination, but when the old man signified that we were approaching the butcher's shop on Pedro Gil Street, it seemed rude to disembark. At that point, the whole Jeepney was engaged in a mass sing-song to Stewart's maritime classic, complete with arms held aloft, waving in unison. I signalled two minutes to the old man and he nodded his agreement. As the song ended, he banged on the roof, our driver pulled into the kerb and we climbed off to begin our walk back to the butcher's shop, as the whole jeepney burst into applause to hail their own performance. The journey had taken us an hour longer than it would have in a taxi, but it was well worth it!

A twenty minute walk brought us to a non-descript building with a dimly lit sign which we very nearly walked past. The sight of a three-foot tall bouncer in a black suit and tie caught my eye though, and something told us this must be the place.

"Welcome Sir, Madam!" the friendly doorman greeted us as he stood in his tip-toes to reach the door handle, and admitted us to the bar's dark interior, where a standard sized Filipino man was strumming a guitar on a stage to our right. I was immediately disappointed, as had expected a hobbit-sized band, handling acoustic guitars like double-basses, and playing saxophones in the style of alpine horns. We headed to the bar where a rowdy group of young Americans were whooping and hollering as only drunken Americans can. The bar's walls were adorned with Hobbit movie paraphernalia, but having never seen the film, I was unaware of what a hobbit actually looked like. The posters on the walls indicated either a wild haired leprechaun-like figure, or a bald, shrunken headed creature with large eyes. This was confusing as none of the Hobbit House staff looked anything like that. In fact, they looked like they'd burgled a children's fancy dress shop before starting their shift.

The bar was tended by a two-foot-tall cowgirl in a five-gallon hat, and a diminutive superman, whose outfit was potentially created from a little boy's cast-off pyjamas. The Americans were arguing over which cocktail they should order, and the debate seemed centred around which spirits were on the highest possible shelf, thereby requiring the bar staff to employ a small step ladder to reach the optics.

A waitress appeared at my waist and offered to show us to a table. She was dressed as a grey rabbit, with her hood-head hanging limply over her right shoulder, like she'd just yanked herself free from a snare to serve us. She showed us to a table and took our order, whilst watching the proceedings at the bar with some trepidation.

"American sailors. US Navy." She wrinkled her nose, and I wasn't sure if that was as sign of disapproval or an attempt to remain in lapine character.

A relatively tall dwarf appeared at the door and surveyed the scene with an air of concern. I assumed he was the manager, as he was casually dressed in jeans and a checked shirt, though with hindsight, his outfit could easily have been a half-hearted attempt at a mini lumberjack. He signalled to the guitarist, who began murdering Manilow's Copacabana, as the tiny manager strode purposefully towards the bar.

We were momentarily distracted as the flop-headed bunny delivered our drinks, and when we next looked towards the stage, were surprised to see the manager dancing a fast waltz in the arms of a tattooed, shaven headed sailor, as his shipmates whooped their approval.

It seemed clear that the sailor was taking the lead, as the little man kicked his legs and wriggled in a futile attempt to escape the musical bear-hug he was experiencing. Meanwhile, our bunny waitress had been intercepted on her way back to the bar, and tucked under the arm of a large black seaman, who was delighting his pals by threatening to put her in a pot and turn her into stew. To his surprise, he was thwarted by the arrival of the muscular little bouncer who wrapped his arms around the sailor's thighs and began to headbutt him in the nuts.

At the bar, an eighteen stone female crew member had positioned the barman on her knee like a ventriloquists dummy, and was ruffling his hair as he grimaced and swore in Filipino, while struggling to escape her ham-hock arms. The guitarist clearly felt that a slower pace was required to calm things down, and switched effortlessly to 'Guantanamera', as two tiny chefs appeared from the kitchen wielding ladles, which they swung to good effect on the shins and knees of the dancefloor Hobbit-molestors.

In the melee, the waitress managed to slip from her bunny suit and crawled squealing across the dancefloor, clad only in a black bra and pants, as her captor held her rabbit skin aloft like a hunting trophy.

"Well, this place certainly hasn't disappointed," Kirsty observed, as the chefs finally retrieved their boss from the clutches of his dance partner, who had retreated to a booth clutching his spoon-battered shins.

Order was eventually restored by the appearance of two full-sized security staff from a neighbouring establishment, who made it clear that the bar wasn't intended to be a hobbit petting zoo, and that a look-don't-touch rule was now in force. The Americans were determined to make the most of their last night of shore leave though, and began drumming the bar with their beer bottles while chanting 'Shots! Shots! Shots!' I noticed the manager putting a crash helmet on, and was unsure whether he was about to make his getaway on a small scooter or was preparing for the rest of the night by donning riot gear.

A final memory of Hobbit House was rekindled as I watched the drunken Aussie teenagers teetering on the table in front of us in Fiji. As we'd left after an eventful hour, I'd glanced back to see the rabbit waitress being snagged by the ears and hoisted onto a table, where her sailor friend was dancing and swaying precariously. At that point, everyone in the bar, small people included, were being roped into a seemingly endless round of shots and we'd decided to make our excuses and gone to work out how to take a Jeepney back to our hotel.

***

The rain got heavier, our umbrella began to leak as the Aussies' singing got worse, and we had a rental car to collect early in the morning to begin our Fijian exploration. Luckily, on this occasion we only had to walk upstairs to reach our beds, although I knew that if a chrome covered, light flashing, music-blasting Jeep had pulled up outside at that moment, I'd need no encouragement to jump aboard.

South Pacific

Day 47- RakiRaki, Fiji

The nation of Fiji is actually an archipelago of over 300 islands, of which 106 are inhabited, with around 90% of the 800,000 population living on the two main islands, Vanua Levu and Viti Levu. The latter accounts for 60% of Fiji's land mass and is the location of the small capital city of Suva. Measuring just 150km in length and 100km in width, we'd decided to rent a car and explore the largest island at a leisurely pace, rather than spend time at ferry ports and airports to undertake an island-hopping agenda. We were, however, aware of some tiny islets lying just off the coast, which we felt may be worthy of a visit.

Online research had indicated that most of Viti Levu's road network was paved and in a reasonable condition. I'd therefore employed my usual tactic of requesting the smallest, oldest, and obviously cheapest rental car available, when I'd emailed some local companies from Christchurch.

I'd had a reply from Sammy, who promised me that no one would undercut him on price, and his daily rate did seem suspiciously low in comparison to the other responses I received. I'd hoped this would mean the car would be suitably battle-scarred, reducing the risk of a penalty for any additional damage I managed to inflict, and hadn't been disappointed when Sammy had arrived at our hotel in Nadi.

The car was an aubergine coloured Nissan Tiida, which I was pleased to note was liberally adorned with a patchwork of dents and scratches. I was less impressed by the fact that for some inexplicable reason, someone had decided to fit a full body kit to the 1200cc vehicle, including a side-skirt which left about 6 inches of clearance between car and road. I winced as I considered the pot-holes and hidden speed bumps we'd be likely to encounter on our circumnavigation of the island, but Sammy was unconcerned.

"The roads are fine! The car is funky! It's no problem! ...Just don't drive at night.'

We'd headed south from Nadi intending to drive around the island in an anti-clockwise direction, which is a 500km journey. At a push it could be achieved in a single day, but we'd given ourselves a week to take our time and get a feel for the place, well away from the offshore, paradise tourist resorts. It was my first time in the South Pacific and my initial impressions were of an unusual cultural soup - The infrastructure and laidback feel of a large Caribbean island with a heavy antipodean influence and a population dominated by people from the Indian subcontinent. The weather left us in no doubt we were in the tropics – night time temperatures rarely fell below the mid 70's and 80% humidity made for sticky days, even though the skies were filled with brooding dark clouds.

We spent a few days idling along the south coast, staying at Air B+B homestays in a couple of small towns, before arriving in the capital, Suva, on a Saturday afternoon. We stayed in the cellar of a decaying old colonial house which had been turned into an eclectic hostel, with skinny roaming dogs, Himalayan prayer flags and a sitting room full of cadaverous Fijian pensioners who seemed understandably confused by our presence. Our room was dark and damp, with no windows and a mildew encrusted cold-drip shower. It had a vaguely cave-like ambience but was a surprisingly welcome respite from Suva's steamy streets.

We wandered into town and witnessed the longest ATM cashpoint queues I'd ever seen. Every bank was easily spotted, due to a line of around a hundred people, most sporting straw hats and multi-coloured shirts snaking from its doors. I asked a shopkeeper whether the cashpoints were always so busy.

"No, today is Saturday sir. These are people who have just come in from the bush," he explained, which left us no wiser.

There weren't many 'must-sees' in Suva. We poked around a dilapidated museum and watched wedding guests dancing in a tent in the scrubby grounds. We called for an expensive glass of coke at the Grand Pacific Hotel where Prince Harry and his new bride Meghan had stayed a couple of months earlier, after almost being overwhelmed by crowds in the local market. We had hoped to watch the sunset from the hotel's terrace, but the bar prices and stalking security staff led us to seek out a more authentic local option. A few hundred yards along the road was the Suva Crown Green Bowling Club, with floodlit astro-turf greens, and outdoor tables perfectly placed to watch a kaleidoscopic sunset framed against a row of swaying palm trees. An elderly organist in a white stetson was crooning some Fijian hits of yesteryear, and a handful of late sixties couples were jerking around on a makeshift dancefloor. It was clear that the elderly Fijians took their bowls night seriously, and Kirsty and I seemed to be the only ones present not wearing a luminous colour-coded outfit to denote which team we belonged to. We ordered a couple of bottles of Fiji Gold and some pizzas and savoured the strangely unique atmosphere of a Saturday night in Suva.

The following day we were up bright and early for a three-hour drive along Viti Levu's east coast, towards the small town of RakiRaki in the far north east. The sun was shining, and it seemed we were the only car on the road, as we passed through a lush green landscape of grazing dairy cattle and suited-and-booted families heading to church. Without fail, every group we passed shouted out a greeting of 'Bola!' as we slowed down and waved. Like most island capitals, Suva had been somewhat underwhelming, but now, in the countryside, the pastel painted wooden houses, with vibrant, flapping lines of laundry lining the Wainibuka River, suggested the tropical idyll that most people associate with Fiji.

Accommodation options were limited in this part of the island, so after a few nights of budget rooms, we decided to treat ourselves and splash out. The BoliBoli resort wasn't just the best hotel on this stretch of coast, as far as we could tell it was the only hotel for miles around. We were checked in efficiently by a smartly dressed receptionist, and shown to a spacious oceanfront bungalow by a liveried porter, who demonstrated the features of the room, most of which we'd not experienced since arriving in Fiji, with air conditioning being the most welcome addition. We had a walk on the white sand beach and a dip in the bathwater-warm sea, before adjourning to the pool, where I engaged in a conversational Travel-Top-Trumps contest with a know-all Canadian scuba diver.

We had a few beers by the pool and a couple more on our room's patio, and by 8pm were starting to feel peckish. We'd seen a sign saying it was barbecue night and headed to the almost empty poolside restaurant, where upon arrival we were seated by a bow-tied waiter.

"Tonight is our special barbecue night," he announced with a flourish, and pointed towards a flaming pit of glowing embers. This was a 'lovo', a traditional Fijian method of cooking, in which meat and vegetables are wrapped in banana leaves, and placed in a firepit filled with white-hot rocks. Beyond the lovo was a long table filled with silver tureens, lit by harsh spotlights under which clouds of giant moths were being flapped at by two junior waiters wielding towels.

"We have pork, beef, chicken, sausage, burger, and all the veggies and salad are all included. All same price, just eighty."

"Sorry, eighty? Is that Fiji dollars? Per person? " My brain was attempted to compute what seemed like an unfeasibly large amount for a barbecue.

"Yes sir, eighty Fiji dollars. But you can have everything, as much as you want. Pork, beef, chicken..."

"What if I only want some chicken, or a burger?" Eighty Fiji dollars was about £30, and I was struggling to envisage eating enough meat to make that worthwhile in the whole of the next week. When travelling, I always try to avoid calculating what I feel the local price should be, and instead consider whether I'd consider the cost fair at home. In this case, I was left thinking that thirty quid was bloody expensive for a barbecue wherever in the world it was.

"Sir, you can have pork, beef, chicken..." smiled the waiter as he glanced towards his colleagues, who were now attempting to incinerate the swarming moths using flaming torches from the barbecue pit.

"But we only want a burger each. Or some chicken. How much would that cost?"

"No sir. Not possible." I realised I was asking the waiter to break his employer's rules, so asked to speak to the manager, and a sturdy woman in a floral dress was summoned from behind the bar. She swept towards us like a galleon in full sail, while flashing us a pearl-toothed grin. Her face had an air of excited anticipation, as if she was about to open an intriguing birthday gift.

"Sir!" she exhaled theatrically and closed her eyes whilst maintaining a serene smile. I realised this was my invitation to speak, so started to explain my issue.

"Your waiter explained that tonight is barbecue night and..."

"Sir. We have pork, beef, chicken, sausages..."

"Yes I know, I can see it and it all looks very nice but we don't want that much. We just want a burger, or maybe a piece of chicken and some salad?"

"...Sausages, burgers, all the veggies and salad are included in the price sir." The manageress's eyes remained closed and I assumed this rendered her deaf to customer complaints.

"But we're not really that hungry. We only want a burger or some chicken."

"That's fine sir. You can eat as much or as little as you like." She held her arm aloft to indicate my route to the barbecue.

"But I don't want to pay eighty dollars for a burger! That would make the cost of two burgers about the same as our room. Surely, you can reduce the price and just put us a couple of burgers on a plate?"

The manageress sighed and closed her eyes again and smiled enigmatically.

"It's not possible sir." She flashed me a winning smile, as if she'd just delivered some fantastic news.

"So what if we don't pay the eighty dollars. What else can we eat?"

"I can enquire with our bar manager," she paused as if to consider a range of options. "He may be able to provide you with some nuts."

"Nuts?"

"Nuts... which you may eat in your room. It's not possible to eat nuts in the restaurant on barbecue night sir."

If Kirsty was asked to comment on one of my most annoying characteristics, cutting my nose off to spite my face would surely rank high on the list and, true to form, I sprang into action and figuratively began hacking away at my hooter with a now obsolete steak knife.

"Come on, we're leaving." I noisily pushed back my chair, and the still smiling manageress stood aside to let me know that she had no intention of stopping me.

"But what are we going to eat? We've had nothing since this morning, we can't live on nuts." As usual Kirsty was allowing common sense to cloud my lack of judgement.

"We'll go out in the car and find something. There must be a town nearby." I stormed past the manageress, whose eyes were closed again, though I detected the serene smile struggling to contain a smirk.

Half an hour later, I was regretting a number of things. One was not swallowing my pride and paying thirty quid for a burger. Another was drinking six bottles of strong Fijian beer before deciding to eat. Finally, I wished I'd paid a bit more for a 4x4 with adequate headlights, instead of a tiny Nissan with a custom body kit, but lights which only illuminated the pitch-black road for five feet in front of us.

We bounced and scraped along a rutted track at 10mph, through dense jungle which clipped our windscreen and snagged on our side mirrors. The cousins of the barbecue moth swarm careered headlong into our windscreen, leaving dusty impact marks which further obscured my vision, and the track was carpeted with a legion of tiny, hopping frogs trying in vain to evade our wheels. We were heading blindly towards some distant lights which I hoped would be a village, but suspected may prove to be yachts moored in the bay. We had no idea where we were and as the track narrowed, I began to fear that it would terminate in a jungle cul-de-sac and we'd be forced to retrace our route in reverse.

It came as some relief then when our headlights settled on a strip of tarmac ahead and we reached a small road. I stopped the car, and we consulted a phone, but were surprised to discover that according to Google maps, the body kit had seemingly granted the Nissan amphibious qualities. The flashing dot on the screen indicated that we were about a mile offshore.

As I tried to locate the lights we'd been aiming for, a set of headlights appeared from around a bend in the road ahead and a vehicle approached slowly. I wound down the window as the car crawled towards us, hoping to ask for directions to the nearest source of food. It was a 4x4 land cruiser with powerful headlights which blinded us as it approached to draw level with our car.

I looked up at the two bemused, dark faces regarding us suspiciously, and immediately spotted the epaulettes on their shoulders. Suddenly conscious of my beer breath, I quickly closed my mouth and smiled. The way the night was progressing, it would be just my luck to get busted for drink driving by the only police patrol for miles around. We both waved at the scowling officers to indicate that all was fine, we needed no assistance, and that creeping around dark country lanes in the middle of nowhere was a perfectly normal way to spend a Sunday night in rural Fiji. Obesity is a big problem in the South Pacific Islands, with 30% of the Fijian population classed as overweight, and the middle aged officers both appeared to be pushing the twenty stone mark, with enormous, foot-wide heads and multiple chins resting on impressive bosoms. They weighed us up, as if considering whether we were worth the considerable effort of hauling their two fat arses from their seats, so I made the decision for them by smiling and waving before accelerating away. Thankfully, their lights remained red in our rearview mirror, and eventually vanished into the gloom.

Further along the road we again spotted the elusive 'village' lights and headed towards them, along another rutted track, through a large gate and along a drive, to arrive at what looked like a hotel. Single storey buildings were scattered around a swimming pool and a handful of cottages in manicured grounds extended up a hillside. We parked the Nissan to be greeted by a grinning elderly man in a boilersuit striding towards us shouting "Welcome! Bola!"

He introduced himself as Timi. 'I am Head of Security," he beamed proudly.

"What is this place?" We looked around. Everything was pristine. The pool shimmered, illuminated by underwater lighting, the lawns were trimmed to perfection, and bougainvillea perfectly framed the doorway of the wood-decked building Timi led us towards.

"This is Bluewater Cove. A brand new resort, only open for two weeks!" Timi was clearly thrilled with his new position and bounded excitedly ahead of us.

"It seems very quiet...Are there any guests?"

"No guests yet! Advertising is only now beginning. Come, come!" Timi led us through reception to a bar area with outdoor seating, where half a dozen uniformed staff were standing around a table, which contained nothing but a blue plastic bucket. They smiled and 'Bola'd' our arrival, but shifted uneasily, like schoolkids hiding cigarettes behind their backs.

"Is the restaurant open? We're looking for some food...any food." I explained our plight, which broke the ice, and we were ushered over to shake hands with Vivian the waitress, Sandy and Nihola the cleaners, Brandan the bar manager, Thomas the Gardener, and most importantly Isaac, the chef who was more than happy to christen his new kitchen by knocking us up some chicken roti's.

It was clear that our arrival had interrupted the staff's enjoyment of their pre-operational downtime, and furtive glances were cast in our direction, as Brandan delivered a couple of Fiji Gold's to our table. The remaining staff skulked uneasily around the table, occasionally glancing towards the bucket, and we began to feel guilty that they were unable to continue whatever they'd been up to, since our arrival. After a few minutes of speculation, which ranged from magic potions to drowning kittens, my curiosity got the better of me and I strolled over to the table to investigate.

Vivian, Sandy and Nihola stepped back nervously as I approached, but Thomas the gardener stood his ground. It was obvious he was the guardian of the sacred bucket, and nodded his encouragement as I tilted it towards me, unsure of what to expect. I was unable to detect any eye of newt, toe of frog or wool of bat, nor were there any young cats floundering in the pail, only several inches of grey, muddy water with a half coconut shell slopping around in the gloopy mixture.

My confused expression prompted Thomas into an attempted explanation.

"Yaqona....grog....kava?" I recognised the final word. Kava was widely viewed as the national drink of Fiji, though was banned in many countries, Australia included. Made from the ground root of the Piper Methysicum plant, kava is a mild narcotic which slows down the transmission of signals between brain and body, leading to a feeling of relaxation. It also leaves the lips and tongue numb, so a kava session can leave you feeling like you've been to the dentist for a mouthful of fillings.

I'm always keen to experience unique customs, but looking at the contents of the bucket, I wasn't sure whether I wanted to experience this local cocktail. It wasn't difficult to imagine that one of the cleaners had just squeezed her mop out in the bucket after cleaning the bathroom floor.

It was no surprise therefore when Thomas dipped the coconut shell into the slop and slowly pushed it towards me, as his colleagues giggled their encouragement.

"You first." I was aware that there was an etiquette surrounding a kava ceremony, and was also keen to avoid falling for the old 'make-the-tourist-drink-toiletwater' trick. I wanted to see someone else taste the foul looking concoction before me.

Thomas handed the shell to Brandan who raised it aloft. Thomas clapped his hands and accepted the shell back. He bowed towards it, downed it in one and clapped again while shouting 'Bula!' as the rest of the staff applauded loudly and slowly three times.

Kirsty had by now made her way over to us, with the familiar look of resignation she employs when she knows she's going to be immersed into some bizarre ritual, whether she likes it or not. She grimaced at the mud spattered bucket of grey slime on the table, and gave me a 'WTF' look, as Thomas dipped the shell into the bucket and asked me "High tide or low tide?"

Brandan squeezed my bicep and answered for me. "High tide for the gentleman!"

"High tide! High tide!" chirped the ladies, and Thomas immersed the half-shell into the bucket and raised it towards me, filled to the brim with a muddy, grey semi-liquid which looked like ready mix cement.

"High Tide!" He beamed mischievously.

Eager to get my initiation over with, I reached out to take the shell, but a nudge from Brandon reminded me of the ritual. I clapped once before taking the cup from Thomas.

Kirsty gave me the special look she reserves for when I'm about to perform a ridiculous life-threatening act, as I raised the shell to my mouth, tipped it back, and downed the whole lot in one, as is the custom. It looked worse than it tasted. It had the texture of chalky water and a vaguely minty taste, like indigestion tablets that have been put in a washing machine. Not something I'd drink all night, but I'd had worse.

"Bula!...It was okay that actually." I licked my lips as I clapped slowly three times to conclude the ritual.

"Where do you think they got the water from?" Kirsty whispered, and I realised I hadn't considered that. It was unlikely to be Evian, and drinking local tap water was a definite no-no.

"Madame now." Brandon was keen to get Kirsty involved, and I agreed. If one of us was catching dysentery, we might as well share the pain.

"Low tide for lady," chorused the female members of the party and Kirsty agreed.

"Very low tide, please."

Thomas sloshed around in the bucket and emerged with a half-filled, low-tide coconut shell. Kirsty began the clapping ritual as my tongue began to sprout fur. She knocked back half a shell, clapped three times, shouted Bula and stifled a retch. Meanwhile, I was enjoying the slow creep of paralysis which was extending from my tongue to my lips. My mouth tasted like I'd been sucking a pocketful of coins coated in chalk. It was a feeling I decided I liked, and as the coconut shell was passed around the circle, I surprised myself by assessing how many more 'rounds' were in the bucket. Plenty was the answer.

"Same again Thomas," I smiled as Kirsty shook her head. "High Tide!"

At some point our chicken roti's appeared and we munched on them between rounds from the bucket. They might have been incredibly tasty. They might have been totally rank. Our tastebuds had been numbed to the point that they no longer functioned. Our tongues felt like they'd doubled in size and I was sure my lower lip was drooping towards my chin like Homer Simpson's. None of us really cared though. We all stood around the bucket and grinned through grey, grit flecked teeth.

At some point Kirsty reminded me that we needed to drive back to the hotel on a pitch-black, rutted track, dodging frogs and police patrols while massacring squadrons of moths. She was right and we had one more high tide and a low tide for the road, washed down with Fiji Gold, then waved goodbye to our new friends.

I don't remember much of the drive back to the hotel. Only that the car windows were wide open, and we had a local radio station on playing some of the local, ukulele-heavy 'Vude' music. Also, that the little frogs now seemed to hop higher and more slowly than before, and sometimes the moths seemed to be smiling at us as they hurtled into the windscreen, to transform themselves into a pleasing kaleidoscopic explosion of dust. I had a feeling we'd sleep well that night.

The Rock

 Unsurprisingly, we slept heavily after the kava session, and I was woken by a dream in which I was slurping from a bucket of porridge with a froglike mouth which stretched right across my face. I got out of bed and rubbed at my teeth which felt like they belonged to someone else, most likely a horse. Thankfully, the Kava infusion had obviously nullified any waterborne diseases and we were surprisingly free of any intestinal disturbances.

I opened the patio doors and stepped out into the greenhouse warmth of a tropical morning, while gurning and chewing my numb lips to try and stimulate them into life. My tongue felt furry and my mouth was filled with a vaguely chemical taste, like I'd licked a newly painted door. The complementary buffet breakfast was less than appealing, especially after I'd created a scene by rejecting the delights of barbecue night in favour of an evening drinking muddy water from a plastic bucket.

I fired up the laptop, inserted the Thai USB stick and clicked into the Windows photo app. After a couple of no-show missing files, a dark thumbnail image told me the next file was a 'hit' and after a couple of seconds, the laptop screen was filled with a simple, yet striking image. The dark silhouette of a man, striding up an incline against a backdrop of the sun's faint glow. I recognised it immediately. It was taken as dawn broke at the summit of Uluru, or Ayers Rock, the 350 metre sandstone monolith rising from the Northern Territories desert, in the dead centre of Australia. It would be convenient to pretend that the shadowy figure in the photo was me, but in reality, I had no idea who the subject in the frame was, as I lined up a sunrise shot while being buffeted by gusty winds in the chill of first light. I was alone at that point, feeling exhilarated to have reached the summit of the rock, but nervous about the approaching descent.

It was November 2000, and my partner Karen and I were nearing the end of our three week trip, and our fifteen year

87

relationship. She'd moved out of the house a couple of months earlier, but we'd remained friends, and with the Australia trip planned and paid for well in advance, it seemed stupid not to go.

The familiarity gained through spending most of our adult lives together to that point soon outweighed any awkwardness, and we enjoyed our whistlestop tour of the highlights of Australia. It was clear though, that three weeks was in no way enough to even scratch the surface of the huge country. I promised myself that I'd return at some point in the future, to spend a few months exploring properly.

The fact that we were no longer a couple probably had a bearing on my decision to climb Uluru alone. We stayed at one of the cluster of hotels at the purpose built 'Ayers Rock village', 15km from the site itself, and took organised coach tours to the rock to see the sunset and the following day's sunrise. I hate travelling as part of a tour group and my frustration was increased by the attitude of our designated coach driver. Mid 50's, with the remnants of a lank quiff suggesting a past-life as an antipodean teddy boy, Colin had been afflicted by some form of facial palsy, which caused the left side of his face to droop an inch lower than the right. A permanent angry sneer made him resemble a bad-tempered John Merrick, with slightly better teeth and marginally worse hair.

It was clear that Colin had little sympathy with the native Anagu people of the Northern Territory, who had retaken ownership of the Ayers Rock site from the Australian government in 1985.

"They say the rock is sacred to the Abo's so they don't like people climbing it. That's bullshit. They're just scared of lawsuits when some bugger falls off and dies," he explained, in answer to a question from an elderly American schoolteacher.

"And believe me, lots do fall off!" Colin's sneer slipped momentarily as he chuckled at the thought of some bloody tourist plummeting a thousand feet to their death on the desert floor.

If his first assertion was doubtful, the second was factual, and was proven by a swathe of brass plaques attached to the rock, commemorating those who had plunged to their deaths while attempting the climb over the years.

Reading the plaques during our 'Uluru Sunset' tour the previous evening, Karen looked up at the exposed, almost vertical incline which was the climb route, and shook her head.

"No way I'm doing that. I'll walk around the bottom instead."

We'd listened as a more helpful tour guide explained the Sunrise tour options to his group. A 10km circumnavigation at the foot of the rock along a well-defined, but snake infested path. Or a 2km clamber up a sometimes near vertical rockface, to watch the sun rising over the desert from the summit of Uluru. This option was not for the faint hearted or the unfit. Those scared of heights. Anyone with a heart condition, epilepsy or pregnant. Anyone with mental health issues or those prone to panic attacks.

"A lot of people find coming down worse than going up," he explained. "I've known people shuffle down the whole way on their arse. And it's a bloody long crawl! They have to call the chopper out a couple of times a year, and you don't want that." He rubbed his thumb on his forefinger to emphasise the Aussie dollar impact of a sudden case of vertigo at the summit.

I felt bad about abandoning Karen and had we still been a couple, I may have forfeited the chance to scale the rock and accompanied her on the base walk. However, I decided that this was likely to be a once-in-a-lifetime chance, so I decided to proceed as I would if I'd been on the trip alone.

When travelling, an alarm sounding in the dead of night causes momentary confusion, as you try to remember where you are, and why you've been roused from a deep sleep. Then you remember, and question the wisdom of the ridiculously early bus, train ,flight, or excursion to witness some early morning phenomenon. Our 3.30 alarm was no different.

Colin had made it clear that the bus would leave at 4am and anyone not on board would be left behind. He had an unhealthy obsession with being the first bus to arrive and the first to leave, which was annoying as he sounded the horn with the sun still dipping towards the horizon on the sunset trip, but could be a benefit in order to catch the sunrise.

It was still dark as we disembarked, shivering in the chill desert dawn, amidst a choke of diesel fumes from buses which disgorged bleary-eyed passengers, who involuntarily peered upwards at the rocky monolith looming above them. We'd been informed that the sun would make its appearance above the eastern desert horizon at 5.50am, and that the climb would take between forty five and ninety minutes, depending on weather conditions and the fitness level of the climber. It was approaching 4.30, so anyone at the lower end of the fitness scale was already likely to miss the main event.

I bade farewell to Karen, who understandably looked less than happy as she embarked on her solo walk on the dark path around the rock, especially as she seemed to be the only person who'd gone for the low-level option.

I set off at a brisk pace along the initial, gradual incline of the rock, eager to warm up, as a chill wind whipping in from the north left me regretting not wearing an extra layer of clothing. A head torch was also a notable omission on my part, and I quickly caught up with a couple of torch beams bobbing along ahead of me, who revealed themselves to be two career-break twenty-somethings from Southampton, Max and Phil. My initial quick pace slowed as the gradient began to increase, causing the climbers ahead to slow, and by the time we reached the first steep section where the climb was assisted by a chain, a human traffic jam had formed behind a gaggle of middle-aged Koreans.

Eager to keep moving, the Southampton lads and I decided to overtake and began to scramble up the 30% gradient slope.

"Be careful guys." An Aussie voice stalled us as we passed a group of six, and I recognised the tour guide from the previous evening. "It can get frustrating, but you should stick close to the chain. The wind is really getting up and a strong gust can literally blow you away as you get higher."

We dropped in behind the group and the guide introduced himself as Gavin, who worked out of the backpacker resort at Ayers Rock village. As we waited for the Koreans to haul themselves along the chain, he explained some of the debate around climbing Uluru. Contrary to the teachings of Colin the coach driver, the rock is indeed sacred to the Anangu aboriginal people, and they are generally unhappy with visitors climbing it. They believe that the earth and its people were created by ancestral beings during a time called the Dreaming. Sacred areas were designated by landmarks such as Uluru, which was created by the actions of ten of the most important ancient beings. Gavin began to expand on the tale, which involved battles between snake spirits and a cast of characters including ghost dingoes, a woman called Willy Wagtail, and fantastical creatures such as marsupial moles and hare wallabys. Such a tale deserved to be told around a desert campfire, accompanied by a few beers, or possibly more appropriately, some hallucinogenic Pituri bush leaves. It was harder to appreciate while clinging to a chain on a dark mountainside, while being buffeted by 60mph winds.

"We're coming to the steepest part of the climb," Gavin shouted to his teenage group who were scrambling ahead on hands and knees. "Keep hold of the chain."

"I'm surprised they've let us climb today. This wind is too strong and it's getting worse." He turned to check on the three of us and spotted Max breathing heavily. "Stick together and stay close to the chain."

The steep gradient and the curve of the rock disappearing into the darkness ahead prevented us seeing what was holding us up, and we seemed to be stationary for increasing periods of time. This became more unnerving as we were rocked by gale force gusts sweeping in from our left. It was becoming clear that someone ahead of us hadn't listened to the 'fitness' briefing. At least our stuttering progress had allowed Max to catch his breath, and the three of us embarked on an incongruous discussion about Leeds United's unexpected success in that season's Champions League, while clinging to a rusting chain in order to avoid being blown off a mountain into the dark Australian desert.

The steep gradient meant that my head was level with the knee of Phil, who was ahead of me, and Max's head was positioned at the level of my shin. We were debating Leeds' chances of gaining a point in the San Siro against AC Milan, when I saw Max's eyes widen and his gaze extend upwards to our left. The incline and curve of the rock meant that our field of vision was limited to around thirty feet, and initially it was hard to establish what was moving in the darkness. What was clear was that whatever the shape was, it was in a precarious position and was moving quickly into further danger in the form of a near vertical ascent. It took a couple of slow-motion minutes for my eyes to focus and the shocking realisation to dawn that the figure was human, walking jerkily with arms extended ahead, while forced to lean backwards by the severity of the gradient.

The clamour of voices ahead was suddenly breached by the high-pitched scream of a woman and shouts of alarm uttered in an undecipherable language. I peered into the darkness as the wind made my eyes stream, and at first thought the staggering figure was a child, but I made out a pair of khaki combat trousers and matching anorak and recognised one of the Koreans from the group ahead of us - a slight man in his mid-fifties with dark mop-top hair and glasses, who'd grinned a toothy greeting as we assembled in the car park.

"What's he doing? Where's he going?" Max's shout summed up what we were all thinking. It's strange how witnessing the imminent death of a fellow human can cause a wave of panic to engulf you, but we all clung harder to the chain and crouched as low to the rock as possible, as the man rocked and swayed in the wind, while standing on the lip of a thousand foot drop with arms now outstretched, as if he was about to take flight.

There was more screaming from the Korean group and another dark shape began to move from their midst along the rockface.

"No! Stop!! Get Back!!" Gavin was now scrambling urgently forward, waving his arms and indicating that the would-be rescuer return to the relative safety of the chain. We heard a muffled discussion and more wailing, then a figure which we assumed to be Gavin, scuttling crab-like across the rock towards the man, who had now turned and seemed to be holding his head in his hands, suddenly surprised to find himself standing exposed on a rock precipice above the Australian desert. There followed the sounds of a scuffle as the Korean was wrestled to the ground by Gavin and held there, struggling and shouting.

The Southampton lads and I clung to the chain and watched for what seemed like several minutes as Gavin attempted to pin the flailing man to the rock.

"Shit, this is bad. We'd better go help him." Phil was right. It seemed highly likely the man could break free at any point and propel himself and Gavin into the dark void below us. I forced myself to release my grip on the chain and, gingerly, the three of us began to edge along the rock face, bracing ourselves against the gusting wind.

"No! Guys get back! Go down the chain and find another tour guide. Tell him to get up here. Hurry!" Gavin's panicked voice sent us scurrying into reverse and we began to edge downwards, only to be met after twenty feet by a bearded man in a bush hat, who was engaged in a rapid crawling ascent.

"What's the hold up?" he yelled, and we blurted out a garbled account of the drama taking place above us.

"Stay here. Stop anyone coming past." We heard a radio crackle into life, and he was off, scurrying up the rock like a four-limbed tarantula.

We spent an uncomfortable few minutes crouching on the dark mountainside with a large queue forming on the chain behind us. The wind chill began to take effect and we were all shivering when a shape appeared from above. It was Gavin.

"Okay, they're going to try to take him down. We need to get everyone moving up the rock. It's too dangerous to turn everyone round now."

We scrambled along behind him, passing the bearded guide who was holding the distressed Korean in a tight bear hug. Eventually we cleared the steep, chained section to begin an uphill climb which allowed us to catch our breath, while Gavin explained that the man had become disoriented, possibly due to ascending the rock too quickly and affecting the levels of oxygen reaching his brain. He'd seemingly blacked out and had no idea where he was, as he staggered towards a vertical rock face.

"Approaching someone in that state is very dangerous." Gavin inhaled deeply and took a swig from his water bottle. "They tend to go over the edge, and take whoever is near them along for the ride. He was very lucky. And so was I."

They haven't got him down yet, I thought, as we quickened the pace to get to the summit before sunset. The final section was easy after the steep, gale blown ascent we'd experienced, and once at the summit, I split from Phil and Max and wandered the strange lunar-like surface, as the eastern sky began to take on a purple hue to indicate the imminent arrival of a new day.

As Uluru is the only distinguishing feature in the desert landscape, watching the sunrise is more of a personal, perhaps spiritual experience than a photographic opportunity, due to the lack of anything to frame in silhouette against the sun's light. I watched as an orange glow emerged quickly on the horizon, but resisted the urge to reach for my camera. In those non-digital days, it was hard to take good sunrise photos without an expensive SLR camera which I didn't possess, but that didn't stop numerous point-and-shoot flashes exploding around me. Knowing the resulting images would show very little, I kept my camera in my backpack until I spotted a lone figure striding purposefully along a ridge ahead of me.

A twenty yard jog to my left got me ahead of the lanky figure, and I was able to position myself to capture him with my trusty little Canon, as he ascended a small slope with the sun's glow behind him. I took a handful of shots, to increase my chances of at least one working out. In those days of 35mm film, it was impossible to know what you'd taken until your photos came back from Boots or SupaSnaps!

I'd heard that many people viewed the descent of Uluru as scarier than the ascent but in the post-dawn light, with the earlier wind having subsided, the main issue I faced was new climbers ascending the rock and hogging the chain. I therefore found the best means of descent was to walk forwards while leaning back to counter the gradient. This worked well until the steepest section, where I felt I was leaning back so much that I could almost touch the rockface behind me with my hands as I walked. After a brief period of arse-shuffling, I reached the bottom to find Karen waiting for me. She was pleased to have completed her circumnavigation of Uluru but had been plagued by snakes slithering across the path for the duration of the walk.

"Did you get to the top? Enjoy it?" She enquired.

I wasn't sure 'enjoy' was the word I'd use, but on balance I was glad I'd done the climb. At the time I'd felt it was a once-in-a-lifetime chance, and this was proven correct, when climbing the rock was banned in October 2019, with the restless spirits of the Anangu ancients finally left to rest in peace.

✳✳✳

I looked up from my laptop as Kirsty emerged from our Fijian hotel room.

"I can't feel my teeth." She slurred while licking her grey lips and gums.

"My mouth feels like suede," I agreed. "I do feel quite lively though. I actually didn't mind Kava, but don't think I could drink a whole bucket."

Kirsty shook her head and rubbed her teeth with a furred tongue. "Come on, we've got a boat to catch."

Castaway

Day 50- Nananu-i-Ra, Fiji

M ost visitors to Fiji fly into Viti Levu or Vanua Levu, before moving quickly on to one of the 300 islands to the north and west. These range from backpacker focused camps with $10 a night dorm rooms, to all-inclusive five-star resorts on the outlying islands, aimed firmly towards the lucrative honeymoon market.

Neither appealed to Kirsty and I, but after a couple of months of being on the road, the idea of spending a few days on a quiet tropical beach was appealing, so we'd spent some time researching on Google and seemed to have found what we were looking for. Nananu-i-Ra was tiny – about 3km long and 1km wide, with no roads or cars and just a couple of low-key accommodation options offering beachfront cottages at a reasonable price. Importantly, it was only 3km off Viti Levu's north coast, meaning no long, return boat journey which would have seriously reduced the time we could spend on most of the other islands.

Neither of the guest houses on the island had a website so I'd resorted to phoning to make a reservation. No one had answered the phone at our first choice, Malcolm's Cottages, so I'd telephoned the only other option, Benson's Beach Cottages.

"Hello?" Enquired the voice of an elderly lady, who sounded like she was answering a dusty phone which had just rattled into life for the first in many years. I'd enquired about the availability of a cottage, and she'd seemed vaguely amused at the possibility that there could ever be a period of full occupation.

"A cottage? Yes, yes of course. How many weeks do you need it for?"

"Erm...just a couple of days really, maybe three?" I offered apologetically, and this amused her even more. It was clear that not many independent travellers arrived on the island at this time of year, if at all. The lady, who'd introduced herself as Nia, quoted me a price and agreed to send a boat to Ellington Wharf to collect us at 9am on the day of arrival.

Having skipped breakfast and driven away from the BoliBoli Resort, we speculated on the likely cost of a couple of coffees, as Ellington Wharf sounded like a slick, super-yacht mooring. We needn't have worried. The wharf was a dilapidated wooden pier which had collapsed on one side and now floated precariously in the aqua-marine waters. There was a rusting shipping container, and, alerted by a yapping, scab encrusted puppy with a dislocated hip, its occupant emerged, naked to the waist and rubbing his eyes.

"Going to the island? You need me to watch your car?"

I was well versed in the 'mind your car' protection racket operated around many inner city, English football stadiums by enterprising urchins. Failure to pay generally meant some misfortune befalling your vehicle while you were at the game, and the scam spawned the apocryphal tale of the supporter who guarded against a break-in by leaving a large Rottweiller in his passenger seat. When approached by the kids offering to watch his car, the fan says he doesn't need their help and points at the slavering hound. 'Must be a clever dog that mister,' observes one of the youngsters, 'if he can work a fire extinguisher.'

With that in mind, I agreed a price with the Fijian entrepreneur, who demonstrated his brain to limb dexterity by simultaneously scratching both his crotch and armpit while flicking a kick towards the sickly pup.

We slumped on our bags and enjoyed the comfortable low-80's morning temperature, as we watched multi-coloured fish swarm in the water below the dock. Eventually, we heard the buzz of an outboard motor and a small fibreglass craft, piloted by a baseball cap wearing teenager, appeared around the headland.

We threw our rucksacks aboard and clambered in after them. Minutes later we were skimming across the open sea and Nananu-i-Ra was immediately visible as a low-lying, palm covered strip of land ahead. The water was as calm as the swimming pool its colour suggested, and we made good progress, soon approaching a white sand beach, fringed with tilting coconut palms, where a large, dark skinned lady and two dogs waited to greet us. Her cliched appearance in a tropical floral dress was granted an air of authenticity by a grubby apron and a bucket containing cleaning detergent and a mop. We splashed through the shallows and she introduced herself as Oni, the sole member of staff, and explained that Nia had returned to the mainland to deal with a 'family crisis'.

As we walked the twenty yards to our cottage, Oni explained that Nananu-i-Ra means 'daydream of the west' in Fijian, and first impressions were certainly of the type of desert island idyll that Europeans hanker for in the dark days of winter. It was late February at home, but the damp chill of Yorkshire felt a world away, as we crossed a fifteen foot strip of flour-like sand, then ten feet of lawn and entered the breeze block, single storey building.

Oni began to show us around the large, family sized cottage and took particular pride and care in demonstrating the full kitchen facilities. It was while she was going into some detail on the complex process required to light the oven, that I uttered a phrase which stopped her in her tracks.

"Don't worry, we won't be cooking anything."

Oni was bending down, attempting to get the oven to ignite with a lit match, and seemed to freeze as I uttered the words. With the match rapidly burning towards her fingers, she slowly turned and looked up at me.

"What?" She stood and blew out the flame.

"We're not planning on doing any cooking. We don't have any food to cook anyway."

Oni's eyes widened and her mouth fell open. She dipped her head toward me as if to speak, but no words came out, leaving her resembling a five year old watching an amazing magic trick. She seemed to be struggling for words and an awkward silence descended, as Kirsty and I stood smiling at her, delighted to have fallen so lucky with our island retreat.

Oni blinked rapidly and shook her head. "Did you speak to Nia?"

I confirmed that I had.

"Did she not tell you that there is no restaurant here?"

"No, she never mentioned that." I was still upbeat, having read good reviews of the restaurant at Malcolm's Cottages which was a five minute stroll along the beach. "Don't worry though, we'll eat at Malcolm's."

Oni cringed visibly and blinked even harder. "Malcolm's is closed sir. There is no restaurant."

"Is there a shop?"

"No shops."

"Where do the villagers buy supplies?" The potential problem of spending three days on a tropical island with no food was now looming large in our minds.

"Not many people live here all year. Those that do, go to Ba Town for shopping once a fortnight." That was a boat ride and hour-long car journey away.

"What do you eat? Is there not a freezer somewhere at the guest house?"

Oni looked uncomfortable with the direction I was attempting to steer the conversation toward. She was a large lady and the suggestion that she share her supplies with two ill-prepared tourists obviously didn't appeal.

"We do have a small shop here, but it hasn't been opened since Christmas. I don't know what we have in there." As a diversion tactic it worked, and I suggested we go check what provisions were available immediately. Oni said she needed to find the keys, though I suspected she wanted to hide her food stash, in case I tried to exercise a search warrant on her kitchen.

We unpacked our rucksacks and made friends with the two dogs who had followed us into the cottage and were enjoying the coolness of the tiled kitchen floor. Kamo was a young ginger cross-breed, with an inquisitive face and a tail which twitched into an immediate, involuntary wag upon eye contact. Milly was an elderly wolfhound/alsatian cross with an aloof nature, more cat-like than canine. It was clear she barely tolerated Kamo's childlike exuberance, and he therefore correctly identified us as likely playmates. Where we went, Kamo followed for the duration of our stay, which suited us just fine. Having a desert island to ourselves complete with a borrowed hound was our idea of heaven.

I eventually spotted Oni struggling with a padlock on a small cabin opposite our cottage, and headed over to perform a stock check which, for us, was the difference between a journey back to the mainland, going hungry or going home early.

I leant over the counter as Oni delivered her good news/bad news summary. The good news was the freezer had been left on. The bad news was that it only contained three loaves of white bread. The good news was that there were also a dozen rusty tins of food at the back of a cupboard. The bad news was that the labels had peeled off nearly all of them, so it was impossible to tell what the contents were. Further bad news was that they were hidden away behind some Christmas decorations which Oni regarded with some concern. I spotted some New Year bunting which she rapidly hid, leaving me to suspect that it was probably celebrating the end of the 1970's and the tins had been put there before then.

Flinging open a cupboard, Oni let out a whoop of delight and produced two bags of dry pasta, which she held aloft like trophies. Things were looking up.

"I also have eggs!" Oni announced triumphantly, "but not many." I suspected these were from her private food stash and she'd calculated she could afford to offer some up.

I'd spotted an unlit drinks fridge and on the basis that being hungry for three days is bad enough, but being hungry and sober is borderline intolerable, I requested an investigation.

"Beer!" Oni held up a slightly rusted can of Fiji Gold, and confirmed there were about twenty cans present. Not ideal, but better than nothing.

I said I'd take the lot and Oni loaded it into a cardboard box, while painstakingly writing out every purchase on a pad, which she then slowly totted up with a calculator and told me she'd bring to our cottage later. When I saw the amount we'd been charged, I understood why she felt the need to deliver it under cover of darkness!

The sea, rippling just yards from our room was crystal clear, still as a millpond and as warm as a bath. We quickly forgot our food mishap, as we floated in the shallows under a cloudless sky, with Kamo joining us to partake in his favourite pastime of angling. For an animal that had been born on a beach and had never been away from the sea, he was surprisingly fascinated by fish. He'd patrol the waterline, his gaze firmly fixed on the water, until he spotted a shoal of tiny angelfish, at which point he'd spring forward, landing with a splash, head submerged and jaws snapping. He'd then lick his lips and paw at his snout several times, until he was satisfied that his assault had been unsuccessful, before starting the whole process again. He was the most attentive, affectionate dog imaginable when on dry land, but once in the water he became a laser focused fishing machine, albeit a very unsuccessful one!

On our first evening, Kirsty and I settled down on the sand with a beer and watched an amazing sunset. As is often the case in the tropics, late afternoon cloud served as an inky backdrop to a blood red sun, which shimmered as it descended, then seemed to melt into the horizon in a blaze of crimson and purple. I grabbed my camera and caught some spectacular images of a silhouetted Kamo enjoying his favourite hobby in the foreground, beneath a blazing orange and red sky.

After the sun had set, we eagerly embarked on a task we'd saved as a special treat – identifying the contents of the labelless tins. We had some clues – The majority of tins were of the same size and one had retained a label identifying it as chopped tomatoes. Four were a third of the size of the rest, and we suspected these may contain tuna. That was the obvious place to start and Kirsty was already working out how far she could make four small tins of tuna stretch as I opened the first tin.

She looked on expectantly as I delivered the verdict.

"Broad beans."

"Shit!"

"A small tin of broad beans." I began to consider the taste sensation which broad beans on toast could represent. Kirsty was eagerly twisting the tin opener to reveal the contents of one of the larger tins.

"Chopped tomatoes." She half-smiled like a child at Christmas, opening an X-Box shaped gift and finding slippers.

It was my turn next, and this time I hit the mother lode with one of the smaller tins.

"Tuna! It's bloody tuna! Gettttiinn you beauty!" I punched the air and Kirsty clapped jubilantly.

With one of each tin size opened, the inventory was complete. We had two bags of pasta, twelve eggs, two loaves of bread, three small tins of tuna, eleven tins of chopped tomatoes and a tin of broad beans. And now only eighteen cans of beer, which had to last us three days and nights. I cracked open another Fiji Gold as we contemplated three days of tomatoes on toast.

"Let's view it as a desert island detox. People pay thousands for that." I tried to look on the bright side.

In the morning, our rations were boosted by a doorstep delivery of six fresh coconuts from Lala the gardener and speedboat skipper, who'd just shinned up a palm next to the cottage and macheted them off for us. That unexpected bonus was negated when Kirsty cracked the last of six eggs into a bowl to make a breakfast of scrambled eggs. An unbelievable stench immediately filled the room, making us both gag. We couldn't believe our bad luck that the final egg introduced into the mix was rotten, rather than the first, therefore contaminating the whole lot. I carried the bowl outside to dispose of the vile liquid and Kamo came bounding over, seemingly driven into a frenzy by the smell. As I headed towards a drain near the shop, he leapt to almost head height, salivating and eyes wild with excitement. He managed to get his head under the bowl as I tipped it down the drain, and lapped open-mouthed at the revolting slime which splashed all over his head and neck. The smell was indescribably terrible, and I retched as I turned away clutching the empty bowl. As I walked back to our cottage, I noticed Oni peering from a window in the main building. She looked from me back towards Kamo, who was desperately trying to lick the liquified egg from his own head, and gave me a hard stare, obviously baffled as to why I'd taken our limited food supply and smeared it all over a dog.

Whereas Kamo seemed to adore me and followed me everywhere, my relationship with Milly was more problematic. Our interactions ranged from her totally ignoring my clicks and whistles as she strolled past us on the beach, to two full blown, unprovoked attacks. On both occasions I was seeking Oni out at the main house, when Milly spotted me and charged towards me, snarling and with teeth bared. In both instances I managed to stand my ground and stall her with raised hands and stern words, but I was shaking as I retreated to a safe distance. Kamo seemed confused and almost embarrassed by these incidents, like a bloke who's invited his best friend to a works Christmas party, only for him to punch the boss. He'd climb up on my knee back at the cottage and give me a lick and a look which seemed to say 'women eh?!'

After travelling hard for the best part of two months, it was great to suddenly have nothing to do. We had toast and coconut for breakfast, a small portion of scrambled egg and toast for lunch and tuna pasta for our evening meal. We didn't find a use for the broad beans, and our meagre beer stash meant we were on rationed alcohol. Days were spent laying on the beach, then shuffling into the shade of a coconut palm when the heat became too much, or helping Kamo on a fishing expedition. The water was so still and clear that the fish would actually swim into your cupped hand if you remained still. Our canine friend looked on enviously.

This was the first proper downtime we'd had since setting off on our trip, and was a perfect opportunity for me to make some serious progress on The Two Week Traveller. I'd envisaged my laptop photo collection serving as a memory-jog for aspects of stories I couldn't recall, but it was obvious now that it wasn't going to work like that. Unable to easily locate the relevant photos, I was forced to leave gaps when my memory failed me, knowing I could check my facts when back on my home computer with its well-ordered photo files. The random images thrown up on my laptop screen brought an unexpected benefit though, in that they rekindled some long-forgotten memories, and my notepad of anecdotes and incidents was expanding daily, to the point I now felt confident I'd have more than enough content for the book. Kirsty had been keeping a journal of our travels to date and she spent her time tidying this up and adding details, with the intention of emailing it to her family and friends once we were back in the land of broadband.

We're both iPhone step-counter addicts, but the size of the island meant it was difficult to achieve our usual ten thousand steps a day. That didn't stop us setting off to explore though. The north side of the island, barely a kilometre from our tranquil bay, was a surprisingly different environment. Exposed to the wind, it boasted white-capped waves and the rutted sands were strewn with driftwood and other seaborne detritus. There was a rustic, run down resort hidden in the trees. which seemed totally deserted, and it was tempting to wonder how long it would be possible to stay in one of the cabins there without anyone noticing.

Kamo was our constant companion on these island explorations, and one afternoon we were walking along a sandy strip of beach facing the main island, three kilometres distant. As usual, Kamo was patrolling the shallows looking for fish, when he stopped and sniffed the air. Something had piqued his interest and caused him to pause and look out across the water. Up to this point, he'd restricted his aquatic activities to wading with the water at chest height, causing us to wonder if he could even swim. He now answered that question emphatically and plunged forward, paddling along with head bobbing above the small waves. At first, I wondered if he'd spotted something floating in the near distance and was heading out to investigate, but as he passed a marker buoy twenty metres out, it became clear where he was heading – Viti Levu, the main island.

Having lost sight of the small ginger head, we scaled a rock outcrop and eventually spotted him again, around two hundred metres from shore and still swimming in the same line. We were now concerned. The dog never strayed from the cottages unless he was accompanying us, and we wondered if he'd ever been to this beach before. Perhaps he'd never seen the main island and had decided to set off to seek his fortune like a canine Dick Whittington. More likely he'd caught the scent of a bitch on heat, drifting across the strait from one of the farms in the hills behind Ellington Wharf.

Three kilometres of sea swimming was a tough ask for a young dog, but like most teenagers, Kamo was obviously a risk taker and was oblivious to the danger he faced from passing boats or sharks. I was more concerned about how we would explain his disappearance to Oni. We began to shout his name until we could no longer see him. We scanned the water from our rocky perch but there was nothing. He was gone. We had to face facts - we'd taken someone else's dog for a walk and allowed him to drown. We slumped on the rock and debated whether to come clean or deny all knowledge, and say we hadn't seen him that afternoon. Recalling that the last time Oni saw me with the dog, I was pouring rotten eggs over his head, I suspected the latter explanation was unlikely to be accepted.

We set off trudging sadly back towards the cottages. Fijian mythology holds that Nananu-i-rah is the point of departure for disembodied spirits leaving this world for the afterlife, and it seemed that Kamo had chosen to follow them. I resolved to try and steer clear of Oni when we arrived back at the cottages, which was always going to be a difficult task when we were the only guests. I then realised we only had four cans of Fiji Gold beer left, so I braced myself for some awkward questions on Kamo's whereabouts, and set off to find her, to ask if there was an additional secret stash of alcohol anywhere.

Oni greeted me with an excited smile and told me that two unexpected guests would be joining us, and that Lala had taken the boat to Ellington Wharf to collect them. Unfortunately, there was no more beer, but given our unfortunate misunderstanding with Nia, she'd made sure they understood they had to bring their own provisions, and had instructed them to stop at the supermarket in Ba Town on their way from the airport. I asked what nationality the newcomers were and Oni's shouted answer of 'Australians!' was good news. Surely Aussies wouldn't arrive without a healthy supply of 'tinnies.' Thankfully, the new visitors seemed to have distracted Oni's attention away from Kamo's absence, and she didn't ask if I'd seen him.

Kirsty and I sat sadly outside our cottage enjoying the warmth of the late afternoon sun, until the buzz of the approaching speedboat saw me nervously scanning the beach. I envisaged the dog's shark ravaged corpse making a gruesome re-appearance on the evening tide as the new arrivals disembarked, to spoil Oni's welcome party.

I heard the kitchen door slam, and cringed as I heard Oni calling the dogs to join her on the beach to greet the new arrivals. There was bound to be an inquest when Kamo was a no-show, and Kirsty and I shuffled guiltily into the cottage.

We heard Lala kill the outboard motor, then some shouted greetings and the unmistakable sounds of dogs being petted enthusiastically. Given that Milly was more likely to take the hand off a new guest than respond affectionately to being stroked, this was strange. I poked my head round the corner of the door and spotted the unmistakable leaping, rolling, ginger blur that was Kamo, acquainting himself with his new friends.

"He's back!" I shouted to a relieved looking Kirsty. "And the new Aussie kid has just carried a big crate of beer off the boat." Things were looking up.

I let our new neighbours settle in for all of twenty minutes before I took a tactical beach stroll in front of their cottage, and waved a cheery greeting. They introduced themselves as Gabby and Tim, a late twenties couple who had come on a five day break to the island. It was Tim's first trip outside Australia and he complained about the 'long three hour flight' from Brisbane. He screwed up his face in horror when I told him that a direct flight from London to Nadi took about twenty hours, but as such a route didn't exist, you could easily add another fifteen hours travel time to that. He was similarly unimpressed when I told him of our enforced detox diet of toast, tuna and pasta. They donated some baked beans and fruit, and more importantly a dozen cans of Fiji Gold from Tim's stash.

We only had a day left on the island and during that time Kamo soon worked out which cottage had the best food, and subsequently spent most of his time hanging around with Gabby and Tim. Only when we went for a walk did he decide to join us, though we were now careful never to take him within sight of the main island, in case he caught the scent of his lady friend again!

On the day we left, Oni, Tim and Gabby plus Kamo, the little traitor, turned out on the beach to wave us off, as Lala tugged at the outboard motor cord. Milly watched from a distance, obviously glad to see the back of me. We lay on our backpacks as

Nananu-i-rah shrank away on the horizon and we sped towards the main island. We'd enjoyed our few days of relaxation but now it was time to get back on the road.

After settling up with our car minder at Ellington Wharf, we set off along Viti Levu's North Coast road towards Ba Town. We were due to fly from Nadi, 70km further along the road in a couple of days, but before then, I'd spotted an interesting diversion from the main route. Navala is viewed as the last traditional village in Fiji, having been protected from the advances of the modern world by its location deep in the remote Nausori Highlands. The thousand strong population live in traditional thatched huts known as bures, which are constructed from clay, straw, and wood from the surrounding forests, and the only stone structure in the village is a small Catholic church.

I'd seen photos of traditionally dressed villagers and scattered huts set against a lush mountain backdrop, and decided that a glimpse of pre-tourism Fiji would be an interesting contrast after a few days on an island. The problem was likely to be getting to Navala. Photos of tour groups who'd made the journey showed mud spattered landcruisers labouring along pot-hole riven mountain tracks. With its full body kit, the Nissan Tiida may have cut a dash in downtown Nadi, but it wasn't the best choice of vehicle for a tough mountain ascent.

We arrived in Ba Town with a steady drizzle falling, and I headed to the most likely source of up-to-the-minute local knowledge, the bus station. I parked the Nissan and strolled over to a gaggle of loitering taxis, their drivers smoking, chatting and lounging with legs extended from driver's doors.

My question of whether it was possible to reach Navala in a non 4x4 vehicle sparked some lively debate, especially when I pointed to the little car parked up on the roadside. The sight of the side-skirts, which lowered the vehicle's clearance to about six inches, swayed any waverers in the debate, and the general consensus was delivered via laughter and vigorously shaken heads. There was only one dissenting view. Another Nissan driver, sporting a silky purple shirt and looking like he'd just left a disco, took a final drag on his cigarette and flicked it towards the gutter.

"It's no problem. Take it slow and you'll be okay."

There were some muffled giggles and uneasy head shaking, but no one argued. I took it that 'purple shirt' was a respected authority amongst the other drivers.

"Thanks. I will," I said and headed back to Kirsty who'd been watching the exchange.

"Well?" she asked as I turned on the ignition.

"They said it's fine, no problem," I lied, and we set off.

The road into the mountains was fine as we departed Ba Town, with a new asphalt surface lulling us into an early false sense of security. That ended abruptly at a T-Junction about 2km out of town when the concrete turned to gravel, then quickly deteriorated into a mixture of mud and stones.

"How far is it on this road?" Kirsty enquired, and I mumbled a non-committal 'twenty minutes-ish' rather than tell her it was actually 20km.

There was really no need for the taxi driver to advise me to take it slow, as I was unable to do anything else. It didn't take long before I was lurching between first and second gear as I negotiated a route around large rocks, small crevasses and foot-deep tyre grooves, to an alarming accompanying soundtrack of scrapes and bangs from the Nissan's undercarriage.

The mountain scenery was stunning but although we were travelling at a maximum of around 10mph, I had to keep my eyes firmly fixed on the track ahead. On a couple of occasions, we found ourselves grounded upon a large stone, and I exited the vehicle to work out the best way to extract us, before rolling backwards or inching forwards, with the underneath of the car crunching and grinding its way free of the obstacle. My twenty minute estimate had long faded into the realms of fantasy, when we stuttered to the brow of a hill to see the Ba River in the valley below and wisps of smoke rising from the hills beyond.

"That must be Navala, we're nearly there!" Again I was guilty of over optimism and it was another half an hour before we crossed a causeway over the fast flowing Ba river, to arrive at the gates of the village, which was announced by a hand painted sign advising us of the rules we must follow to be admitted. First, we were to wait until a villager arrived to escort us to the head man's hut for an audience with the village elders. This meeting is to request permission to visit the village and, traditionally a 'Sevusevu' gift or token is presented to the chief. For Fijians this is usually a quantity of kava root, but for tourists the preferred offering is, not surprisingly, Fijian dollars in cash!

No sooner had I turned off the engine, than a smiling , plump lady appeared, and summoned us forward, introducing herself as Sera, who would be our guide. Kirsty was presented with a floral sarong which she was to wear to protect her modesty, and we were led through the village for our interview with the chief, as large drops of warm rain began to patter around us, and distant thunder rumbled along the valley.

The bures were constructed in neat rows with a low door frame and few windows. Their design was unchanged for hundreds of years, with the huts built around a central timber pole with interior walls woven from split bamboo, and earthen floors covered with mats made from woven coconut leaves. Meals were prepared on stone hearths which billowed smoke through makeshift chimneys in the thatched roofs, and toddlers with soot darkened faces peered with large eyes from doorways as we passed.

Sera cast a wary eye to the mountains in the east as we arrived at a large central bure.

"Rain is coming soon."

The spots were large but infrequent and dappled the dusty ground of the chief's enclosure as they landed with an audible splat, and we were glad to be ushered into the bure away from the coming storm.

We had to crouch to enter through the three-foot-tall door frame, but the hut was surprisingly spacious inside, with a tall ceiling and little in the way of furniture. The corners of the room were lost to the gloom, but three elderly men were easily identifiable in the glow of the central hearth and one gestured us to join them, cross legged on the floor.

The chief was a weighty gent in his late sixties, wearing a freshly laundered white shirt and a patterned burgundy sarong. He regarded me with disinterest, like a depressed silverback gorilla in a failing zoo. The sidekicks on either side of him were of a similar age, and displayed the same lack of interest in our presence. One seemed mesmerised by the flickering flames in the hearth and the other picked absentmindedly at a troublesome toenail. Eventually the chief spoke and I assumed he was greeting us in his own language, so Kirsty and I nodded respectfully and smiled. He then repeated the sound he'd made, and we guessed he was asking us a question.

"Awwoe-his-hoe-connshee?"

The chief had very few teeth and a large mouth housing an even larger tongue. Using the old wartime adage, this old man's loose lips could have sunk a whole convoy of ships. Having travelled so far it would be disappointing to be refused admittance to the village due to failing our entrance interview, and Kirsty and I looked to Sera for a translation.

"Country? What is your country?"

"Ah, country! England. We are from England," we announced proudly. Fiji was a British colony up to 1970 and elderly citizens of Crown colonies often speak affectionately of the Queen, but if we were hoping this would establish some rapport with the chief, we were to be disappointed. He nodded without emotion and was handed a pad and biro by one of his unsmiling attendants, which he passed to Sera.

"The chief says you are welcome to visit our village." She smiled softly and I wondered how I'd missed that. "It is customary to bring the chief a token."

At this point, I wished I'd brought some Kava from Ba market, just to see his face.

"If you have no token, he will accept Fiji dollars. Twenty five per each person." That was almost £10 each, which was roughly the cost we were paying for a room per night. I blinked and felt Kirsty tense beside me. I quickly tried to concoct a reason not to pay, but under the stern gaze of the village elders, and with Sera holding out her hand, I was lost for words, and reached reluctantly for my wallet. The cash was swiftly handed to the chief, who stuffed it into his breast pocket and waved a hand to dismiss us.

"Enshoy-wissit-my-wiiillish." He slurred as we stood up and I detected a half smile on his rubbery features.

Sera was already looking at the sky as we crouched to exit the chief's bure. The large raindrops had stopped, and it seemed to be brightening up, but her gaze was fixed on the distant hills.

"Big rain now in the mountains. Problem," she muttered, and gestured for us to follow her, as we began our tour of the village. We'd read accounts of visitors taking part in kava ceremonies and being invited into local homes for traditional meals with the villagers; being shown round the school and chatting to local farmers; even helping with the construction of new bures. We'd therefore expected to spend a few hours in Navala, and although the cost was more than we'd expected, I was sure it would be worth it as a unique experience.

The first item on Sera's agenda was a visit to her sister's bure, from where she emerged with an umbrella. "Rain is coming," she reminded us again. We then set off on a haphazard meander around her neighbours' huts. There were few people on the muddy streets and little activity for me to photograph. In remote villages, it's usual to be followed by a gaggle of excited children asking for sweets or pens. I like to take a picture of them then watch their reaction when I show them their image on the digital screen. Here the kids all seemed confined to their huts and watched as we passed, as disinterested in us as the village elders were. I suspected the village was suffering tourist fatigue, with an increasing number of tour groups making the journey to see Fiji's 'last undiscovered tribe'.

Navala was undeniably picturesque, set in a verdant valley, surrounded by mist shrouded peaks, and the architecture and a lack of motor vehicles did make it authentically photogenic. We called at a number of bures and all of Sera's neighbours greeted us warmly and showed us their homes before casting a wary eye to the east before uttering dark forecasts of 'big rain in the mountains'. I suspected there was an agenda at play to worry us about the imminent rain, and Sera seemed to be getting increasingly agitated, and called over a boy on a bike and despatched him on an urgent errand. I took the bait and asked what was happening.

"When it rains on the mountain, the river here will flood in maybe one hour, maybe two. I sent this boy to check the causeway."

"If the causeway floods, is there another road back to Ba town?"

"No other way out, there's only one road. You would have to stay here."

The prospect of being stranded in a remote mountain village living in medieval style dwellings was quite appealing, until I considered how much the chief would most likely charge us for an overnight stay. Then when Sera told us that visitors had been trapped in the village on numerous occasions, once for five days, I began to reconsider. We had a flight to catch !

The boy returned, looking agitated, with his little legs a blur on the pedals. He breathlessly jabbered a Fijian equivalent of a breakfast radio traffic bulletin, and Sera inhaled loudly and shook her head.

"The causeway is still passable, but only just. It's better if you leave now, if you don't want to get stranded here."

We'd been in the village for less than an hour but the thought of five days all-inclusive at the chief's room rates convinced us we needed to escape as soon as possible.

Sera looked unimpressed with her tip, which reflected her limited tour guiding abilities and the extortionate 'Sevusevu' I'd paid the chief, but she waved us off surprisingly enthusiastically. We then realised Kirsty had forgotten to hand back her borrowed sarong and it was that which was causing Sera's frenzied arm waving. The waters did seem higher as we edged across the causeway, but the river was still a foot short of flooding the road, and I was left wondering whether we'd been the victims of a well-rehearsed hoax, in order to limit the time we spent in the village.

We made painfully slow progress back to the main road along the rutted mountain track, and reflected on the fact that there are very few places left in the world that remain totally untouched by the impact of mass tourism. It was perhaps unsurprising therefore, that a village which is reachable from a main road in just over an hour in an aging Nissan Tiida with a customised body kit, is not one of them!

The Balloon Man and the Undertaker

We were back in Bangkok, at the guest house near Soi Samsen, after flying from Fiji via Auckland. It was a Saturday in late February and, a couple of months into our trip, we'd decided to break up the homeward journey from New Zealand with a few weeks back in Thailand. No plans, no agenda, no real rush to see anything in a country we'd visited before. It felt good to have no pressure to keep moving, in order to make sure we saw everything we wanted within a tight timescale. We knew the local area now - where to eat and drink, where to wander during the stifling hot days and where to simply sit and watch the world go by.

A favourite spot was a small restaurant with a balcony overlooking the khlong where we'd seen the giant, drainpipe-dwelling monitor lizard on our first visit. They did a passable Western breakfast, and unlike some of the other neighbourhood eateries it was generally unbusy, so there was no hurry to vacate our table. They had efficient Wifi too, which enabled us to catch up on the news from home and send Kirsty's journal and some photos to family and friends.

I finished off the chapter of The Two Week Traveller I'd begun writing on the flight from New Zealand, and flicked to my laptop's photos app, for some entertainment in the familiar form of the scattergun slide show of USB stick images. I scrolled through a couple of blank files, then an Eastern European cityscape with onion dome churches and ugly high rises, which could have been Minsk or Budapest or Gdansk. The next photo held my attention for longer. A large, lime green, patterned balloon was the obvious focal point. When I say large, I mean four or five feet in length. The balloon is being held by a moustachioed, dark skinned man who is sat cross legged on a small skip of rubble. He has removed his flip flops and they lay on the ground in front of him, and he's smiling and seems to be in conversation on a mobile phone. Although I'd obviously taken the photo, it wasn't one I immediately recognised, and it took me a couple of minutes to place where it was and what was going on. Then I remembered, and suddenly his contented expression took on a somewhat sinister quality.

The photo was taken in Mumbai, the mega city of 18 million on India's Western Coast. We'd been travelling in Kerala and Goa, and having never been to India's largest city, we decided to stay for a few days before flying home. With its tropical beaches and Bollywood celebrity enclaves, if Delhi is India's New York, then Mumbai is definitely its LA. Boasting more millionaires and billionaires than most western capitals, a good night out in the hotspots of Juhu or Bandra West would set you back more than in the most exclusive areas of the US or Europe.

The city is also famous for its Victorian architecture, which includes the Chatrapati Shivaji Terminus, looking more like an ostentatious gothic cathedral than a railway station. Kirsty and I made a point of visiting at evening rush hour and found a relatively quiet corner to watch the daily commuter chaos. The days when passengers were shoe-horned into carriages by burly guards, and latecomers travelled on the roof are unfortunately past, but the 5pm rush still made the London underground look like a sleepy rural branch line.

Leaving the station, a short dash across a two lane, wacky races style highway filled with honking black and yellow taxis and buzzing tuk-tuks, brought us to the Oval Maidan. This scrubby, dust field with occasional patchy grass is the spiritual heartland of India's greatest love – cricket. At any time, up to one hundred games will be taking place simultaneously here. We walked the length of the ill-defined boundary line, behind a long row of crouching wicket keepers, and watched a fat man in a green tank-top pitch a tricky googly at an opponent wearing shiny patent leather shoes and beige slacks; an outswinger from a slight teenager with a bum-fluff moustache, swang out too far and nearly dismissed the batsman in the neighbouring game; a plump millennial in double denim delivered a vicious beamer which by-passed the batsman and nearly took out a pensioner walking a dust covered chihuahua. The games ranged from serious tournaments played by athletic looking young men in rip-off replica IPL kits, to school games where tracksuited masters barked out instructions to their young charges. Players spanned the social spectrum from bespectacled clerks in shirts and ties, to barefoot street hawkers swinging homemade bats fashioned from fence slats or packing crates. It was unclear where the outfield of one game merged with its neighbouring contest, and some of the fielders seemed to be taking part in two games at once. The common denominator was that every game was taken deadly seriously. From wealthy entrepreneurs in pristine whites to ragged tuk-tuk drivers, and from geriatric fielders with spindle legs to eight year old street urchins rolling in the dust to prevent a ball reaching a boundary, it was clear that the games all meant something. In a land, and city, divided by huge wealth and extreme poverty, it was great to see cricket in its role as a unifying force, bringing all sections of society together on one patch of scrubby earth.

Mumbai is famous for being the wealthiest city in India, but it is also home to one of the world's largest slums, Dharavi, setting for the 2009 film Slumdog Millionaire. With a population of around a million, living in an area of less than three square kilometres, it has a mind-boggling population density of around 350,000 inhabitants per kilometre. Some people refer to tours of slums, Brazilian Favelas or African townships as 'poverty porn', but my view is that if a sizeable percentage of the population live in those areas, you aren't really experiencing the place if you ignore them. We therefore arranged a tour with a young Dharavi resident who was recommended on the Lonely Planet Thorn Tree message board.

Ikram was a university student, and met us in the reception of our guest house with the polished, well attired air of a young man who was unlikely to be living in Dharavi for much longer. His new Nikes certainly seemed far too white for a life treading dusty slum streets. He had a taxi waiting, and soon we were crawling through a fog of exhaust fumes in bumper to bumper traffic. Our car had air conditioning, but I usually enjoy travelling with the window open to fully appreciate the smells and sounds of a strange city. Not here, as I was suffering badly. Both Kirsty and I had stinging eyes and a sore throat from the pollution, but my sinuses seemed to have reacted to the overload of airborne toxins by shutting down completely. It felt like my nasal membrane had swollen to the extent that both nostrils were totally sealed. I couldn't breathe through my nose at all and sounded like the kid on the Vicks advert who couldn't do his exams 'with his nose blocked up like this.'

Ikram was studying economics and had seen a gap in the market to become one of the first guides to offer slum tours, and fell lucky with the timing of Danny Boyle's movie. He established his tours before a number of other operators set up with similar offerings after the film's release. Just about every tour company in Mumbai now offered Slumdog Millionaire location tours, but Ikram was from the area, so was able to offer access to the real Dharavi and the people who lived and worked there. He told us that in contrast to the general image of a slum being an area of high crime and low employment, Dharavi is something of an economic powerhouse, with a turnover of more than £500m per year. An estimated 15,000 single room 'factories' churn out produce twenty four hours a day. Textile manufacturing and workshops creating leatherwear, ceramics and jewellery are big business, as is recycling. A regular sight on India's roads is a skinny man pedalling a cycle rickshaw containing a ten-foot tall hessian sack, filled with plastic bottles and containers. He's the middleman in a recycling chain which ends in the melt-down factories of Dharavi, and begins with barefoot urchins begging empty water bottles from foreign tourists. Dharavi's residents earn, on average, between $500 and $1500 per year, which is a meagre wage by Western standards but with rent on the cheapest shack starting at around $5 per month, that potentially leaves them with more disposable income than most UK mortgage holders!

We began our tour on a railway bridge overlooking the Dhobi Ghats or open air laundries, where more than two hundred 'dhobi-wallah' families ply their trade. A warren of single storey, tin roof shacks surrounded rows of concrete washing pens, where men, women and small children soaked, starched, bleached and rinsed Mumbai's soiled linen. It was then hung out to dry and the view from the bridge was a riot of colour, as thousands of bed sheets, towels and items of clothing fluttered on lines in the breeze. Clearly, each dhobi wallah had a specialism, with one washing line filled with bedding, another with chef's aprons, one with pillow cases and one curiously replete with hundreds of pairs of purple trousers. Ikram explained that all the big hotels send their laundry here, and it was strange to think that guests staying in the top suites of the Taj Mahal Palace Hotel, would be stepping from their jacuzzi to dry themselves on a towel which had hung in the diesel scented breeze, beside a railway line in a nearby slum.

Next, we wandered Dharavi's back alleys which were a hive of industry. Tailors sewed cross-legged in corrugated iron boxes; blacksmiths hammered glowing rods on primitive anvils; girls in brightly coloured sarees wove on clattering looms; schoolkids in lovingly patched-up uniforms darted past skinny donkeys laden with plastic bottles. Ikram led us up a rusting stairway to the flat roof of a two storey building, where we squeezed past sacks filled with yellow jerry cans, to arrive at a vantage point overlooking neighbouring rooftops and yards. As far as the eye could see was a panorama of garbage. One roof contained disembowelled TV's and computer monitors, broken keyboards, circuitry and tangles of wire; its neighbour was home to a never-ending pile of multicoloured plastic components of some unidentifiable machinery; next, blue and red crates were stacked twenty feet high in a precarious tower, beside a wall of car batteries. The air was acrid and tasted of chemicals, and our eyes stung as we headed back down to ground level and into a muddy alleyway, which saw Ikram tiptoeing gingerly to avoid soiling his perfect Nikes.

He served warning of what to expect next, by producing a handkerchief which he wrapped around his mouth and nose, Mexican bandit style, before ducking through a low arch into a dark workshop. We followed and were immediately plunged into a toxic netherworld, as we identified two slight figures stooping in the glow of a furnace ahead. Ikram shouted an instruction in the local Marathi dialect and two small boys approached us through the gloom, brandishing armfuls of electrical cable. Ikram selected a length of cord and peeled back the rubber insulation with his nail to reveal the copper wire within.

"They recycle the copper here," he explained "by burning off the rubber in the furnace."

It was dark, stiflingly hot and the air was filled with choking chemicals. Our eyes began to stream, and my throat seemed destined to join my nose in sealing up completely. We struggled to the door, where we gulped in the comparatively fresh outside air like fish on a riverbank.

"Those boys will work in there for fourteen maybe fifteen hours a day, seven days a week. There are thousands like them here. Some have even more dangerous jobs."

It was a sobering insight into how millions of people live and work every day around the world, in conditions we can't imagine in the West. Returning from trips to places like Dharavi always makes me appreciate how much we have, simply due to our good fortune in being born in a wealthy country. Those who dismiss tours like Ikram's as 'poverty porn' miss the opportunity to learn an important lesson in appreciating how lucky they are!

The taxi dropped us off near the ceremonial archway of the Gateway of India, and we stopped to watch one of Mumbai's unique street performances, performed by a five year old girl on a tightrope strung between two trees on a traffic island. The child was sporting her best tartan party frock and a pair of stripey, multi-coloured leggings. She was blindfolded, had a stack of five golden bowls balanced on her head, and was carrying a large section of scaffolding pole, as she teetered along the high wire around eight feet from the ground. Her mother passed among the watching crowd with a bowl containing a handful of small denomination rupee notes. Such a performance in Europe would no doubt attract the attention of child protection services, but compared to the boys we'd just seen working the Dharavi furnace, this youngster had an enviable career ahead of her.

That night we headed out to sample some of Mumbai's more low-key nightlife. The rooftop cocktail bars and nightclubs of the Bollywood glitterati weren't our scene, and we stepped over dozens of sleeping bodies in the arcade beneath the opulent Taj Mahal Palace Hotel, to arrive at a small bar with a balcony facing the choppy waters of the Arabian Sea. It was a perfect spot for people watching with a beer, and in India, there's never a shortage of people to watch.

I'd just slurped the froth from my second large bottle of Kingfisher, when my attention was drawn to a fire engine with lights flashing, which had stopped opposite the bar. Four firemen emerged, dressed all in black with over-sized helmets, their uniforms looking strangely archaic compared to the high tech, Hi-Vis outfits worn in Western nations. They strolled over to meet two police officers who were loafing on the sea wall. The group entered into a huddled conference, while looking out across the rocky foreshore. One of the firemen retreated to their vehicle and returned with a length of rope attached to a four-pronged grappling iron, and they all made their way down a flight of stone steps towards the shoreline. Kirsty was reading, and I sipped my beer while monitoring their progress. It was low tide and the beach was made up of craggy rocks of varying sizes, so I was unable to see exactly what was happening, but it soon became clear that the emergency services were engaged in some form of fishing exercise. They took it in turns to toss the grappling hook into the sea then hauled it in without getting a bite.

When anything whatsoever of note happens in India, a crowd of onlookers quickly forms. I've seen crowds gather to watch parking tickets be issued, roadkill dogs being scraped from roads and that undeniable highlight for Indian loiterers, a tourist looking at a map or guidebook. A fire engine, a police car and six officers throwing a hook into the sea was a sight too good to miss and a crowd of a dozen men had gathered on the sea wall to observe the proceedings. (99% of Indian onlookers are men, and 99% of them have a moustache.)

I took a swig of my drink, picked up my camera and told Kirsty I was going to investigate. My appearance and progress down the stone steps to the beach was closely observed by the onlookers and I heard a murmur of excitement as I descended, nearly slipping on the moss-covered surface. One of the firemen noticed me approaching and alerted his colleagues, who looked round momentarily, then carried on slinging the hook into the sea. I clambered over the rocks, intending to ask if I could have a go at hooking whatever they were trying to catch...until I saw what it was.

The corpse was floating about ten feet away from the rock which the officers were casting off from. Clearly a young man, wearing a burgundy shirt and blue jeans, he rose and fell on the incoming waves in a crucifixion pose, with arms extended in a 'ten to two' position. One of the firemen turned to me and grinned.

"Body," was his unrequired summary. I watched a couple of unsuccessful attempts to snag the cadaver, but then grew concerned that they might offer me a go. I couldn't imagine the frenzy it would cause amongst the growing crowd if a foreign tourist managed to line-catch a dead body on a Mumbai beach.

I headed back to the balcony to finish my beer. It took another half an hour for the angling skills of the emergency services to come to fruition, and an audible clamour of excitement from the now sizeable crowd announced that the body was ashore. My morbid curiosity got the better of me and I strolled back down to see what was happening. I arrived at the sea wall to see the four firemen struggling to lift the corpse up the steps, each holding a dripping limb, while the police officers literally refrained from getting their hands, and uniforms, dirty by bringing up the rear.

In Europe, such a scenario would be classed as a potential crime scene and the body would be left in-situ on the beach, surrounded by screens, while forensic officers began a fingertip examination of the corpse. In Mumbai, it was hoisted through the jostling crowd and laid on the pavement while the firemen caught their breath.

The crowd closed in, chattering excitedly and pushing to get the best view of the body. The police officers sat on the bonnet of their car while one spoke on his radio, and the fire crew hosed down their kit, their job obviously complete. None of them made any attempt to shield the corpse. The crowd now numbered around eighty and word was spreading. The original onlookers were being joined by family groups who came running, alerted by text messages from friends. The mood was carnival-like. Kids were hoisted onto fathers' shoulders to get a better view; young couples bent down to achieve a better angle for their stiff-selfie; teenage girls giggled at the undignified pose of the deceased.

Being around a foot taller than most present, I was able to easily see over the crowd of bobbing heads in front of me. The man was in his early twenties, and looked pale skinned, though that could have been due to the effects of the salt water, with collar length hair and a stubbly beard. He was rake thin. His shirt was unbuttoned and his jeans, which looked many sizes too large, were bunched up below his knees, revealing a pair of grubby brown underpants. He was barefoot and his right eye was swollen and bloodied.

It was a strange feeling to observe the scene. The crowd were in holiday mood - laughing, joking, jostling, pushing little boys towards the corpse to scare them, taking close-ups of the dead man's face on mobile phones. And there he lay. Someone's son, someone's brother. Maybe a street person, maybe a foreign sailor. Maybe murdered, maybe committed suicide. No one knew, and no one cared. All he represented now was an opportunity for half an hour of fun. A cheap distraction from a tough existence for those present and witnessing his return from the sea.

The crowd had attracted hawkers aplenty. Barefoot boys sold toxic-looking coloured drinks in plastic bags; an aged hunchback pushing a cart, sold peanuts and water melon; youths sold plastic toys which flew into the air propelled by spinning rotor blades. Trade was brisk but no one was as popular as the balloon man. Wearing a loud, striped shirt, with the ubiquitous moustache of the Indian thirty-something, he carried a large black holdall from which he produced a battery operated tyre pump and strips of multi-coloured rubber. Once inflated, these were transformed into something magical – enormous balloons, in green, pink and blue. As tall as a ten-year-old and twice as wide as the floorbound corpse, the balloons were a sensation. Fifty rupees was about the equivalent of 50p, and represented a perfect opportunity for Mumbai's lower middle class to flex their financial muscles and give their pleading offspring a spectacular treat. A little girl struggled to wrap her arms around her new toy as barefoot street urchins squealed with delight and attempted to gain an illicit, fleeting touch of the balloon, which cost more than their family's daily food bill. The balloon seller was almost overwhelmed by customers and resorted to sitting on his holdall while he inflated another sale, to prevent nimble fingers pilfering his stock.

As the fire engine left, a black van drew up to the kerb and two men in white overalls got out and approached the police officers. After a brief discussion they retrieved a cardboard crate from the rear of their van and pushed through the dwindling crowd surrounding the corpse. Distracted by the activity, some of the balloon seller's customers drifted back to watch the body being loaded into its makeshift coffin, giving him time to carry out an impromptu stock check. The satisfied smile on his face as he reviewed the contents of his holdall told me he'd had a very good day.

With the body safely loaded on the van, the crowd began to disperse. The municipal undertakers sat in their cab while the driver wrote on a clipboard, and the balloon seller strolled towards them as I headed back to the balcony. He was still deep in conversation with them when I rejoined Kirsty and picked up my drink. The undertakers' van eventually departed, and I watched the balloon seller cross the road to assume a sitting position in the alleyway next to the bar. He rummaged in his holdall and removed a polythene bag of multicoloured rubber. The satisfied expression on his face suggested it was his last bag of stock, and he'd had an excellent day's trading. Delving into the holdall, he located a long, lime green strip of rubber and attached it to his battery pump, then watched as it slowly inflated until it was nearly as big as he was. He regarded his product with pride, then secured it between knee and elbow as he poked an old Nokia into life, and I lifted my camera to capture the image.

I watched as he jabbered away excitedly. I imagined him telling his wife to get the kids ready. He was coming home from work early so they could go out to celebrate a great day at the office. He'd sold two days worth of stock and what's more, made a deal with the council undertakers. They'd tip him off to the location of bodies, because where there are corpses, there are crowds, and crowds mean customers! Maybe they would take a rickshaw along Marine Drive and buy the kids ice cream at Chowpatty Beach, and later stop for Keema Pav at Crawford Market. He grinned and his head waggled happily as he spoke, and just when it seemed things couldn't get much better, he had to momentarily put down the Nokia as a smartly dressed woman approached with a wide-eyed boy and purchased his last balloon.

The balloon seller resumed his conversation, laughing as he spoke, and although I couldn't understand a word he said, I didn't need an interpreter to decipher the message.

"This time next year Roshni, we'll be millionaires!"

Night Train to Trang

Day 55 – Bangkok, Thailand

B angkok was as hot as Hell. The stifling humidity was compounded by uninterrupted sunshine, though the narrow streets around Soi Samsen, and the constant blanket of smog went some way to reducing the strength of the sun's rays. We'd made no plans, but it was clear we needed to get out of the city. We were mindful of the fact that after returning to England for a couple of weeks, we'd be setting off again for two months of tough travel in South America. Neither of us felt like doing anything too adventurous. After multiple flights between the UK, New Zealand, Fiji and Thailand, we'd also had enough of planes and airports. I had my eye on a train journey.

If I had to name my favourite mode of transport when travelling, I'd have to opt for the night-train, particularly in Asia or Eastern Europe. The start of a twelve hour train ride across strange lands still conjures up a sense of journey and adventure. I like to get to the station early, to get established in my cabin or secure the best bunk. To watch the comings and goings of fellow passengers, while I unpack my provisions for the night ahead. Plenty of water, snacks and alcohol. A torch, toothbrush and toothpaste, and some deodorant for a freshen-up in a stinking toilet cubicle in the morning. Some ear plugs and reading material. Then all that's left to do is settle back and await the guard's whistle, before sticking your head out of an open door or window to watch the sun set as you chug out of the station.

I knew that Thailand was a great place to travel by train, with an efficient country-wide network with links to neighbouring countries. Express trains from Bangkok headed south to Hat Yai, then on to Penang and Kuala Lumpur in Malaysia; east to Ban Klong Luk and across the border into Cambodia; north to Chiang Mai and the mountainous Golden Triangle region, and west to Kanchanaburi and the Bridge over the River Kwai. Long distance trains are of reasonable quality and fares are cheap – a 48 hour 1200 mile journey from Bangkok to Singapore would set you back just over fifty quid!

We'd enjoyed our time on Nananu-i-Ra in Fiji, and decided that a few more chill-out weeks on a beach would be a good option, as we wouldn't be seeing the sea again until the end of our upcoming South America trip, and Thailand is blessed with a multitude of islands. We decided that isolation of the kind we'd experienced in Fiji might become tiresome after a few days, but we were also keen to avoid the other end of the scale –waving glow sticks while dancing to trance music under a full moon on Ko Pha-Ngan held little appeal at our age.

I consulted the Thailand Lonely Planet which provided a good summary of each island. We wanted somewhere authentically local where people still lived and worked, as opposed to a large manufactured resort; small enough to get around by scooter, without encountering major towns or cities, but large enough to move on every few days and experience different areas.

We were sat outside the monitor-lizard bar when I thought I'd spotted an ideal location.

"Sixteen miles long and four miles wide," I read out to Kirsty.

"Sounds about the right size," she agreed.

"One main town which has two roads, and a total population of about 7,000. Seven villages and eleven white sand beaches, set against a backdrop of rubber trees and palms, mountains and jungle."

"Sounds nice. What's it called?"

"Koh Lanta Yai. Looks like we can get a night train part of the way there too. Fifteen hours!"

A fifteen hour journey by train might not sound like something to look forward to, but for us it killed two birds with one stone – It was taking us most of the way to Koh Lanta, and saving a night's accommodation too. We set off to book the train.

The streets surrounding our guest house were a warren of local housing and businesses, with home laundries figuring prominently. These were generally operated by old ladies who charged around thirty bhat per kilo of washing, which equated to around 75p or $1. Our bin liner stuffed with road-weary t-shirts and shorts was handed to an old crone with teeth like dry-roasted peanuts, and we agreed a price of eighty bhat to wash and dry the lot. We arranged a collection time by pointing at the hands of my watch, and set off to Hualamphong railway station to buy tickets to take us to Koh Lanta, or, more accurately, in the direction of Koh Lanta.

We knew that the N83 Express would only take us as far as the city of Trang, from where we'd need to take an hour long bus journey to the ferry port at Ban Pak Meng, followed by a two hour ferry. The train left Bangkok at 17.05 and arrived in Trang at 8.05 the next morning. There was only one ferry a day to Koh Lanta and that departed at 1pm, meaning we'd arrive on the island at about 3pm. All in all, it was going to take us a lot longer to get from Bangkok to Koh Lanta than from Thailand back to the UK! We were in no rush though and I was looking forward to a night train journey.

The following day we had a leisurely breakfast, with time to kill before making our way to Hualamphong station for the train at 17.05. We collected our now rejuvenated clothes, while wishing that UK pensioners would launch a similar home laundry service, and then called into a Seven-Eleven supermarket to purchase our provisions for the train. A five litre bottle of water and some Pot Noodles and crisps were placed in a basket and I headed towards the fridges containing the beer, only to be stopped in my tracks by the sight of chains and padlocks through the door handles. I'd been to Thailand a number of times, but it was clearly the first time I'd attempted to purchase take-away alcohol between the hours of 2pm and 5pm. Had I tried previously, I'd have been aware that an obscure law prohibits the sale of alcohol to be consumed away from licensed premises in the afternoon. This was a blow. A night train journey without a drink isn't much fun. The alcohol also helps ensure at least some sleep as the train bumps, lurches and grinds its way through the night. Our fifteen hour journey started to look a lot less appealing.

We collected our bags and jumped in a tuk-tuk to the station as I tried to concoct a plan to overcome our likely beer drought. We arrived half an hour before the scheduled departure, and I immediately spotted a Seven-Eleven over the road from the station, and began some mental calculations. We found the N83 express on Platform 1, and located our carriage. First class was only a couple of hundred baht more than second class and guaranteed us our own compartment, so we'd opted for that, rather than risk being separated from a serial snorer, farter or talker by only a thin cloth curtain in second class. The air-con in our compartment was set to gale-force and the windows were sealed shut, so we sat and shivered for a few minutes before I set off to explore. I found the 'restaurant car' and established that their alcohol range only extended to a six pack of warm Singha lager. The carriage door was open, and I leant out, feeling like I'd walked into a warm greenhouse on a freezing cold winters day. I looked down the platform to where three barbers had set up their chairs and were trimming and shaving commuters amidst the rush hour throng. Beyond them was a set of double doors leading to the street and a four-lane highway, with the Seven-Eleven on the far side of the road. I estimated that one minute should be enough to run up the platform, thirty seconds from station door to road. The unknown was how long it would take to cross the busy highway. I could buy beer at 5pm. The train left at five past. I was going to be cutting it fine. The next train was lunchtime tomorrow and if I didn't get aboard in time, Kirsty would be making the trip to Trang alone. It was obviously nonsensical to attempt the five minute beer-buy-and-sprint.

"Who dares wins." I muttered to myself.

Fifteen minutes later I was standing in the Seven-Eleven. I'd explained the situation to the perspiring, bespectacled manager who was more understanding than Kirsty had been. We'd agreed a strategy. He'd unlocked the fridges and allowed me to load up a small rucksack with cans of Chang. The problem was that the till system wouldn't allow the sale to be recorded until 17.00. We'd worked out the price, and the cash was already on the counter, but the manager told me that company policy dictated that he had to issue a receipt. At 16.59, service to a queue of commuters was suspended, and all present stared at the LED displaying the time on the till. The check-out clerk was a pimple faced youth with a name badge saying Dang. He bit his lip nervously like a sprinter awaiting the starters gun, as his manager coached him on the plan. Scan the Chang barcode, add x20, ring through the sale, print the receipt. He nodded solemnly.

The shop fell silent. The only noise was the honking traffic streaming past on the road outside, and the hum of a slush drink machine. I silently wondered if the clock had stopped and glanced nervously at my watch which was edging towards 17.01. Then, with the queue of commuters beginning to shuffle impatiently, the display silently replaced 16 with 17.

"Go!!! Go!!!" The manager was waving his arms and Dang fumbled the bar code and forgot how to key in twenty, before the till whirred and pinged and he thrust the receipt towards me as I took off towards the door.

I met a small, professional looking woman teetering on high heels coming the other way, and removed her from my path by gripping her shoulders and grinning manically as I guided her away from the door while shouting 'Sorry! Emergency!'

I'd already decided that there was no point waiting to cross the road conventionally, and that I would approach the obstacle as I'd learnt to in nations such as Vietnam, which view pedestrian crossings as an unnecessary indulgence. I strode purposefully into the oncoming flow of cars and tuk-tuks, taking one lane at a time. The idea is to pick an appropriate gap in the traffic and make eye contact with the oncoming driver to let him know that you don't intend to stop. Raising your hand in a 'halt' signal can also assist, as you march forward towards the white line denoting the lanes. Then start the process again for each lane until you reach the far pavement. Displaying any hesitation or nerves, or worse still taking a step backwards is likely to result in becoming an unusual Tuk-Tuk mascot for a few minutes at best, and truck roadkill at worst.

Staring down a cavalcade of rush hour traffic is an unnerving experience at the best of times, but doing it while lugging a backpack full of beer in a race against the clock increases the pressure substantially. The thought of Kirsty's likely reaction if I missed the train spurred me on and, after a near-miss game of chicken with a psychopathic pensioner in a Honda Civic in lane three, I reached the far pavement and charged towards the station doors. I noticed the large hand of the station clock positioned midway between 12 and 1, meaning I had about 2 minutes to cover the last hundred yards.

My obstacles were now human, and I was forced to adopt a 'survival of the fittest' policy, in that I only swerved to avoid the old, infirm or children. Anyone else was fair game for my flailing arms, barging shoulders and swinging rucksack. A smart-suited city type was despatched back into the barber's chair he'd just vacated as I flew past, with the train guard slamming shut the final door and raising his whistle to his lips.

There was no way I was going to reach our carriage, so I leapt aboard the first one I reached, which luckily had no door, as the train creaked and slowly began to roll forward. The third-class coach was full, and all aboard craned their necks to observe the sweating, panting foreigner, who was doubled up in the aisle, trying hard not to vomit. I just hoped Kirsty had seen me approaching and hadn't jumped off herself.

I made my way down the train and found Kirsty shivering in our compartment. She'd been monitoring my progress, waiting at the carriage door, preparing to throw our bags off and jump after them if I hadn't made it.

We cracked open a beer each and sat at the open door in the corridor, legs dangling above the tracks, enjoying the warmth as the sun's strength reduced, with darkness falling quickly. Dusk and dawn are my favourite times on a night train journey, and our clattering, slow pace through Bangkok's sprawling outskirts and satellite towns allowed us to share in the early evening routines of those whose homes sit alongside the tracks. Fathers tinkered with scooters, children played, mothers prepared food and bathed infants in tin tubs. A railway line seems to pass almost unnoticed, intimately closer to bedrooms, kitchens and toilet shacks than a road can ever be. The fact that those observing from a train have no way of stopping to breach the layer of anonymity, to actually meet the occupants of trackside homes, seems to render them invisible as they roll past and onto destinations hundreds of miles away.

We visited what was optimistically referred to as the 'restaurant car' to get some boiled water for our pot noodles. It had bench seats and an open kitchen, staffed by a chef from a bad comedy, with food stained 'wife-beater' vest and tight sports shorts straining obscenely beneath a bulging gut. The carriage had open window frames with no glazing, which allowed the warm night air to circulate as a pleasant breeze, far preferable to the icy chemical flow in our compartment. The only other occupants were a middle aged German couple who chain smoked and drank coffee while playing cards, so I retrieved some cans of Chang, and we sat and dodged giant moths and bullet-hard crickets which dive-bombed through the open window as the train trundled along.

The train was almost full with mostly local passengers, and we wondered aloud why none were choosing to sample the Thai Railways cuisine. Our explanation was soon forthcoming, as we watched the chef stirring a sizzling wok of noodles while balancing a cigarette between his lips, which boasted an impressive, inch long tail of ash. Predictably, and in keeping with the sitcom tone, he overdid the balancing act and didn't flinch as the burnt residue fell into the pan. He just carried on stirring. No need for black pepper in this dish! The noodles were duly dispensed into a polystyrene container which was collected by an unsmiling waitress, and transported to some unwary take-away customer further down the train.

The chef packed up at around 9pm, pulled down a shutter, turned off the lights and curled up on a camp bed behind the counter. The Germans finished off the remainder of the forty cigs they'd gone through during the evening and departed, and left Kirsty and I in the dark, clanking through the Thai countryside with the warm night hair blowing on our faces like a hair dryer.

I woke at first light in the morning, shivering beneath a thick blanket with the air-con in our cabin pumping out arctic blasts. My bones felt stiff and my eye was crusted from a typhoon strength vent directly above me. I picked up my camera and headed for the restaurant car to warm up.

The chef was already up and about, pans were sizzling and his first cigarette of the day was already threatening to make an unwelcome contribution to the breakfast noodles. A couple of middle-aged Thai men drank coffee alone, yawning and smoking. The sun was edging above the horizon to our left and I shivered as the first rays began to warm the carriage. I leant out of the window and clicked away as we passed through towns and villages, each one getting progressively busier, until by 7am every level crossing we passed, was six rows deep with motorbikes, scooters and tuk-tuks, revving their tinny engines and jostling for position at the barrier. A new day dawning, and for us, only another eight hours until we reached our destination!

The Day of the Beast

I winced as Jackson's Billy Jean pulsated from the large speaker four feet to my right, and a Dutch couple slurped and slobbered their way through a shared bowl of over-priced noodles on our left. I looked out at the calm waters of the Andaman sea and spotted the outline of Ko Muk to the south, and the limestone outcrop of Ko Ngai ahead. 30km to the north was our destination, Ko Lanta, and I willed the late running, inbound ferry to appear. It was already past our scheduled departure time of 1pm and the ferry dock at Ban Pak Meng was rapidly losing its appeal.

The small port was at the end of a road to nowhere with a scattering of marine workshops and boatyards. Someone had had the foresight to set up a small bar and shop, and the current proprietor clearly had ambitious plans to expand his business beyond snacks and beer. The chubby, floppy-haired twenty something was a jack-of-all trades and flitted effortlessly from barman to tour guide, as he dispensed advice on activities on the islands, supplemented with handfuls of 'friends' business cards. He also seemed to be the unofficial representative of the ferry company, as he shouted out regular updates on the boat's progress to the assembled backpack-toting masses gathered at the dock. Most annoyingly he also fancied himself as a party DJ specialising in 80's classics played at ear splitting volume.

I'd opened my laptop with the intention of beginning the next chapter of my book, but the first blasted chords of Cher's 'Turn Back Time' caused my mouse to shuffle across the table of its own accord, and I quickly developed writers block. I reached for the USB stick and clicked on the photos app, and my screen began to fill with thumbnail icons, some blank, others with intriguing images which invited a double-click.

One such image was of two figures on horseback, which I initially took to be Kirsty and I enjoying one of our ill-fated equine adventures. Opening the image to its full size, instead revealed two cowboys sat astride chestnut mounts on a dusty country lane.

Closer inspection showed a man in his forties and a boy in his early teens, most probably a father and son team. Both are wearing wide brimmed, navy blue sombrero style hats, and the horses' tack is adorned with multiple brightly coloured tassels.

I recognised the photo immediately, and involuntarily ran my fingers over my shins to feel for the scars that were inflicted on that day almost fifteen years ago, in the countryside near San Juan Del Sur in the Central American nation of Nicaragua.

We'd been travelling in neighbouring Costa Rica, but I'd been eyeing its more populous neighbour to the north. Nicaragua had formed part of the cultural backdrop to the late 1970's and early 80's and had sounded dangerous and exotic to my teenage ears, as I watched footage of the civil war on UK news bulletins. Even the players in the drama sounded like characters from a far-fetched banana republic spy parody – Sandinista rebels, Somozas, the Contras, Iranian arms dealers and Oliver North nearly bringing down the Reagan administration. When I realised our location in Costa Rica's Monteverde region was only a hundred miles from the border, I cooked up a plan.

It wasn't possible to take our hired car into Nicaragua, so we headed to the northern Costa Rican city of Liberia and parked up near the border. There was a regular direct bus service between Liberia and our first Nicaraguan destination, the city of Granada, and we crossed the border at Penas Blancas, and arrived in the old colonial city on the shores of Lake Nicaragua in the early afternoon. Granada is viewed as one of the architectural highlights of Central America and the cobbled streets lined with pastel shaded buildings were certainly atmospheric. However, the lakeside was litter strewn and underwhelming, with a few neglected cafes, and a kids' playground which was a health and safety risk of minefield proportions. The town centre itself boasted three magnificent 16th century churches, and Spanish influenced plazas with the usual cast of somnolent pensioners on benches, peanut vendors and toddlers chasing pigeons, but I couldn't help but feel that staying in the tourist-trap city wouldn't allow us to see the real Nicaragua. We scoured our guidebook, and I spotted a small fishing town, San Juan Del Sur, which had become popular with surfers, and was two hours and just two dollars by bus from Granada.

Kirsty recognised the name immediately from the Lonely Planet's Thorn Tree forum. The previous year a young American ex-pat, Eric Volz, had been jailed for the rape and murder of his ex-girlfriend in the town, even though his supporters claimed to have proof that he was in the capital, Managua, at the time of the crime. Volz had narrowly avoided being lynched outside the courtroom by a hostile crowd of locals, and later successfully appealed against the conviction and wrote a book, Gringo Nightmare, describing his ordeal.

We arrived in San Juan the following afternoon and immediately liked the feel of the place. The compact village centre had dusty gravel roads lined by brightly painted clapboard houses of Victorian vintage. Narrow 'panga' canoes bobbed on a perfect sea in a horseshoe bay backed by lush vegetation, and old men with lined, nut-brown faces mended fishing lines as surfer chicks in hot pants wandered past barefoot.

We booked into a bright green guest house with a fruit laden banana tree shading a scrubby garden, and set out to explore. In addition to the white sand beach in front of the town, we'd read of a number of spectacular and isolated coves to the north, so my intention was to rent some form of transport to explore the coastal backroads. It was clearly siesta time as we strolled through the quiet streets, with most of the businesses in town having already pulled down the shutters for the afternoon. A white rastafarian on a rickety cycle with cow-horn handlebars pedalled lazily past us, and I watched as he pulled up outside an open storefront ahead, where a couple of other bikes were propped against a wooden handrail. A hand painted sign spelled out 'Bike Rentals' in daubed burgundy letters, and though I didn't fancy a long distance cycle ride in the heat, I was hopeful they may have some motorised options available.

"Sorry dude, we don't do scooters or motorbikes. Just pedal power." A pony-tailed youth in jeans cut-off at the knees, and with an elaborate Incan sun tattoo spreading across his shoulder and chest delivered the unwanted verdict.

"Anywhere in town where we could rent one?"

"Not officially...but, just give me a minute." He headed back into the shack from which he ran his business, and returned after a couple of minutes with better news.

"My friend Armando is a mechanic. He usually has some bikes that he's working on or looking to sell that he doesn't mind renting. He's got something you can borrow."

As is usually the case in these situations, Kirsty's well placed common-sense kicks in to derail my ill conceived plans, and as we sat on the kerb waiting for Armando, she began to wonder aloud about details such as insurance or a rental agreement if we were to be stopped by the police.

"It will be a crappy 50cc scooter, worth a couple of hundred dollars. I doubt anyone will be bothered." I did my best to convince myself, while Kirsty looked dubious. Minutes later we were enveloped in a dust cloud, as a powerful quad bike roared up the little street at 40mph and executed a stunt-class U-Turn to pull up in front of the shop.

"Dickhead." I muttered as a muscular Hispanic twenty-something in a Chicago Bulls vest cut the engine and nodded a greeting.

"Armando! Yo!" The pony-tailed proprietor bounded out and fist bumped his friend as Kirsty gave me a 'told you so' look.

I looked at the quad. It was blue and chunky, and heavy looking, more like a small armoured car than a bike, with thick ridged tyres better suited to a tractor, and an ominous '500' beneath the saddle. A 500cc vehicle wasn't what I'd been expecting. Armando had also added some personalisation in the shape of a sticker proudly announcing the vehicle's name - 'Beast'. I correctly guessed it wasn't an automatic. I'd only driven a manual geared bike once before, and that was a little 125cc trials bike on a Thai island with no traffic.

Armando tossed me the key and asked how long I wanted the bike for. A sensible person would have explained that they only really wanted a battered little Chinese scooter to putter around on at 20mph, and decline the kind offer. My macho pride would obviously not allow that though, and I found myself agreeing to rent it for a couple of days for $10 a day. Kirsty's sharp elbow in the ribs reminded me to enquire about paperwork.

"No need man. The police around here know it's my bike. It's no problem."

"And....erm, I guess there's...erm no..." I knew how stupid it sounded before I said it. "Insurance?"

Armando and the bike shop owner smirked and gave me looks which said 'what do you think Gringo?'

"It's no problem dude, just drive slow. You'll be okay."

"But, if something did happen...?"

"Then we sort something out between us. Don't worry." Armando waved his hand dismissively and I couldn't help thinking about Eric Volz's courtroom welcome. This probably wasn't the best place to get on the wrong side of either the law or the locals.

Kirsty wisely refused to get on the bike until I'd ridden it up and down the main street a couple of times to get the hang of it. The gear change was a pedal-click down to engage first, then upward clicks for second, third and fourth. Fine for someone wearing motorcycle boots but in open toed sandals the sharp underside of the gear pedal would soon take its toll. I resolved to stay in second as long as possible as I cruised the dusty street, smiling confidently to show Kirsty I was in full control of 'the beast', though I found that the throttle was overly sensitive. Turning it a centimetre too far hinted at the vehicle's power and it lurched forward with a whiplash inducing turn of pace.

Eventually my performance somehow convinced Kirsty it was safe enough and she straddled the wide saddle to get on behind me, and we bunny-hopped our way out of town.

We headed north on Route 72, then turned off down a sandy track, heading back towards the coast and the hidden bays and beaches of Marsella, Maderas and Mathilda. Recent years have seen a development boom along the Pacific coast, with million dollar condos springing up amongst the pine forested hills overlooking the ocean, but ten years earlier when we explored the area, the coastal backroads still felt rough and untamed, with little motorised traffic. A handful of machete wielding campesinos bumped past us on ancient cycles, and we pulled the 'beast' to the side of a narrow track to allow a farm cart laden with sugar cane to pass. It was drawn by two unsurprisingly despondent Ankole cattle, with a thick wooden yoke, fashioned from a large tree branch, secured to the animals by a thick rope knotted around their enormous horns, in a manner unchanged for centuries.

Soon after, we came across the father and son cowboy double act trotting towards us on a quiet, tree lined stretch of road. I was concerned that the 'Beast's' throaty roar might startle the horses, so stopped and turned off the engine as they approached, riding side by side. Both animals were tacked up in the local 'vaquero' style, with the metal 'bit' replaced by a rope headstall, and were adorned with multiple flowing leather tassels which deter flies and stimulate the horse.

The highlight of the social calendar in small towns across Nicaragua is the annual Hipica or horse parade, and San Juan del Sur is no exception. Farmers from the surrounding area converge on the town with their prize mounts decked out in full traditional regalia, with manes groomed and styled and tails braided. There are floats, loud music and plenty of alcohol and the highlight of the festival is a dancing competition for horses!

I produced my camera as the cowboys approached and gestured to ask if they'd mind me taking a picture. The boy grinned shyly, and his Dad nodded his agreement. Then as often happens in many parts of the world, their friendly smiles disappeared as I raised my old Canon, and they assumed the persona of two stone-faced desperados. As soon as I'd clicked the shutter, the smiles reappeared, and I ambled over to show them the image in the LCD display.

We'd been on the quad bike for a couple of hours and I felt I was getting the hang of it, but Kirsty was still choosing to jump off to walk up particularly large hills, or over sections of the track with thick tyre ruts. I was generally travelling in second or third gear and maintaining a steady pace. We splashed through a small river with no problem, and picked up speed as we approached an incline curving upwards into the trees ahead. In anticipation of the hill, I remained in second gear and twisted the throttle to increase our speed. The track was sandy gravel with occasional large rocks hidden beneath the surface, which caused me to focus on the terrain beneath the Beast's wheels rather than the road ahead. It was only as we rounded the bend that the hill's gradient became apparent. What had begun as a gentle slope now turned into a steep 1:3 challenge, made more difficult by a marked deterioration in the road surface. I momentarily hesitated and considered whether I should stop to let Kirsty get off, but felt the bike begin to stall, so I dropped to first gear, and increased the gas a little too sharply, which caused us to lurch forward and bounce out of a large pot hole.

With the tyres spinning on the dusty surface, I glanced to the right to see the river far below us, at the foot of a steep slope which fell away sharply from the road. A barbed wire fence was the only barrier to a one-hundred-foot tumble down the ravine. Kirsty was struggling to stay on the pillion due to the increasing gradient, and the rough surface meant I was unable to gain enough speed to maintain our momentum. With a splutter and a clunk the engine cut out as I stalled the quad, and we began to slide backwards.

"Jump!" I yelled, but Kirsty had already leapt clear and landed in a heap in the dust. The Beast was now tilting and rolling slowly backwards towards the fence and the hillside beyond, so I applied the brakes. The wheels stopped turning and the quad halted momentarily before resuming a backwards slide with both wheels locked.

I heard Kirsty yelp in terror as the bike and I gradually slid towards the drop. As I usually do in such situations, I quickly considered the worst thing that could happen, and my mind was flooded with possible outcomes, all pretty terrible. The fence was constructed of thin wooden posts and two strands of barbed wire. It was highly unlikely to withhold the weight of the Beast, so would serve only to tear open my flesh as I crashed through it, at the beginning of a rapid descent down the hillside. Even if I managed to fall clear of the tumbling quad bike, and escaped with only several broken limbs, we were miles from anywhere. It would be a long ride back to town on an ox-drawn cart. And then, in my hospital bed, I'd be visited by Armando and his associates, come to 'sort out' the compensation for the deceased Beast.

I was now around two feet from the fence and, over my shoulder, gained a stomach churning view down the near vertical slope which I was perilously close to. It felt like the end of 'The Italian Job' with the getaway bus suspended over a cliff.

I felt exposed sitting on the bike, which was still sliding slowly backwards, so I calculated that if I got off the saddle to put my feet on the ground, but kept holding the front brake, that would buy me some time to consider what to do.

I immediately knew I'd made a mistake as my feet touched the dirt. My weight must have been anchoring the quad in position and now I'd got off, it again began to slide more rapidly towards the fence. I dug my feet into the gravel, gripped the handlebars and braced my arms to bring it to a halt. Fortunately, Armando had fitted the Beast with some rugged front mud-guards and these came to rest on my shins, therefore providing another braking method. Unfortunately, they were sharp and rusted and my lower legs were now bearing the weight of a 300KG bike. I howled in pain and felt a warm tickling sensation on my feet as blood trickled into my sandals. I gripped the front brake and locked my arms, having to push with all my might on the handlebars just to hold the bike in place. I was trapped, and I knew I couldn't hold it for much longer.

They say your life flashes before your eyes in such situations, but in this case, time seemed to stand still. Kirsty moved to help support the quad from behind, which reduced the weight I was bearing. I looked around and decided that if the terrain had contributed to our unfortunate position, it could maybe also help us out of it. I nodded towards a large stone which was half buried in the gravel and deployed Kirsty to excavate it and roll it across to the bike. Then another small boulder and a large tree trunk were retrieved and wedged beneath the back wheels of the Beast, while I continued to hold it in place, a couple of feet from a one-hundred-foot drop, with muscles straining and blood pumping from my lacerated shins. To our relief the quad remained in position. We both sank to the ground. Kirsty looked like I'd been towing her behind the bike for the afternoon, perspiring and covered in dust, with bloodied fingers and holiday nail-job destroyed. My arms throbbed and my shins were badly bruised and bore two bloody gashes inflicted by the Beast's mud guards.

"Maybe I'll tell Armando we only want the bike for one day." I stated the obvious as I started the ignition, and turned the Beast around, careful not to dislodge the makeshift barrier holding the back wheels in place. We limped back into town and dropped the quad off at the bike shop. The youth with the ponytail greeted us as we pulled up, and asked where we'd been. I muttered that we'd had a nice afternoon at one of the beaches as I handed over the keys, leaving him looking unsurprisingly bemused as he noticed the state we were in.

＊

Back on the ferry dock at Ban Pak Meng, I decided not to draw Kirsty's attention to the photo of the Nicaraguan horsemen. Our intention was to rent a scooter to get around on Koh Lanta and I didn't want to risk any post-traumatic flashbacks scuppering the plans if none were available and we had to resort to another quad bike!

At that point the owner of the bar interrupted a speaker-busting 'Born in the USA' to ring a clanking bell and trill over the microphone.

"Boat is coming! Boat is coming! Bon Voyage! Boat is coming!"

We picked up our rucksacks and shuffled along in a line of Western tourists and a smattering of locals. It had taken the best part of twenty four hours, but we were finally on our way to Koh Lanta.

Eyeland Life

Day 73 – Koh Lanta, Thailand

We soon settled into life on Koh Lanta, which was a melting pot of Buddhists, Thai-Chinese, Muslims, and Chao Leh sea gypsies. The Islamic influence was immediate as we stepped from the ferry to be met by a commotion of hooting tuk tuks, which were actually better described as a large motorbike and sidecar. A metal frame with a single wheel, bench seats and a canopy was welded to a standard motorbike, and at the ferry dock, 90% were driven by young Muslim women sporting an array of brightly coloured headscarves. In many Islamic countries, it would be frowned upon for an unmarried woman to even be seen in the company of male non-family members, but Koh Lanta's version of Islam seemed very relaxed. The girls were cheeky and chatty, like male taxi and tuk tuk drivers around the world.

A smiley late-teen girl skillfully negotiated the pot-holes to deposit us at the only accommodation we'd arranged on the island, a $10 'bungalow' at Klong Dao beach which we'd booked online in Fiji. In our previous guise as two week travellers, this place wouldn't have even been considered. With limited time in a beach location, we'd generally try to secure a beachfront, mid range option. Travelling for months rather than weeks meant that money became a key consideration, and we'd budgeted on a $15 per night average for Thailand. That would hopefully position us somewhere above dorm rooms and shared bathrooms with squat toilets, but we knew it also meant less sea views and no air-con.

Our bungalow was along a dirt track just off the main road. It was a single room bamboo construction boasting a small wet-room bathroom with Western style toilet, and a shower head positioned directly above the pan. If you so desired, you could combine a sit-down toilet visit with a shower and halve the time you spent on your ablutions! We had a small balcony with hammock which could double up as storage for our unpacked rucksacks, as there was no hanging space in the room and floor space was seriously limited. The picture-perfect, palm fringed beach and aqua-marine sea were a five minute walk away through a cypress fir wood. There were plenty of bars and restaurants with a chilled, traveller vibe pumping out a steady stream of Ambient House classics, but on the first night I caught the lazy beat of Marley's 'Natural Mystic' above the buzz of scooters on the main strip, and dragged Kirsty along a dark track to investigate.

We found an open plan, multi-level bar which looked like it had been constructed using the booty from a raid on a pallet factory. It was adorned with the green-yellow-red of the Rastafarian flag and imagery of the Lion of Judah and Emperor Haile Sellasie, with beanbags strewn around the various decking areas in lieu of seating. A young Thai Rasta with knotted dreads was manning the decks, which, as is usual nowadays, was a laptop hooked up to the powerful speaker system. We ordered drinks and flopped onto a couple of large cushions, and it wasn't long before Kirsty gave me a knowing look, reached for her book and said 'Go on then...'

Wherever I am in the world, I chat to reggae DJ's. We generally start by comparing our collection of tracks, and I always have artists on my phone which they've never heard of, mostly gathered from similar conversations held in bars around the world. Every country produces its own brand of reggae music, with its own unique styles and homegrown artists, and the young Thai asked me if I'd heard anything by Srirajah Rockers from Bangkok, and summoned up a track on the sound system. I nodded my appreciation, but it was a bit 'poppy' for my taste. Ras Muhamad from Indonesia was undeniably catchy but not something I'd want in my iTunes Library. Next up was Cambodia's Dub Addiction which was a bizarre confluence of traditional Khmer music and Reggae Dubstep. I liked it.

"Can you copy me this or Bluetooth me it?" The young DJ grinned and nodded and we set about pairing my iPhone with his laptop. Another addition to my collection. Next it was my turn.

I flicked through my library, by-passing the too-obvious offerings of commercially successful artists such as Marley, Culture and Black Uhuru. I needed something more obscure to prove my credentials, but didn't want to bamboozle him with a foreign language track initially, so flicked through my playlist until I found that under-rated classic 'None a Jah Jah Children' by Ras Michael and the Sons of Negus. Next, I flicked down to a couple of Spanish language offerings I'd picked up in Honduras, by an artist called Don Patero. By the time I knocked out a track by an Algerian band called Intik, which I'd picked up in West Africa, the DJ was visibly impressed and was writing down names and searching out You Tube clips. Then, as often happens, he thrust the USB cable in my direction to hand over control of the sound system. I linked up my phone via Bluetooth and went back to join Kirsty, wondering whether any passing British visitor would be baffled at hearing a Yorkshire reggae homage to the Chapeltown area of Leeds, blasting from a speaker on a small Thai island.

I was relieved to see that scooter rental was widely available for around 200 baht, or just over £4 a day, so there would be no repetition of our quad bike near-miss. Our daily routine was to have a leisurely breakfast, then attempt to escape the stifling heat in the sea, although this was easier said than done. The water was so warm on most of the beaches that it was like stepping into a recently run bath. We also had to contend with annoying little parasites known as sea fleas. Resembling tiny prawns if viewed under a microscope, they're carnivorous crustaceans with a voracious appetite for human flesh. They struggled to attach to a moving body, but if you remained still for a few seconds, you'd begin to feel the sensation of hundreds of tiny pin pricks. They were most prevalent when the sea was calm, and a dip in the appealing blue waters then, felt like being thrashed with a handful of nettles.

When it got too hot on the beach, we'd hop on the scooter to explore the island. If we found a beachside village we liked the look of, Kirsty would retire to a café and I'd go door-knocking to find a room for the following night. Then the next day we'd throw our bags into a tuk tuk and move down the coast to the next location. The face to face approach allowed me to negotiate with guest house owners and we secured some bargains, with most of our subsequent rooms directly facing a spectacular beach, and at much lower cost than that which appeared on booking engines.

At the most southerly beach on the island, Klong Jak, there was a high-end resort on a bluff, which was clearly beyond our price range, and a couple of low-key wooden bungalow complexes hidden in the trees facing the bay. Kirsty and I entered reception to find a late-twenties couple chattering excitedly with the receptionist. They were slim, tanned and good looking. Both were barefoot and swigging from bottles of Chang, and the 'ripped' young man was shirtless. The girl shrieked and giggled, and he spoke loudly in perfect, German-accented English. I took an immediate dislike to them, probably because he was breaching one of the rules by which I live my life - Never conduct business with exposed nipples.

They'd asked to view the rooms available, and the lady on reception dispatched a loafing youth to conduct a guided tour. The girl gave Kirsty and I the once-over, and sniffed disdainfully as she passed, clearly unimpressed by our road-dusted clothing. I approached the desk and asked the same question. The receptionist was a plump, jovial, Muslim lady called Soo, who told us to follow the other couple to have a look at the rooms.

"We only have two rooms left for tomorrow. The one at the front facing the beach has only a fan and is 500 Baht, the one at the back has air-con and is 600," she shouted after us as we left reception.

The couple were mauling and slobbering over each other on the balcony of the beachfront room when we caught up with them, to the obvious embarrassment of the boy who was showing them around.

"So cute! We love it!" squealed the girl.

"May as well check out the other room anyway." Her boyfriend took her hand, and their young guide led the way towards the rear of the building.

Kirsty had barely stepped onto the wooden balcony before I'd stuck my head round the door frame, quickly retracted it, and set off at speed towards reception. She followed me just in time to see me handing over a thousand baht to Soo.

"Yes, we'll take that one for two nights, maybe three."

Soo took the cash, gave me a receipt and said she'd arrange for her sister to collect us on her tuk tuk in the morning. I was just explaining where to pick us up when the annoyingly exuberant couple burst back into reception, the girl whooping with delight as her partner playfully nipped her skinny arse.

"We're going to take the seafront room Soo," the girl yelled over my shoulder. "I want to write poetry as I watch the sunset."

"Oh...." Soo's face fell as we walked away from reception.

We paused after rounding the corner and smirked as we heard the mood turn ugly.

"Those people have taken our room Soo...how on earth did that happen?!" I was tempted to poke my head back round the corner to offer some advice. 'You snooze, you lose. And keep your nipples out of sight when conducting business son!'

We spent a couple of weeks moving between the island's beachside villages, then decided to spend our final nights in Lanta village on the East Coast, known locally as 'Old Town'. We'd visited on our scooter and found a single dusty street, lined with local shops and a smattering of tourist focused bars and restaurants. Behind the main drag were a series of wooden docks and traditional stilt houses. A ten minute wander along the piers had led us to a room for rent overlooking the water, with distant views of the tiny island of Koh Por and the Thai mainland beyond. The room was cheap, and we slept well, listening to the waves below us, but the stilt houses were something of a photo highlight and I had to refrain from sitting on the balcony in my undies, in case I was inadvertently captured by the long lens of a passenger on one of the passing ferries.

The village had a pharmacy, which was useful, as I'd developed a lump on the lower lid of my right eye. This had deteriorated from what I'd assumed to be a small stye, into a large red swelling which had become quite painful. The pharmacist peered at it for a few seconds and shook his head.

"Not stye. Insect bite. Wear this." He produced a tube of antibacterial gel and waved me on my way.

Overnight the swelling and the pain increased, and when I awoke it looked like I'd been poked in the eye. I returned to the chemist and was greeted by a different pharmacist, this time younger and female.

"Not bite. It's maybe stye or cist. Keep clean and use these." This time I was handed some antibiotic drops and suspected that the original pharmacist was hiding behind the counter, eager to sell me as many eye remedies as possible.

A day later and things had taken a visible turn for the worse. My lower eyelid had begun to fill with pus and throbbed beneath the sun's glare. Tellingly, Kirsty had taken to grimacing and turning away when I asked her what it looked like.

We rode the scooter to the main town of Baan Saladan, where I hoped there would be a better qualified range of pharmacists to assess the problem. There were certainly a lot of pharmacists, and they all had an opinion. Unfortunately, none were the same.

Abcess. Stye. Cist. Dirt in eye. Infection. No infection. Conjunctivitis. Definitely not conjunctivitis. Insect bite. Poke in eye?

Remedies also ranged from drops and ointments to oral antibiotics; drying it in the sun to keeping it out of the sun; cleaning with salt water to keeping it away from the sea.

What they clearly did all agree on was that my eye was disgusting. They all visibly blanched at the sight of it, and when usually nonchalant medical staff do that, you know you have a problem. By our last day on the island, my lower eyelid was now a pus-filled carbuncle, which was weeping and had started to attract flies. Cleaning it with cotton wool soaked in cold water seemed to bring some temporary relief, but I now had to contend with a near twenty-four hour journey by boat, bus and train back to Bangkok. Access to clean water was going to be a problem.

As we waited on the boat dock for the ferry back to Ban Pak Meng the following day, I began to notice other travellers recoiling in horror at the sight of my eye, and Kirsty could no longer look at me. I'd also started to notice a strange smell amongst the diesel fumes and unwashed tourist aromas surrounding me. I began to suspect that my eyelid was rotting. Maybe an insect had laid eggs in the wound, and its spawn would hatch spectacularly from my eye socket as the guard stamped my ticket on the Bangkok Express. On a brighter note, it was my birthday!

I rarely wear sunglasses and had none with me in Thailand. Stupidly, I'd also not thought to buy any from a tourist shop on Koh Lanta, so Kirsty leant me hers, to prevent me contributing to any feelings of sea sickness on the ferry. I sat feeling sorry for myself with Kirsty's glamorous, oversized tortoiseshell shades concealing the abomination that was my pulsating eyelid. I looked like a low-rent Jackie Onassis drag act on a very bad day, but at least I wasn't scaring any children.

When we arrived in Trang, I left Kirsty sat outside a café at the station and went to buy some more appropriate sunglasses. I got some strange looks as I wandered the main street wearing obvious ladies' shades, with a drizzle of discoloured liquid weeping down my cheek like a septic tear. Trang was a workaday sort of town. With no tourist draws, it was really just a place for travellers to pass through. Therefore, there were no shops selling tourist tat. No fake Tag Heuer watches or rip off European football kits. No deep fried grasshoppers and seemingly no sunglasses!

I walked up and down every shopping street under a blazing sun, and trailed through every street market, before I was directed to a shop selling cheap household goods. I was dubious upon entering, but after pointing to Kirsty's shades, I was led along a dusty aisle by an equally dusty old man, who pointed to a shelf which was too high for him to reach. I extended my arm and located a cardboard box, which I pulled from the shelf as the shopkeeper nodded.

The box had been there for some time, and he brushed a layer of accumulated grime from the lid and opened it. We both peered inside, at which point I deduced that these sunglasses must have been purchased from the wholesaler when the pensioner was in his late twenties, and had seen Elton John performing Rocket Man. They were thick, square framed, silver in colour and had blue tinted mirror lenses. I scrabbled through the box, but they were all the same in their uniform ugliness. The old man nodded enthusiastically, then recoiled at the sight of my putrescent eye as I removed Kirsty's glasses. Clearly once I'd tried his pair on, there would now be no chance of not buying them.

Kirsty was finishing her coffee as I arrived back at the station. She watched me approach as I crossed the road sporting my newly acquired shades, and tried unsuccessfully to stifle a smirk as I handed her sunglasses back.

"What? At least they cover my eye up." I was anticipating sporting the spectacular eyewear until we got back to England for a proper diagnosis, so was hoping for some encouragement.

"You look like..."

"What? These were all they had...what do I look like?"

"You look like a really bad sex tourist. Like one of those old perverts you see with Thai teenagers."

I caught sight of my reflection in the café window and had to agree. I was more Gary Glitter than Elton John. If I landed at Heathrow wearing these, I'd be on a register before I left the terminal, but hopefully the regulars on the train we were catching would be more used to people like me. I picked up my rucksack.

"Come on. Let's go to Bangkok."

Sharia Cocktails

"This is the 09.33 GNER service from London Kings Cross to Leeds, calling at Steven-age, Peter-borrow, Grant-Ham, Noo-wark Nort-gate, Doncaster..." I smiled at the familiar 'Asian-with-a-hint-of Yorkshire' accent that crackled from the speaker above our heads. It was a pleasant March Saturday, and we were on our way home for a couple of weeks before setting off again on our travels. I'd sought out a more professional looking pharmacy in Bangkok and been prescribed some strong antibiotics for my eye infection. For once, the white coated medic behind the counter didn't even attempt to diagnose the problem.

"It's badly infected, and it's nasty!" was her summary.

Two days later and my eye's appearance had improved to the point that I didn't feel the need to wear my child-molester shades, though I did catch a couple of passengers on the tube from Heathrow give me a second glance before turning away in disgust.

The 200 mile train journey home from London, after an all night flight from a steamy tropical city such as Bangkok, is always guaranteed to leave you disorientated. After travelling more or less non-stop over a number of days from somewhere like Koh Lanta, it's especially perplexing for mind and body. Kirsty snoozed, but I was on Thai time and it was late afternoon, so I felt a strange combination of physical fatigue and mental liveliness. I opened my laptop and clicked into the photos app.

The first thumbnail image to appear was a graffitied building pockmarked by bullet and shell fire. Mostar in Bosnia was easily recognisable. Next, an old Chinese man on a bike wearing a baseball cap. The bike had a wire basket on the front containing a large white rabbit. Sun Moon Lake, Taiwan. I remembered wondering whether it was a pet or his dinner. I was on a roll here. The next click was a 'file not found'. I clicked again and a photo of a petrol station appeared with the yellow and red livery and logo of the Shell oil company. I was about to click the mouse to move to the next image, but wondered what had caused me to photograph a gas station, so double clicked on the file. It was at that point I noticed deep water where a road should have been, and recognised it as one of the unique floating petrol stations in Bandar Seri Begawan, capital of the Kingdom of Brunei.

'Where is Brunei?' is one of those geographical quiz questions which catches a lot of people out. Just as people tend to locate Guyana in Africa, most would point to the Middle East if asked to locate the oil rich sultanate. I would probably have given the same answer, until a trip to Borneo, when my atlas had revealed the tiny 2000 square mile enclave surrounded by the Malaysian State of Sarawak. I knew nothing about Brunei, but when our flight schedule provided the opportunity to fly home through the country, it was a no-brainer. If a new country is easily reachable during a trip, and it's officially one of the least visited nations in the world, why not visit?

A quick Google search revealed Brunei to be a nation with one of the world's highest standards of living, thanks to its bountiful oil and gas reserves, and the fact that Bruneians pay no income tax. A British Protectorate until 1984, the country is now ruled as an absolute monarchy by the Sultan, Hassanal Bolkiah, who is rumoured to be one of the world's richest men. Indeed, his lavish lifestyle is the stuff of legend, with an airbus A330 which he pilots himself, and a two thousand room palace with a garage large enough to house his collection of five hundred Rolls Royces.

I read that Brunei is deemed one of the safest countries in the world, with a justice system based on an uneasy mix of British law and strict Islamic Sharia. Punishments seemed to lean towards the latter, with limb amputations for theft and stoning for adultery. It didn't sound like electronic tags and ASBO's had really taken off in Brunei.

The mention of Sharia set alarm bells ringing and as I read on, I detected a potential problem. I'm not an alcoholic, honestly. But I do like a drink, especially when travelling. For me, the best part of a day, especially one which has involved some form of adventure or life threatening situation, is to sit back and reflect on it as the sun sets, with an ice cold beer in hand. I don't need to get drunk to have a good time. In fact, as I've got older, the pain of the following day tends to outweigh the enjoyment of the night before a little too much, but I do like a couple of 'sundowners' and a drink with a meal. Brunei is a 'dry' country, in fact, arid is probably a better word to describe it.

I'd assumed that, as in many Arabic countries, bars and restaurants wouldn't sell alcohol, but large hotels would have a discreet room hidden away, with a tiny bar, visible through a fug of cigarette smoke, with men in cheap suits and large moustaches and dark eyed woman in short skirts, with slightly smaller moustaches. No such luck. Nowhere sold alcohol in Brunei and the penalties for locals caught drinking were severe – whipping with forty lashes for a first offence, eighty if you didn't learn from that, and two years in jail if you still felt inclined to have a crafty can of Carling before evening prayers. Rules were fortunately less stringent for foreigners, and it was permissible to import two litres of spirits and eight cans of beer. However, imported alcohol could only be drunk in private, in a hotel room or private residence, and only in the presence of non-Muslims. Drinking or being intoxicated in public was deemed a serious offence, punishable by a fine of $8000 and up to two years in prison. 'Pre-loading' in a hotel room felt a bit desperate to me, like a junkie shooting up in a back alley, but I purchased a litre of vodka before we left Kota Kinabalu anyway, thinking it might come in handy.

We had a couple of days in the capital, Bandar Seri Begawan, which felt a little like a model town in a theme park. Streets were spotless, a huge golden domed mosque surrounded a lagoon with ornamental fountains, and air-conditioned shopping plazas were filled with affluent looking ladies in colourful Islamic head scarves, and skinny men in tight suits and 'songkok' fez hats. The city centre felt like an even more sterile version of Singapore and held little appeal, so we headed towards the river and Kampong Ayer, which is BSB's old town. Known as the original 'Venice of the East', Kampong Ayer is the world's largest floating stilt village, though a population of around 30,000 probably qualifies it as a stilt city!

The Brunei River has reputedly been home to a floating settlement for over a thousand years, and Kampong Ayer is actually made up of over forty separate villages, connected by a network of 38km of wooden walkways and bridges. This sounded much more appealing than the gleaming city centre, so we jumped aboard one of the ubiquitous speedboat taxis and headed across the water.

This was a different world to the city just across the river. Timber houses, some dilapidated and sun faded, others freshly painted in lilacs, greens and pinks, sat alongside mosques, schools, shops and restaurants. Old men cycled along the wooden boardwalk streets, dodging schoolkids casting makeshift fishing lines into the river on their lunchbreak; three old ladies watched a Malay soap on a blaring portable TV, a reminder that every house had electricity, as well as running water. The river was alive with speedboats – city slicker commuters in sharp suits heading home for lunch; women with chainstore carrier bags stuffed with sale bargains; and the local police force working their beat in a powerful craft with dual outboard motors and flashing blue lights.

We wandered the labyrinth of boardwalks for hours, not having a clue where we were, though we didn't need to. When we decided to head back to our hotel in the city centre, we simply stuck out an arm and waved down a taxi, Brunei style. Hundreds of speedboats ply their trade around Kampong Ayer, and we were soon skimming across the river at 30 knots in one of the most exhilarating 'taxi' journeys I'd ever experienced. We also experienced the floating petrol station, which I'd snapped as our driver stopped for a fill-up en-route.

Back at the hotel, I eyed up the litre bottle of vodka while Kirsty was in the shower, and considered my options for the night ahead. I'd read on the Lonely Planet forum about a couple of semi-mythical and highly illicit 'speak-easies' which supposedly served alcohol, if you could find them. However, their location was an ever changing and closely guarded secret, which was hardly surprising when a night out and a few beers could result in being stretched over a rack in the local cop shop, then whipped to within an inch of your life. Also, in my experience, illegal drinking dens sound glamorous and exciting, but generally lose their appeal after the first drink or two, and can often turn into a 'Hotel California' style experience, where the 'lock-in' is literal, and you're forced to stay for the long haul whether you want to or not.

I therefore decided that Bruneian drinking dens were probably not going to deliver a fun packed night, and began to decant the vodka into two empty plastic water bottles. Kirsty exited the bathroom and gave a quizzical look when she saw what I was up to.

"We might find somewhere quiet where we can slip some into a glass of coke." I felt like a secret alcoholic being caught putting vodka into my breakfast orange juice, but justified it by telling myself I was on holiday so deserved a drink, and swigging full fat coke all night would keep me awake and rot my teeth.

"But you don't even drink Vodka." Kirsty shook her head in the way she does when she anticipates trouble ahead.

I'd read another thread on the Thorn Tree forum which suggested that certain Chinese restaurants sold beer disguised in teapots, and the code to indicate that alcohol was on offer was a menu containing pork dishes. The old teapot trick is well used around the world and I've enjoyed a beer in a porcelain tea cup or a logoed mug more suited to a builders brew, in various cities in India and Syria. The giveaway in those countries was that the terraces of the restaurants in question were full of glassy eyed Westerners apparently slurping their way through multiple pots of frothy chai. In Brunei, there were no other tourists to provide us with a clue, so I was going to have to make some subtle enquiries myself.

We passed a couple of Chinese restaurants and I cast an eye over the menu as we passed, but didn't spot any swine based cuisine. I was beginning to think the tale was an urban myth, when we arrived at a slick looking establishment, brightly lit and with large picture windows facing the road which ran parallel to the river. A red leather-bound menu stood on a lectern by the door and I flicked through the laminated pages until I spotted the words 'Char Siu' under the 'special barbecue' section. I had a feeling that Char Siu was pork, and maybe the fact that it wasn't spelled out as such was a ploy to deceive the authorities. If illicit pork was on offer, then surely a teapot full of ice cold Anchor Beer, smuggled over the border from Sabah would be available to wash it down.

The restaurant was around half full and a young waiter spotted me hovering in the doorway and approached, smiling. He had a long thin mouth, extending almost to his ears, and small pointy teeth which made him look like a bottlenose dolphin in a polo shirt.

"Table for two person?" He seemed proud of his English.

"Maybe." I replied cryptically and lowered my head towards his.

"Do you sell....Pork?" I pronounced pork slowly and carefully and looked deep into the waiter's eyes while raising my eyebrows quizzically.

"Pork sir?"

"Yes. PORK." I emphasised the word and nodded. And winked. I looked round the restaurant but couldn't see any teapots on the tables.

The waiter retreated to the bar, from where he retrieved a menu, which he began to thumb through.

"Char Siu, sir, it's pork dish, I think. Pig?"

He wasn't taking the bait, so I decided to take the bull by the horns, and leaned in towards him.

"Do you....sell beer here?" I winked again and made a tea-drinking gesture, even extending my little finger to add an air of refinement, but the waiter reacted as if I'd asked to buy his sister. The Flipper smile was replaced by an anxious frown.

"Oh no sir! No beer, alcohol is forbidden here." He looked over his shoulder as if expecting a whip wielding constable to appear from the kitchen.

Again, I felt like a shamefaced smackhead caught injecting in a park by a primary school outing, and shuffled out of the door.

We crossed the road to a small restaurant with a balcony overlooking the river, where I steered us to a quiet corner table away from the few other diners. Unfortunately, as is often the case when you're the only foreigners in town, our presence was obviously seen as a good advert for the restaurant, and a bright spotlight was illuminated behind us, to ensure we were clearly visible to any potential punters perusing the menu. Two attentive waiters dashed back and forth, and delivered what promised to be the first of many glasses of coke.

We ordered stir fried chicken and a side bowl of ambuyat, which the waiter told us was the national dish of Brunei. Made from sago palm tree starch cooked into a white paste, it looked like the 'Gloy' glue used in primary school art lessons in the 1970's, and tasted as I'd have expected, had you been forced to eat some by the school bully. It wasn't a delicacy I could see catching on if Bruneian restaurants ever become a culinary craze in the UK, but the chicken was tasty, the evening was warm, and the view across the river towards the twinkling lights of Kampong Ayer was fantastic. We finished our meal and ordered more coke, as two smartly dressed couples in their thirties smiled a greeting as they selected the table opposite ours. The restaurant was filling up and was clearly a favourite amongst the chattering classes of Bandar Seri Begawan.

The river was a hive of activity, as speedboats zipped back and forth, illuminating the water in the beam of their powerful navigation lamps, and the haunting sound of the 'Isha' call to prayer drifted on the still night air from the minarets of dozens of mosques across the water in Kampong Ayer. It was the sort of place I'd have been happy to spend the rest of the evening, but I was beginning to tire of cola.

I called the waiter over and ordered a bottle of mineral water. Kirsty eyed me suspiciously, and with good cause. I'd noticed that the water served in the restaurant came in a non-descript plastic bottle which was almost identical to those containing vodka which I had stashed in our rucksack. Within seconds of the waiter delivering it to our table, the bottle had been furtively switched with one containing a more potent form of refreshment. I took a swig of coke, then topped up my glass from the 'water' bottle.

"Stop it! That woman's watching you!" Kirsty was nervously surveying our fellow diners, and was clearly envisaging spending the next day applying after-sun lotion to my whip lacerated back. I cast a wary sidewards glance towards the neighbouring table, where one of the women did seem to be taking a keen interest in our European drinking habits. 'They're diluting their coke. The British must not like fizzy drinks,' I imagined her speculating to her friends.

It wasn't long before Kirsty's concern gave way to her asking for a Smirnoff dash to liven up her own glass of pop, and I duly obliged, while continuing to be closely observed by our fellow diners. I'm not usually a spirit drinker, and although the vodka was largely tasteless, it gave the coke a pleasant kick, and I'd soon polished off a glass and was topping up again from the 'water' bottle.

"You might as well fill mine up while you're at it," whispered Kirsty and I poured her a generous measure.

This was more like it, and we began to relax, turning our seats out towards the river and watching the innumerable small craft buzzing by, with our drinks going down very nicely. We ordered a couple more cokes and it wasn't long before we'd finished the first bottle of vodka, and I executed another furtive switch to replace it with the second one from the bag.

One benefit of drinking spirits instead of beer was that the number of toilet visits was greatly reduced, but after about an hour, I decided that a trip to the bathroom was required. I hadn't realised that a downside of drinking vodka is that, unlike beer, which greets you like an old friend, then engages you in evermore entertaining conversation, vodka creeps up on you like a mugger in a back alley. One minute you feel fine, you're enjoying a laidback drink on a scenic riverside terrace and the next...wham! It hits you hard and there's no going back.

As soon as I rose to my feet, I knew I was in trouble. The floor seemed to slope away towards the two couples who were all closely monitoring my progress. The doorway to the interior of the main restaurant was brightly lit by a ring of halogen bulbs, which dazzled me and caused me to blink and rub my eyes. I set off walking towards the door, but my legs felt leaden and unruly and I stumbled, then began to veer uncontrollably to the right. Conscious that I was being watched, I gave the couples a cheery wave to let them know I was okay, and lurched forward.

Two waiters approached as I entered the restaurant, and that further unbalanced me, and I took three steps backwards and crashed into a thankfully unoccupied table. I smiled and asked the way to the toilet, but my tongue suddenly felt too big for my mouth and my lips seemed to move slower than my brain.

"Whuusatoyyatt?" was the sound that I made, and the two waiters stopped and looked at me with wide eyes and perplexed expressions.

"Toyyyat?" I pointed haphazardly beyond the bar and shrugged theatrically.

The waiters looked concerned and one took hold of my arm to steady me, as an older man approached from behind the bar.

"Aaaamorriiite!" I slurred and patted my helper on his back, while struggling to focus as he and his colleague reeled and span in front of me.

"Sir, are you feeling okay? I am the manager here. Is everything alright?" His worried expression befitted a man who had never before experienced an inebriated customer, and therefore assumed he had a tourist suffering a serious medical episode in his establishment.

"Yuusaamfine-arjusneedatoyaat. Please."

The manager shook his head and assigned one of the waiters to look after me. He took my arm and guided me past a table of smartly dressed middle aged men, who stopped eating to watch with concerned faces as I staggered past them. Their expressions suggested doctors on a night out, no doubt wondering if they were about to be summoned to deal with a stroke victim. The waiter pushed open the door to the toilets and stood watching me as I swayed and fiddled with the zip on my shorts.

"Soekay. Yuucangurnow." As soon as he closed the door, I made my way to the wash basins and began to splash my face with cold water. I tried to focus on my reflection, but the bright lights turned the room into a nauseating fairground ride, so I gripped the sink and closed my eyes. I had to sober up quickly. The restaurant staff seemed oblivious to the signs of excess drink, but the couples on the neighbouring table looked more worldly wise. I imagined them on the phone to the sharia police, who would now be speeding to the restaurant in a pick-up truck, menacing in black turbans and with vicious leather whips twitching, ready for action.

After five minutes of face splashing, I exited the toilets and the whole room turned to watch me gingerly pick my way between the tables, nodding respectfully to the worried looking doctors as I passed.

"Could we have the bill please?" I mouthed, slowly and carefully as I headed back to our table.

"Where have you been? Those people started talking to me! Why are you all wet?" Kirsty whispered loudly. Her eyes were struggling to focus on me, and it was clear she was also suffering the effects of our alcoholic over-indulgence.

We'd strolled into the restaurant as two healthy, thirty-something tourists enjoying a night out in an exotic capital city. We shuffled slowly out, arm in arm, supporting each other like a couple of geriatric derelicts who'd been drinking cooking sherry on a park bench. No wonder the manager looked visibly shaken as he bade us farewell.

Even in my drunken state, the threat of the evening ending with forty lashes loomed large in my mind, and we hurried to the nearest taxi dock and flagged down a ride home. If our afternoon speedboat ride had been exhilarating, repeating it in the dark after downing a litre of vodka elevated the experience to white-knuckle ride proportions. Our whoops, yells and screams only encouraged our driver, who cranked the outboard to the max and undertook some hair-raising manoeuvres as we swerved off the river, and along narrow canals flanked by neon lit high-rises and mosques bathed in golden light. Not surprisingly we both had to suppress the urge to vomit as we paid and staggered onto the pier near our hotel.

The following day was too hot for a hangover, and Kirsty and I skulked in air-conditioned malls until the sun set. Not surprisingly, we then decided to avoid the riverside restaurant and sought out the dolphin faced waiter from the Chinese restaurant of the previous evening. He greeted us with a familiar, face-wide grin, and on this occasion I had no need to enter into a coded discussion on the availability of pork or the contents of his teapots. After the previous night's excesses, it seemed only right that we follow the local customs, and for the first time I could remember while travelling, a tea-total, Sharia compliant evening was actually quite appealing.

A Day Trip to Brazil

Day 87- Sao Paulo, Brazil

It was late March and Kirsty and I were sat outside a bar in Brazil. We're weren't meant to be there, and I don't mean in that bar, or that street or even that city. We weren't meant to be in Brazil. We should have been 1500km away in Asuncion, the capital of Paraguay. As unexpected travel diversions go, it was quite significant. Like getting a flight from Manchester to London and ending up in Madrid.

We'd arrived home from Thailand in mid March, and done all the things you do when you've been away for a couple of months. Spent time with friends and relatives; took our motorhome to our spiritual home, the Yorkshire Dales; had a proper pint and a real Yorkshire curry; and I'd temporarily reclaimed my season ticket to see Leeds United's promotion hopes take a predictable hit with a defeat to Sheffield United.

I'd also made sure that I'd successfully downloaded my photo collection before we set off to South America. I was about to bin the Thai USB stick, but in the end I couldn't bring myself to do it. I'd come to enjoy the random, scattergun stream of memories appearing on my laptop screen, and it had actually become an essential part of the trip, to be anticipated and savoured over an evening beer. We expected plenty of long, night-bus journeys on this leg of the trip, and I thought my snapshot collection may prove a welcome diversion from darks nights on Andean mountain roads.

Our plan was to travel overland from Bolivia, into Peru and then on to Ecuador, from where we'd fly home in two months. Before that though, we'd visit Paraguay, a mysterious land which I'd been reading about in John's Gimlette's book, 'At the Tomb of the Inflatable Pig.' What was in Paraguay? Not much really. Why were we visiting? Basically, because it was there. I didn't know anyone who'd ever been to Paraguay, and various traveller forums proved its 'off-the-beaten-track' credentials with only a smattering of posts featuring unanswered questions stretching back a number of years.

Gimlette's book described a nation of jungles, dictators, fraudsters, Nazi war criminals, ridiculous wars and numerous coups. Tellingly, it was one of the few countries in the world without its own Lonely Planet or Rough Guide. When I noticed that Iberia flew there via a daily LATAM Airlines connection in Sao Paulo, it was an obvious place to start our South American odyssey.

Our overnight Iberia flight landed in Sao Paulo at 6am, ahead of a connection to the Paraguayan capital just over two hours later, and the Spanish Airbus A330 was thankfully only half full, allowing us to stretch across a row of seats and get a half decent night's sleep. We emerged bleary eyed into a bright dawn at Sao Paulo's Guarulhos airport, and began scanning the 'Flight Connections' screen for the Asuncion gate. Airlines in South America often operate flight schedules like bus timetables, with various stops en-route to a final destination, so I didn't panic when I failed to spot Asuncion on the board. I kept looking, assuming that the flight terminating in Santiago or Mendoza would suddenly blink, and flick over to show 'via Asuncion', but nothing happened.

We stood and stared at the board until the rest of the passengers from our flight had trundled their wheelie bags along the long corridor into the terminal.

"Hmmm. That's not looking good." I pulled out the boarding cards we'd been handed in Madrid to double check the time. "Definitely 08.15 departure. Boarding 07.30." That was still an hour and a half away.

We wandered through the quiet terminal until we came to a LATAM customer service desk, looking like customer service desks at airports all around the world. Middle Aged women in crumpled clothes with bedhead hair slumping asleep on piled-up luggage; a melee of frowning passengers leaning on the desk, facing nonchalant, uniformed staff with phones glued to their ears; men in suits huffing and puffing, waving sheaths of paper and looking at their watches; a bored toddler crawling on stained floor tiles as his mother scrabbles in an oversized bag for a missing passport or luggage receipt. Airport customer service desks are one of the most depressing places in the world, and the law of averages says if you travel enough, every so often you'll be forced to experience one.

We joined the queue and I heard snatches of conversation in Spanish mentioning Asuncion. The young woman at the front of the queue was pointed towards the bowels of the terminal, and stomped away, shaking her head and muttering oaths of terrible revenge. It wasn't a promising sign.

After half an hour, we reached the front of the queue and were greeted by a swarthy, curly haired employee in a navy blue blazer, with a name badge informing us that he was Lucas. His company-issue tie was loosely knotted, and his top shirt button was undone, hinting that he was at the end of a long shift. Beneath close-set eyes he bore the unfortunate nose of a proboscis monkey, drooping towards his upper lip like a collagen injection accident. His method of greeting dispensed with the need for verbal communication, as he tilted his head upwards slightly and raised his eyebrows, in the universally recognised gesture employed by service staff which loosely translates as 'What the fuck do you want?'

"Our flight to Asuncion..." I began, while brandishing my boarding card at Lucas.

"It's gone." Lucas began tapping on a computer keyboard whilst looking down his bulbous nose at the screen.

"Erm...It's meant to depart at..."

"Yes, but it's gone." Lucas was clearly intent on clearing the queue as quickly as possible so he could go home to bed.

"Gone? Gone where?" I was understandably confused as to how a plane could depart more than two hours early. This wasn't a schedule change that we'd missed, as the departure time was still 08.15 when we'd checked in at Madrid.

"Gone to Asuncion. Where do you think?" Lucas continued tapping away, while shaking his head at my stupidity.

"When? Why?" Lucas's droopy face was perfectly constructed for sneering and I knew I was asking for it.

"It departed at 4am. I have no idea why it did, but it did!" He'd stopped tapping and now stood facing me, holding a sheet of paper.

"That was the only flight to Asuncion today. You have to stay in the airport hotel tonight and fly tomorrow. Here is a voucher. Follow the signs this way. Thank you." Lucas waved a dismissive arm towards the terminal. As far as he was concerned, our exchange was over.

"Not so fast monkey-nose," was what I was tempted to say, but thought that might make the situation even worse, so I only thought it. After missing connections previously, I've managed to get squeezed onto an earlier flight via an elaborate tale involving my non-existent brother's wedding taking place the next day in the location I'm heading to. No such luck this time. I'd just embarked on my tale of woe, enquiring whether there were any possible connections via Argentina or Chile, when Lucas called a halt to the pretence.

"Sir, there are no alternative connections. Here is your hotel voucher. The hotel is in the airport. You don't need to collect your baggage or clear customs."

"What? We have to stay in the airport?" This was even worse. Twenty four hours locked in a sterile space designed to grab a few hours kip on long lay-overs didn't sound enjoyable to me.

"Isn't there a hotel outside the airport we could go to?"

Lucas sighed and frowned. "It's better if you stay in the airport. No need to reclaim your bags or clear customs..."

"I need my bag." Now it was my turn to talk over him. "Medicine...I have to take some medicine within the next hour," I lied.

Lucas puffed out his cheeks loudly, rolled his eyes and wobbled his nose in annoyance. He then picked up a phone, into which he made some obviously disparaging comments, while looking at me like I was something with wings that had landed in his dinner. He then tapped on his keyboard and flounced over to a printer, from where he retrieved a replacement voucher.

"Different hotel. You will have to take a taxi and pay with your own money. Someone will bring your bags." He then treated us to a repeat of his dismissive wave, and we shuffled away from the desk.

An hour later, after pocketing some cashpoint Reals, we were in an airport taxi heading into Sao Paulo, only we weren't. Like 'London Luton' isn't in the capital, Sao Paulo airport is actually in the city of Guarulhos, 25km to the north. A quick glance at Trip Advisor during the thirty minute, rush hour journey, told us that our hotel catered to a very specific customer. Every single review had been posted by someone like us, who had been despatched there by an airline which had cancelled or delayed a flight, or potentially decided to depart four hours early! Consequently, it was a revolving door of single night stays by people who didn't expect, or want, to be there.

Reception was predictably chaotic when we arrived, with yesterday's stop-overs checking out and jockeying for position in a queue for the airport courtesy bus. Other guests replicated the mood of the LATAM customer service desk and paced, frowned and barked into phones, as they tried to realign schedules thrown off kilter by airline inefficiency and Acts of God.

Our room was on the 15th floor, clean, spartan and functional. The bathroom boasted an impressive haul of cheap toiletries, which were an obvious necessity for the high proportion of guests likely to arrive with their baggage still revolving on a carousel, or orbiting the earth at 36,000 feet.

We had no idea where we were, and initially thought we were on the outskirts of Sao Paulo. A quick Google search told us that although we were only 16 miles from the centre of the mega-city, it was likely to take at least an hour and a half to get there in traffic, possibly longer via a complicated bus and train journey. We'd never even heard of Guarulhos and were surprised to learn that, rather than a suburb, it was actually an industrial city with a 1.3 million population. It was quite liberating to have been literally dumped somewhere on the other side of the world, that you knew absolutely nothing about. We poked our heads out of the hotel door and assessed the street scene, knowing from past experience of Brazil that hotels can often be sited close to some very dodgy areas. Shoppers, smartly dressed business people, mothers with pushchairs, a lack of graffiti and expensive cars driving with the windows down, were all good signs and we set off to explore. It was the first day of our South American adventure and we'd been 'gifted' an extra country, so we may as well enjoy it. Tomorrow, we'd try again to reach Paraguay.

Taxi!

Arriving in a new country is, for me, one of the best experiences in travel. You begin to get a feel for the world beyond the terminal as soon as you assemble next to the baggage carousel and take in your surroundings. Is it a bright, air-conditioned hall, with video screened adverts, liveried baggage handlers and computerised display screens listing which conveyor belt your luggage will be disgorged onto? Or maybe there is no carousel, and the bags are tossed through a hatch by unseen arms, to be manhandled into piles by wiry men who resemble the homeless in your own country, and who beg you for tips. The only advert is for a duty free shop you can see in the distance, shutters drawn and rusted, and officials loaf lazily in tatty uniforms, with shifty eyes, hungry for contraband and bribes.

Once out of the airport you're invariably assailed from all angles by touts, moneychangers and taxi drivers. The latter are generally your first experience of a citizen of this new land, and first impressions count. Getting ripped off by the airport taxi via overcharging or the old 'I have no change' trick, will immediately get your back up and set your danger warning antenna twitching. A friendly, helpful driver and a pleasant drive into town makes you warm to a city immediately.

We'd read that although the cost of living and travelling in Paraguay were generally cheap, (Asuncion had recently been named as the world's cheapest capital city) taxis from the airport were disproportionately expensive. As on the first leg of our travels, keeping our costs down would be important, so we'd decided to break from our normal routine and catch a bus into town from Asuncion's Silvio Petirossi airport.

First impressions upon disembarking from the plane were of a modern, clean terminal which felt like the entry point to a small but affluent Mediterranean island, rather than a South American capital city. Our flight had landed on time after the previous day's unexplained early departure, and we retrieved our bags quickly and made our way to passport control. It was only as we filed towards the immigration desk that we realised that our unexpected stay in Brazil could have serious consequences. A yellow sign, written in Spanish and English, listed countries from which passengers needed a valid yellow fever vaccination certificate to enter the country. There, near the top of the list, after Angola and Benin, was Brazil. Kirsty and I looked at each other in panic. Presumably this was the reason Lucas had been eager to confine us to the airport hotel at Sao Paulo. The reason he'd shrugged and sent us into the streets of Guarulhos without telling us that this could prevent our entry into Paraguay, was obviously that he was a total dickhead.

We'd both had the yellow fever vaccine, which lasts for ten years and is a prerequisite for visiting most of Africa, and the cards which act as certificates were stored in a folder along with our passports, travel insurance documents and tickets for upcoming trips. Whether we'd brought them with us to South America was another matter. Kirsty is the guardian of all our important documentation when travelling, so the task of scrabbling frantically through a rucksack fell to her, as I looked on, wondering whether a failure to produce the cards would end in deportation or being shot up with a rusty needle in an airport toilet.

We were next in line to be beckoned forward to the desk, as Kirsty stooped to rustle through the file, before triumphantly emerging with two yellow cards in her hand and a wide smile. We both breathed a huge sigh of relief at what was an enormous slice of luck. Had we realised the cards were there, they'd probably have been left in England, which could have meant a very early forced revision of our schedule!

We walked from the sanctuary of border control into the usual melee of taxi touts offering us a ride to town, but I'd already decided not to get into a haggling battle with them as I usually would, and we bumped through the throng with our backpacks acting as a useful side-on battering ram, to clear a path to the car park. There was no 'official' bus into town, but we'd read that the 'Linea 30' stop was about half a kilometre away so set off walking along a quiet road which led to a large grass roundabout. It was a sunny spring morning and the lack of traffic made it a pleasant walk to a concrete bus shelter, which housed a man of early middle age, who wore a shirt and tie and a long trench coat. He had a vaguely Slavic appearance and brooding, deep-set eyes and was obviously a spy or contract killer.

"Linea Treinta?" I asked and he nodded and lit a cigarette.

The bus was meant to be every twenty minutes, and the spy huffed and puffed and looked at his watch while shaking his head, which led us to believe he'd already been waiting longer than that. Another fifteen minutes passed and our companion had flicked three cigarette ends at the bus shelter to show his displeasure, when a blue 4x4 drew our attention by swerving across two lanes of traffic to pull up on the road ahead of us. It was then crunched into reverse and screeched back to draw up alongside us. A girl in her early twenties wound down the passenger seat window and I assumed she thought we were someone else.

"Hi! You speak English?" She smiled. We confirmed that we did and that, as she'd guessed, we were cheapskate travellers who'd just landed at the airport and were too tight to pay for a taxi.

"Need a lift into town? We're going that way..." I was already picking up my bag, but Kirsty's usual common sense caused her to stall and give me a look which told me she was thinking about South American kidnap gangs. I looked into the car and spotted the bespectacled male driver, who was sporting a freshly laundered polo shirt bearing the Sixt car rental logo. He looked a benign type, and the girl was smiley, curly and looked like a primary school teacher.

"We're not in Bogota," was my verdict and we climbed into the backseat. Beatriz and David confirmed that they both worked for Sixt and had just dropped a car off at their airport depot. They both spoke perfect English, and proudly sold us the delights of their city on the thirty minute drive into town. As first impressions went, we couldn't have asked for much more from Paraguay!

We checked into our small, unassuming backstreet hotel on the edge of the city centre and began to discuss previous airport taxis, and other 'interesting' cab rides we'd had around the world. We laughed about our ill-fated bush taxi incident in Togo, when a highway robbery by a renegade police unit was interrupted by a phone call from my office in England.

"That's it!" I suddenly leapt to my feet and picked up my phone. "That's the perfect story to start The Two Week Traveller. It's a great crossover between travelling and work!" I knew I had some video footage, and a few stills I'd taken on my phone while we were crammed into the back of a Renault estate, with seven locals and a tiny baby. I located the footage on my phone and held it up to show Kirsty the image of a front seat passenger, a man sat on the handbrake beside him, and another who was sat on my knee as we bumped along a West African road, before being held up by gun toting bandits in uniform.

The conversation continued on scary taxi journeys we've experienced around the world – The possessive Albanian with whom I inadvertently started my own blood feud; a Rio boy racer in a souped-up Subaru who seemed to have been trained by Ayrton Senna; and a part-sighted 85 year old lady in a Mercedes in Namibia, were all highly memorable. For me though, the wildest taxi ride of all was one which Kirsty had been fortunate enough to miss.

In the early 2000's, I was working in Marketing for a senior manager whose approach to expenses could have been termed 'living the dream'. Before the financial crash of 2008, and a subsequent takeover which saw belts being tightened to painful levels, I enjoyed 'business' trips to Spain, Greece, Ireland and France, which saw little business and a lot of drinking. Management bonuses were partly linked to staff satisfaction surveys, so our boss, who I'll refer to as 'Paul', cooked up a scheme to ensure he got top marks from his team. The large multinational who had recently acquired our company had a small office in Prague, and Paul made contact with his opposite number there and arranged a fact-finding visit to the Czech Republic. All we had to do, was ensure that our gratitude for a couple of days drinking freebie Staropramen was reflected by top marks in Paul's survey.

Paul didn't do things by halves and after a couple of hours of half hearted, unnecessary meetings with confused Czech staff who did vaguely similar jobs to us, the real business of exploring the bars of Old Town and Wenceslas Square could begin. We stayed in a top hotel, and on the final night Paul relished the embarrassment he inflicted upon us by hiring a fleet of horse drawn carriages, to transport us in a magnificent convoy for a big night on the town. I remember little of the evening. Large quantities of Staropramen and Pilsner Urquell; a meal of pig knuckle and cabbage; a visit to a Hawaiian themed lap dancing bar; and a mild mannered, softly spoken Geordie colleague becoming embroiled in a violent scuffle with a wheely bin, are my hazy memories, before I headed for the hotel in the early hours.

We had a mid-afternoon flight back to the UK the next day, and I was woken around nine by a phone buzzing with text messages from early rising colleagues. Word on the street was that people were meeting for breakfast in a café near the castle, which was a few miles away on the other side of the city centre. After a quick shower, I headed downstairs. It was a bright, sunlit morning and I took a few minutes to breathe in some fresh air to clear my head. Luckily, there was a taxi rank right outside the hotel, with a number of cars parked up, their drivers snoozing, smoking or perusing newspaper crosswords.

I plodded down the steps, feeling the effects of two heavy nights of boozing, and looking forward to some breakfast. I approached the first car in the rank and noticed that the driver was awake, but wasn't smoking, or talking on his phone or doing a puzzle. He was gripping the steering wheel and staring straight ahead. I tapped on the window and he turned to face me, sizing me up with dark eyes beneath a thick mono-brow. His hair was dark, greying at the sides, long and unruly. With a thick moustache curving around his top lip and extending to the middle of his chin and a small 'soul patch' beard nestling beneath his lower lip, he boasted the facial hair of a young Frank Zappa. Any similarity to the American Rocker ended there. In place of Zappa's aquiline nose, the drivers had obviously been broken so many times, it had melted into his bristly moustache like a crushed mouse.

I gave him the café address and he unlocked the doors. I generally prefer to sit alongside the driver in a taxi, to avoid looking like a provincial Lord Mayor in a chauffeur driven limo, or a minor gangster and his minder, so I walked around the car and got in the front passenger seat. The driver seemed perturbed by this and froze. I could sense him looking at me through the corner of his eye, and he breathed noisily as if considering his next move. After a few seconds, he snorted loudly, rammed the car into gear and accelerated away from the rank without checking his mirrors. The streets were cobbled and the whole car vibrated as we sped along a one way street at 50mph. I was pleased that there was no oncoming traffic, but cast a wary eye at the side roads we were flying past. There was no obvious right-of-way and I guessed priority was given to whoever arrived at the junction first...or whoever flew straight through at nearly 60mph. We had a couple of near misses with hesitant pedestrians and a slow turning horse carriage, which caused Zappa to grip the steering wheel and administer a death stare at the oblivious dapple-grey, as we hurtled on our way.

An enforced stop at a red light seemed to escalate his stress levels and he breathed heavily through his nose, while drumming the steering wheel, and staring fixedly at the rear tyres of the bus in front with a look of pure hatred. I decided to lighten the mood with the usual taxi passenger chit chat.

"Lots of traffic today." There was no response, as he continued breathing like a worn-out mule, while drumming and staring.

"Much traffic here." Moving to broken English at least elicited a response and he slowly turned towards me. I smiled, which was obviously the wrong reaction, as his eyes bore into mine and his lip curled in disgust. He looked me up and down and I shrank back in my seat, fearful that he was about to drive his forehead into my face and leave me with me a nose like his. Instead, he shook his head and muttered some incomprehensible words in Czech beneath his moustache. Traffic in the lane to our right began to crawl slowly forward, indicating that the lights had changed, but the bus ahead of us didn't move, so Zappa spat some profanities and forced his way into the line of moving cars while sounding his horn and rocking in his seat like a frustrated bear in a cage.

Soon we were again buzzing at speed over the cobbles, through the backstreets of the old town. I glanced towards the driver and noticed staining on the front of his dark jeans which could have been old urine, but the suicidal driving style preyed on the dark corners of my mind, and I began to suspect it was blood. Was that a spare wheel bumping around in the boot or a previous passenger, bound and gagged and being transported to a Gothic slaughterhouse, along with the next unsuspecting fare, which was me!

The rocking and snorting continued from the driver's seat as we sped across town, and it was now accompanied by a continuous low hum, which I hoped represented a meditational exercise to delay the total mental breakdown which was clearly imminent. At the top of a hill, the road straightened out, and Zappa accelerated towards traffic lights at a junction crossing a busy dual carriageway. The lights were on green and it was clear he was in no mood to stop. I noticed a tiny Fiat 126 labouring through the lights ahead, with its right indicator blinking, and brake lights flashing intermittently. As our speed increased, I noticed the Fiat's indicator switch from right to left and the car began to reposition itself in the road. The driver was clearly lost and was engaged in a debate with himself on which direction to take. We hurtled along at 60mph with the little blue car moving hesitantly ahead of us. Then the traffic lights turned to amber while we were still twenty yards short of the stop line, which caused Zappa to put his foot down hard, and we almost took off as we hit an unseen dip in the road. I was focused on the Fiat, which had now turned both indicators off and was paused in the centre of the road ahead on our right, but Zappa seemed oblivious to it. We thundered through the traffic lights and I spotted the Fiat's front wheels begin to turn to the left. It was obvious to me what was coming, so I braced myself, pushed both feet hard to the taxi floor, extended my arms and locked them on the dashboard while pushing myself firmly back into my seat. This seemed to confuse Zappa, who glanced momentarily towards me, just as the Fiat pulled into our path. The impact sounded like an explosion, and we span in the road like a fairground waltzer, before ending up facing the direction we'd come from. I glanced to my left and saw debris from the Fiat still bouncing down the road. The back end of the little car had been virtually ripped off. I caught my breath and began checking that I could still feel all my limbs. Our car clearly had no airbags, or they'd been disengaged, and Zappa and I seemed unscathed, apart from a large bump which was growing, in cartoon style, above his eye. He looked around, surprised, as if he'd just woken up on a train journey and was trying to work out which station he was at.

A couple of passing cars pulled over to check if there were any casualties, and I spotted a man in a brown leather jacket stumble from the Fiat and put his hands to his head when he saw the destruction wrought upon his vehicle. Zappa rubbed at his bump and scowled at the other driver. He turned to me and growled 'stay', before hauling himself from the car to assess the smashed-in bonnet of his taxi. The man in the brown leather jacket approached with arms spread wide, in a gesture clearly questioning how we hadn't spotted him, but was soon back-pedalling as he was prodded in the chest by the irate, wild haired taxi driver who was clearly in no mood to exchange insurance details.

I looked at my watch. It was approaching 10am. Our flight was at 2pm so I needed to be at the airport for midday. I glanced over to see a smartly dressed lady motorist raising her arms to prevent Zappa from cuffing the Fiat driver, who was attempting to speak into a mobile phone. Clearly the police would be here soon. At best, I'd struggle to provide a statement via a translator at the roadside, would miss breakfast and may just make the flight on time. At worst, the police would find a suitcase full of body parts and a suit made of human skin in the boot, and I'd be forced to spend months in a courtroom for the trial of the Prague Ripper. Neither sounded like a good option.

While the arguments raged twenty feet away, I carefully opened the taxi door and gingerly got out. I stretched and waggled my head, to ensure I hadn't sustained a Bert Trautman style broken neck, and checked that no one was looking. I then walked at speed across the dual carriageway. I'd just reached the other side of the road when I heard a distant roar of "YOU! STOP!" Zappa had paused his attack on the Fiat driver and was staring at me. Faced with a choice of staying to help unravel the legalities of a Czech RTA or eat a hearty breakfast, then fly home, there was only one sensible option. I turned and set off running.

I arrived at the café twenty minutes later and began to tell the story to my colleagues who reacted as they usually did to my travel tales, with a mixture of disbelief, amusement or hungover disinterest.

"Why does stuff like that only ever happen to you?" was a question I was all too used to being asked, by a workmate who clearly suspected I was embellishing the truth for the sake of a good tale.

We finished breakfast and headed back towards the hotel to collect our bags. I was sharing the cab with four colleagues, and was chatting in the back seat, so taking little notice of our surroundings until we slowed at a traffic queue. I heard the driver say the word 'accident' to my colleague in the front, and I peered through the windscreen, as we proceeded slowly past the scene of the earlier collision. The two vehicles were still positioned where they'd come to rest after the crash, and two police cars were in attendance. The taxi driver was seated on a barrier on the central reservation in heated conversation with one of the officers. I sunk low in my seat, but noticed his hands were behind his back and, wondering if he was handcuffed, turned to look. Unfortunately, our new driver had slowed to a crawl, in order to rubberneck and speculate over the cause of the crash, and Zappa's dark eyes flicked towards our vehicle, before locking onto mine. The handcuff question was immediately answered as I saw his arm raise and point towards me.

"Drive! Fast! Now!" I shouted and our confused driver accelerated through the junction towards the city centre. After a couple of hundred yards, the panicked shouts of my colleagues urged him to slow down, and we proceeded to the hotel at a more sedate pace. Perhaps unsurprisingly, it was a different four colleagues who decided to share my taxi to the airport!

Taxi!

***

In Paraguay, I looked again at the photo taken in the crowded Togolese bush taxi and reflected that it may have been hot, smelly and noisy, but the state of the West African roads and the weight of eight adults and a baby, plus our assorted rooftop baggage, at least guaranteed that the old Renault was unable to exceed 30mph. The good news this time was that we wouldn't have to contend with any maniac taxi drivers or overcrowded vehicles in Paraguay - The following day we'd be collecting a rental car to explore beyond the city limits. We were going hunting for the ghosts of Nazi war criminals.

Sleeping in Mengele's Bed

Day 96 -Asuncion, Paraguay

We'd arrived in Asuncion on a Thursday and, as the car rental company was closed on a weekend, had decided to collect the vehicle the following day, then return to explore the capital more fully later in the week. It took some time to locate the 'office' which was hidden in the bowels of a large shopping mall, and we finally found the young female desk clerk crouched at a desk, squeezed beneath a fire escape staircase on the lower level of an underground car park. I squatted to sign the paperwork as she peered from the dark recess like a nervous vole expecting an imminent visit from a passing kestrel.

The little car was worryingly shiny and polished and free of dents and chips, but the driving style was fairly civilised for South America, as we headed south east out of the city. I always like to explore beyond the capital of a new country, as, wherever you are, the largest city is rarely representative of the remainder of a nation, and the lakeside town of San Bernardino had caught my eye.

Paraguay has an interesting, if somewhat dubious modern history of revolution, military coups, dictatorships, civil wars and conflicts with neighbouring countries. It is also well known for its links with early Naziism, and was referred to as the 'Forgotten Fatherland' by journalist Ben Macintyre in his book of the same name. Links with Germany were established in 1870 in the aftermath of the disastrous War of the Triple Alliance, in which Paraguay was unsurprisingly annihilated by the combined powers of Brazil, Argentina and Uruguay. The country was left in ruins, having lost 70% of its population, and was open to investment and emigration from European nations.

One of the first groups of pioneers to arrive, were fourteen German families led by Bernhard Förster and his wife Elisabeth Förster-Nietzsche, the sister of German philosopher Friedrich Nietzsche, who arrived in Asuncion in 1887. The couple were vehement anti-semites, Förster describing the Jews as 'a parasite on the German body,' and his philosophies provided the ideological foundation for the movement Adolf Hitler would later reinvent as Naziism. Their dream was a racially pure, Aryan settlement called Nueva Germania, which was established in the jungle 250 miles from Asuncion. The project was ultimately doomed to failure, with the settlers driven insane by insects, humidity and disease, until Förster committed suicide in 1899, shooting up a lethal dose of morphine and strychnine in Room 19 of the Hotel del Lago in San Bernardino. Guess where Kirsty and I would be staying?

San Bernardino was now a lakeside resort town, catering mainly to second homeowners from the capital, though you wouldn't have known it when we arrived. A single main road ran in a perfect straight line through the town, intersecting a grid of quiet, treelined side streets. There was a smattering of low-key bars and restaurants, most of which seemed to be closed, and quiet streets, devoid of people. There were also very few hotels, and Hotel del Lago appeared at the top of a limited list on all the booking engines.

Built in 1888, the hotel was described as a living museum, retaining most of the décor and features from the period of its construction. The entrance was framed by two turreted towers, housing the best rooms in the hotel. One of these suites became the semi-permanent home of another notable Nazi, a French-German called Hilda Ingenohl, known locally as 'la Tigresa', due to her fondness for heading into the jungle to blast away at a few big cats. The hotel's place in fascist history was then firmly established when the only official Nazi party outside Germany was formed under a tree in the grounds in 1927.

Though we weren't expecting swastika flags above reception and goose-stepping porters, we were pleasantly surprised upon entering through the large wooden front doors. A smiling female employee led us through a cavernous dining room, dimly lit by chandeliers. Polished walnut floorboards creaked and squeaked as we were led to our room to the accompaniment of an operatic aria, and everywhere was dark wood and antiques. Silver framed, monochrome photos of famous guests of years past adorned the walls, and every surface was laden with antique clocks, old gramophones and 1920's vintage telephones. Our room was on the second floor and was approached by a wooden, colonnaded balcony which thankfully led us straight past Förster's ill-fated number 19, to a room at the front of the building, overlooking the tree shaded grounds. Again, dark wood was very much in evidence and the large wrought iron bed looked to have been in-situ for many years, and I wondered about the tales it could tell. All in all, for forty dollars a night, the Hotel del Lago was a bargain.

We headed towards Lake Ypacarai, which shimmered in the early Spring sunlight, and followed a lakeshore path which terminated at a fenced compound announcing itself as the San Bernardino country club. The first visitors from the capital had started to arrive at their weekend retreats, towing jet skis behind large 4x4's, and youths with dark, curly mullets shattered the calm by executing noisy 'doughnuts' out on the water, their distant plumes of upward spray looking like blowing humpback whales.

The town was pleasant enough for strolling, but had the air of an out-of-season seaside resort, and we wondered what would be open on an evening. Appropriately for San Bernardino, we ended up in an establishment with the typically Paraguayan name of Edelweiss. We'd passed it on a side street off the main drag, and spotted an outside table of German-speaking patrons tucking into huge platters of meat and salad, washed down with steins of beer. Other options seemed limited to take away pizza or a white-tablecloth dinner at our hotel, so we ducked into the beer garden and sat down at a picnic bench table, where we were quickly identified as English speaking Europeans, an obvious rarity in San Bernardino.

The restaurant was empty apart from the other table of diners, and they immediately encouraged us to join them. Three men and a woman in their mid-fifties, they stood to greet us formally and shook our hands. Paul and Lina had emigrated to Paraguay in the eighties, a fact which helped explain their fashion sense. I could only assume they'd gone on a spending spree before leaving Berlin in '86 and hadn't bought any clothes since. Their hair styles were also straight out of 'Footloose' or 'Ferris Bueller's Day Off' and Lina's eyelids were heavy with brilliant blue eye shadow. One of the men was older, with a rustic, sun-burnished appearance, and introduced himself as Alex. Marc made up the quartet and told us he was the newcomer, having only been in Paraguay for 16 years. When I asked him what brought him to the other side of the world, he smirked and cast a sideways glance towards Alex and muttered something about a 'disagreement with the government.' All except Paul spoke conversational English, but Kirsty is fluent in German and it wasn't long before she was impressing our new friends with her Wiesbaden-accented chatter.

We ordered Currywurst with potato salad and sauerkraut, washed down with genuine imported Munchen lager, which, at

10,000 Guaranis a litre, was around a quarter of the cost you'd pay in the city it was brewed in!

The beer continued to flow, and we were surprised to hear that we were the first British travellers any of the Germans had met, or even heard of visiting San Bernardino in the time they'd lived there. They even summoned Rolf, the bar owner, to ask if he'd ever met any visiting Brits, but the nearest he could conjure up was a couple of Canadians and an Aussie. They asked what had brought us to town and were perplexed at our lack of a good reason beyond seeing somewhere outside Asuncion. They asked where we were staying and mention of the del Lago resulted in an exchange of looks across the table and a pause, before Alex spoke.

"A very interesting place. Interesting history. You know of it?"

I mentioned Förster, la Tigresa and the Nazis under the tree, and Alex nodded and rubbed his blotchy forehead.

"You know Josef Mengele?"

"The Angel of Death? Of course. But he wasn't here was he?"

"He escaped to Argentina in the late 1940's, then came to Paraguay in '58 when the Nazi hunters were getting too close."

Alex continued in a voice lowered unnecessarily, as there was no one around beyond our table. "He lived in Hohenau, near the Brazilian border, but he had friends here and visited regularly. He always stayed at the Del Lago."

I shuddered as I thought of the ancient bed in our room which surely predated the late fifties. Had the evil physician of Auschwitz slept in our bed?

"Mengeles' time in Paraguay is well documented." Alex was warming to his theme. "But maybe there's an even bigger secret. The biggest..."

Lina snorted and began to laugh and said something to Paul in German. Alex shrugged and the smirk crept back onto Marc's face.

"Go on..." I urged.

"It's nonsense," Lina interjected.

"Hitler died in the Berlin bunker in '45, right?" Alex continued, and I nodded.

"They found his skull with a bullet wound in it, yes?" I was under the impression he'd poisoned himself, but agreed anyway.

"Did you know that a couple of years ago they found out that the skull actually belonged to a young woman?" Alex, sat back and folded his arms as Lina scoffed loudly.

"There's a guy, a journalist from Argentina, who's written a book on what really happened. Your government and the USA didn't want Hitler to be taken by the Russians, so they smuggled him to Spain, then on to Argentina, then Paraguay." Alex took a large swig of his beer before continuing.

"The story goes that Hitler lived here under the protection of President Stroessner, until he died in 1971. Then he was buried in a bunker beneath a hotel, which was then sealed in concrete."

"Which hotel?...You're not saying it's...?" Marc was nodding slowly but Alex pushed out his lower lip and shrugged theatrically.

"Alex knows an old man..." Marc began, but then stopped suddenly, and I sensed that his friend had given him an under-table nudge.

"I guess no one will ever know really..." He smirked again, and we were left wondering about another potential secret in this strange little town.

Back in Asuncion we found ourselves chasing more ghosts. La Recoleta cemetery is a city of the dead. Avenues of huge mausoleums stretch across the scrubby, sun drenched grounds, providing a final resting place for the great and not-so-good of Paraguayan society. In the late 19th century, the size and extravagance of a crypt was an indicator of a family's wealth, so no expense was spared on these concrete constructions, the size of a small detached cottage, and of varying degrees of ugliness. Less wealthy residents were stacked ten-deep on high rise, glass fronted shelves.

Having visited South American cemeteries before, and knowing that la Recoleta held the remains of Presidents, generals, dictators and their mistresses, we were surprised at the general state of decay of the crypts. Glass frontages were cracked and broken, leaving the coffins exposed to the elements. Not surprisingly, some had splintered and others totally collapsed, spilling suit-clad skeletons from their caskets. The local tradition was to place a photograph of the deceased on a shelf above the coffin, and it was eerie to look at a sepia image of a handsome couple in their prime, him sporting an impressive moustache and top hat, she in flowing skirts and a bonnet, while knowing their mortal remains lay decaying in the two shabby wooden boxes before us.

One crypt indicated at an embalmment process carried out by a trainee or maybe not at all, as the floor beneath the casket was stained a rust-coloured red from seeping bodily fluids. We wandered the rows of crypts, and it wasn't uncommon to come face to face with a grinning skull, resting on top of a heap of scattered bones and rotted, splintered wood in a head-height crypt. It suddenly felt intrusive to be there, and we departed, more sure than ever that cremation was the way to go!

Before we'd arrived in Paraguay, I'd found that Asuncion would be playing host to a big football game while we were in town. The Copa Libertadores is the South American equivalent of Europe's Champions League, with 47 teams from 10 countries taking part in a tournament which spans the whole year. One of the capital's teams, Olimpia, would be playing an Argentinian team, Godoy Cruz, from Mendoza. I'd never heard of the visitors, they certainly weren't a team to set the pulse racing as River Plate or Boca Juniors would, but at least tickets should be easier to come by, especially as supporters' groups had been voicing their disquiet at inflated Copa Libertadores pricing. The best tickets for this game would cost the equivalent of $15, which is roughly what you'd pay to stand at a non-league game in England.

I decided to chance my arm and go to the match, hoping to pick up a ticket outside the stadium, but had no idea of likely availability from touts, or what the situation at the ground would be. Kirsty therefore decided that she was happy to spend an evening in the beer garden of an Irish bar in the city centre, catching up on writing her journal. I left her at 6pm, leaving plenty of time to get to the stadium, soak up the pre-match atmosphere, enjoy a few pints of Brahma beer and hopefully bag a ticket.

I flagged down a taxi outside the Irish bar and gave him the details of my destination.

"Football. Olimpia estadio. Copa Libertadores."

The grizzled, middle aged driver gave me the thumbs up and I jumped into the passenger seat. After driving for ten minutes, we began to hit pre-match traffic, and fell into a broken communication of single words and hand signals. As usual in South America, mention of my own team in England prompted a joyous response.

"Leeds United!! El Loco Bielsa!" Our eccentric Argentinian coach, Marcelo Bielsa, had to be one of the most recognisable figures in South America, and in this part of the world had elevated Leeds back to the level of fame we'd enjoyed in the 1970's and all too briefly at the start of the 21st Century. I had no idea how far from the stadium we were, as we crawled along in bumper to bumper traffic, but began to see the first tell-tale signs that we were getting closer, as fake merchandise vendors began to appear by the roadside, and I started to notice a trickle of supporters clad in the black and white of Olimpia, following the traffic flow on foot. It wasn't long before lone figures appeared, skulking in shop doorways or outside bars. Generally middle aged and wearing cheap leather jackets or 80's style shell suits, the ticket touts were scanning the traffic line for likely customers, and my obviously European face peering from the taxi window drew them in like moths to a pyrotechnic flare. Kirsty and I had been learning Spanish using the Duolingo app, and while I could generally communicate in most common situations, I wasn't sure I was up to haggling over the price of a match ticket.

"Cuanto?" was my response as a plump, balding man struggled to keep pace with our vehicle's 5mph crawl.

"Ciento cincuenta mil," was the reply, which at 150,000 guaranis was higher than face value, and I shook my head and wound up the window. This was encouraging. We were obviously still a fair distance from the stadium, the price was only just above face value, and I'd noticed the tout was holding around twenty tickets. Clearly, the game wouldn't be a sell out, and the laws of supply and demand indicated that the price would fall the closer we got to kick off, and the nearer we were to the stadium, with more touts looking to offload their stock onto a diminishing number of customers.

Word had obviously spread that the slow-moving taxi contained a gringo, and before long the car was being trailed by a competing band of touts, all brandishing tickets and quoting terminology that meant nothing to me –'Graderias, Plateas, and Preferencia' were areas of the stadium which all attracted different pricing, which was now ranging from ninety to a hundred and twenty thousand guaranis.

"Noventa mil, es un buen precio!" My driver was impressed, and encouraged me to buy at ninety thousand, but I knew that if that was the roadside price, it would be far lower just before kick off in the streets around the ground.

"A las ocho, no es un boleto, es solo un trozo de papel." I shared my philosophy on purchasing from touts, honed through years of turning up at English grounds without a ticket —'At eight o'clock, it's not a ticket anymore, it's just a piece of paper.' The driver liked that, and laughed out loud, then repeated the mantra quietly to himself 'Es solo un trozo de papel! Bueno.'

Eventually we turned into a brightly lit square with a barrier across the road manned by riot police in full robo-cop gear.

"Aqui. Terminado." The driver made a cut-throat gesture to indicate that he could go no further, and I paid and bade him farewell. I could see the glow of the stadium floodlights a couple of blocks away, so headed in that direction. There were more supporters in the streets now, but less than I would have expected to see in the vicinity of a British stadium, less than an hour before kick off. I assumed they must be crammed into bars near the ground, but upon arrival in the street facing the rear of the stadium, all I could find were merchandise hawkers and vendors selling German hot dogs, corn cobs on sticks and cassava based snacks known as chipa. Ominously, there were a number of prominent signs emblazed with the logo of the Asuncion police force stating 'Alcohol Prohibido,' although the air was thick with cannabis smoke, reflecting the law which stated that up to 10 grams of marijuana (and 2 grams of cocaine) were permissible for personal consumption. This was a blow, as a bar near the stadium is always a likely source of 'spares' from other supporters without having to haggle with touts.

I circled the stadium and it soon became apparent why there were few crowds on the street outside. With a full 45 minutes to kick off, supporters were jogging to the turnstiles as if the game was about to begin, and filing straight into the stands. From the cacophony of chanting, exploding fireworks and the samba beat of a brass band, it was obvious that the ground was already pretty full. It wasn't long before I attracted the attention of the touts who were scurrying back and forth in the shadow of the main stand, bundles of tickets clasped in their hands and with an air of desperation clearly in evidence.

Their gringo antenna was twitching, and I was soon surrounded by a gaggle of reefer toting extras from an early episode of Miami Vice, failing to follow the first rule of touting by demonstrating that supply of tickets clearly exceeded demand. They all had a fistful which they'd clearly struggle to shift. It looked like a buyer's market, and I was the only buyer.

I successfully played off one against the other to drive the price down, before selecting the only vendor with a smattering of English, a prematurely bald fatty in baggy shorts and a stained vest. We settled on a price of sixty thousand Guaranis, which was about £6 and half the face value of the 'Preferencia' ticket.

It was old-school turnstile entry, with a teenager sat on a stool giving my ticket a cursory glance, before clicking the gate to admit me. The stand was similarly archaic, and a far cry from the sanitised stadia we're now used to in Europe. A flight of stone stairs led to a concrete concourse on the lower level, which was empty apart from a stall selling chipa and hot dogs, and a piss-stench toilet which was spewing a river of urine under a graffitied wooden door. I carried on up another concrete staircase to arrive at the upper tier. As I ascended the final flight of steps towards the seated terrace and floodlit, smoke-filled night air, I was struck with a sudden pang of homesickness, with the experience so similar to the walk I've made a thousand times to my seat at Elland Road.

Emerging onto the terrace, any similarity to an English stadium quickly evaporated in the warm evening air. The stand was seating only, but everyone was standing, mostly on their seats, and a fug of smoke from cigarettes, joints and pyro hung like a thick mist over the pitch. The stadium was open to the elements which can often kill any atmosphere, but not this time. Away to our right, in the stand behind the goal, the Olimpia 'Barras Bravas' or ultras groups, were assembled in a ten thousand strong throng. A mass of surging, bouncing, constant motion, they sang their battle anthems literally non-stop. British sports writers often describe a hostile atmosphere as 'non-stop noise', but this was on another level. Complex and choreographed, the number of songs and chants, and their length, with some carrying on for five minutes, was unlike anything I'd ever seen before. Around me, the crowd was a totally mixed demographic – groups of lads, old men, middle aged couples, teenage girls, families with little kids, all were stood, excitedly anticipating the arrival of the teams. Hawkers passed through the crowd, advertising their wares in a shouted sing-song rhyme, and purchases were handed down the stand, with a hot dog probably being touched by thirty people before reaching the mouth of the unfortunate snacker.

Eventually a fanfare over the tannoy announced the arrival of the players, and the entire stadium stood and belted out a staccato anthem, accompanied by straight arm salutes which took on a vaguely sinister air after our few days in San Bernardino.

Pyrotechnic flares were ignited by the Barras Bravas, and thick smoke drifted over the pitch, as the night sky was illuminated by the fizz and pop of thousands of fire crackers. Then from deep within the ranks massed behind the goal, came the plaintive blast of a bugle, to signal the ritual singing of the club anthem, 'Una Tarde Mi Viejo Me Llevo', which translates as 'One afternoon my old man took me', and is a homage to being a true fan, or 'hincha' as it's known in South America, describing a devotion to the club passed down through family lines.

The ten strong brass section of trombones and trumpets, plus an ensemble of booming bass drums kicked in, and the entire stadium bounced and sang along.

'Me enamore de ti tus colores asi yo lo sentí. Una tarde mi viejo me llevo, desde ahí vos sos mi vida y mi passion.'

'I fell in love with you and your colours, so I felt it. One afternoon my old man took me ...from there you are my life and my passion.'

I didn't understand the words at the time, but the tune was undeniably catchy, and to be amongst forty thousand people singing a song that clearly meant so much to them was a stirring experience, even to someone who's experienced the highs and lows of being a football fan for nearly fifty years. Two teenage girls stood in front of me and bounced on their seats as they pumped their fists and sang along, and I noticed tears in the eyes of one, a dark haired beauty in her late teens. I wondered whether it was simply the excitement and emotion of being at a big game, or whether the song stirred memories of her own 'old man' who'd first introduced her to Olimpia. Either way, it was a reminder that although football has been commercialised and sanitised in much of Europe, in its spiritual heartlands of South America it's still more than a game to many.

Olimpia won the game 2-1 and although the standard of play wasn't up to Premier League standards, the experience of watching a big Copa Libertadores match wasn't something I'd soon forget. I left ten minutes before the end to get a taxi, and met Kirsty back at the Irish bar. She'd begun reading 'At the Tomb of the Inflatable Pig', and she remarked on the fact that Paraguay had always been a strange and mysterious place. I couldn't disagree. We'd be leaving the country in a couple of days, and I was left with the unmistakable feeling that I now had more unanswered questions about it than the day I'd arrived!

A Flag of Convenience

" "No te gusta el plátano." I shook my head at the mange encrusted dog which was watching me eat with imploring eyes, assuming he spoke Spanish. I'd never known a dog eat a banana, so was fairly sure he'd turn his scabby nose up if I offered him some. Kirsty arrived back from a toilet visit, pale of face and visibly shaken.

"Don't go to the toilet unless you absolutely have to," she grimaced.

"Bad?"

"You'd be better copying him." She nodded down the road to where the driver of our minibus was exuberantly hosing down a bush shelter, opposite two old ladies who were watching impassively from a bench.

We were in a nameless hamlet in the foothills of the Cordillera Oriental, en-route from Santa Cruz to the village of Samaipata, and were suffering an enforced lunchstop at a greasy-cuchara café on Bolivia's Ruta 7.

We'd flown into Santa Cruz from Paraguay a couple of days earlier, and the plan was for that to be our last flight in South America until we flew home from Quito in around eight weeks – a journey of just over 4000km through the heart of the Andes.

Santa Cruz had been a means to an end rather than a destination we wanted to visit. Flights were cheap and had spared us a gruelling twenty-four hour bus journey from Asuncion through the Chaco desert. Our Air B&B apartment was excellent value at $15 per night and the city also ticked two important logistical boxes. First, it was within striking distance of the mountain village of Samaipata, which is firmly established as a 'must-go-to' on the Bolivian backpacking circuit. Secondly, Santa Cruz is situated in the tropical lowlands of the Andes, at only 415 metres above sea level, and was one of the last low altitude cities we'd be visiting for a few weeks, before travelling on to heights of over 4000 metres, where the risk of altitude sickness was very real. With symptoms ranging from headache, nausea and lethargy, just like a bad hangover, to cerebral oedema and high-altitude pulmonary oedema, altitude sickness or AMS, wasn't something we wanted to suffer in the remote Bolivian Alto Plano. Acetazolamide tablets are the drug of choice to combat the condition, but are unlicenced in the UK, so most GP's won't prescribe them, and if they do it will be on a costly private prescription. Therefore, before travelling I'd despatched our Air B&B host, Guillermo, to a local pharmacy, and our stash of tablets, costing less than a dollar, was awaiting us when we arrived from the airport.

"If you need more, they are called Soroche tablets here," he'd explained. "Soroche comes from the Quechua word 'surúchi', which means tin or lead, as the native people of the mountains believed it was the presence of metal in the rocks which made them sick."

I'd read the English translated instructions on the box of tablets, which is never a good idea. We were warned of 'increased urine production, pins and needles, nausea, vomiting, headache and taste disturbance.' Fortunately, the only side effect we were to suffer was the final one. While taking the tablets, any fizzy drink tasted like battery acid, with a burning, electric shock sensation on the tongue and a vile aftertaste. I was distraught to discover that this also extended to beer, particularly when I found a cheap craft beer joint over the road from our apartment!

Our other task in Santa Cruz was to arrange transport to Samaipata, a distance of around 80km, but a journey which would take three hours on a good day. The bus station had been easy enough to find, with the usual, diesel-cloud belching 'chicken buses', liberally adorned with a surfeit of chrome and religious imagery, and painted names such as 'Christo Rey' and 'Dios es Amor'. As in most of Latin America, drivers working twenty hour shifts on Bolivia's notorious mountain-pass roads relied on divine intervention and a mouthful of coca leaves to keep them and their passengers safe.

We were directed from the main bus station to a sidestreet, where a private company ran daily mini-buses to Samaipata and the mountain towns beyond. The office was empty apart from a sad faced pensioner with laden hessian sacks who'd shrugged and shook her head and looked like she might start crying when I'd enquired of the whereabouts of 'el jefe'.

Eventually a rotund teddy bear of a man in blue shirt and slacks, which he'd obviously bought several diets ago, had bounded through the door and greeted us breathlessly. His already monolid eyes were further concealed within rolls of fat, which made it impossible to see his eyeballs when he smiled, which he did constantly.

Through a combination of hand signals, our limited Spanish and his even more limited English, we'd deduced that there was no booking system, and that buses left when filled to their capacity of seven. It was mid-afternoon, and at that time there were few travellers making the journey south, so we were advised to return around 8am the following morning. Then there would be 'mucho mas de trufi,' he assured us, using the local slang for a mini-bus.

We'd fallen lucky upon arrival just after 8am the next day, and managed to bag the last two seats on a bus. In fact, six people and a toddler were already aboard, so Kirsty and I actually bagged the last half seat, which caused predictable huffing and puffing, not least from the mother of the struggling child who was forced to balance him on her knee in the front seat. Our nearest neighbour was an obese man in shorts, with legs like two hams, who shuffled over momentarily before enveloping Kirsty in blubber as soon as we pulled onto the road. Sharing the front seat with the mother and child was the old lady we'd seen the day before, and I hoped she hadn't spent the night on the office floor waiting for the next full bus, particularly as it looked like she was going to be tormented relentlessly by the inquisitive little boy for three hours.

Our travelling companions now mooched outside the depressing roadside café while the driver stretched his legs, and other body parts. I'd decided not to risk any of the snacks displayed on the flyblown counter, preferring the safe option of bananas and well-stained cups of the strong local coffee, while we sat at a rusting table next to the café door.

There was little going on in the village, except for the occasional truck rumbling along the main road, or an old man on a creaking cycle slowing down to observe the strangers hanging around outside his local. I retrieved my laptop from my rucksack, flipped it open on the table and plugged the Thai USB stick in for a trip down memory lane.

The reason I was still carrying the device was that I'd come to enjoy the anticipation of what would appear on my laptop screen. Often, a non-descript beach or cityscape would cause me to flick straight on to the next image. Sometimes though, the photo was instantly enthralling, causing me to double click to examine its full detail. This was one such picture.

A younger me, seated on a low stool alongside a kneeling, ebony skinned man in a dusty marketplace. His indigo blue robes and turban indicate that he is a Tuareg nomad. The assortment of pills, powders, potions, bird feathers and desiccated animal parts spread on a blanket before him, suggest he is a witch doctor or traditional healer. The tribesman is brandishing an ostrich egg in his left hand. His right hand is firmly gripping my bare knee, which may explain the perturbed expression on my face. Initially, I had no recollection of the image and expanded it to reveal that I'm wearing a T-Shirt made by the Napapijiri brand, bearing a Norwegian flag logo. I immediately recalled where I was, why I'd chosen to wear that particular shirt and what had happened half an hour earlier. For once, when perusing an undated image on the USB stick, I also knew exactly when it was taken - May 2003, in Marrakech, Morocco.

Kirsty and I had flown into the coastal city of Casablanca on the 14th May, and spent a couple of days in the modern port city which felt more like Southern Spain than North Africa. On the 16th we'd picked up a rental car and headed south on the coast road to Essaouira, arriving in the early afternoon. That evening at 9pm, in Casablanca, terrorists from Salafiya Jihadiya, an Al-Qaeda affiliated group, launched a series of attacks. Fourteen young men clad in suicide vests and armed with daggers and hunting knives attacked five locations, all within a one mile radius. All were popular with foreigners, including a Spanish restaurant and a hotel. Thirty three civilians were killed, along with twelve of the bombers, and over a hundred people were seriously injured.

We found out about the attack the following day, and were left reflecting on the good fortune which meant we'd been eating and drinking in that exact area, at the same time, just 24 hours before the attacks. That a different flight schedule or availability of rental cars could have placed us in the path of murderous terrorists, was a sobering thought as we made our way towards Marrakech.

Morocco was on edge, clearly expecting further attacks, and we saw numerous police and army roadblocks, but no other Westerners as we stayed for a few nights in the wilderness of the

Atlas mountains. The Islamic influence was more visible there than in cosmopolitan Casablanca or seaside Essaouira, with women veiled and alcohol unavailable in most restaurants. The attacks left us feeling exposed. The bombers were disaffected young men from Sidi Moumen, a shanty town near Casablanca, and we interpreted the stares from youths loafing on corners of dusty mountain villages as aggression, whereas in reality they were most likely a combination of curiosity and sheer boredom, with more than one in ten unemployed in Morocco at the time.

Our flight home was from Marrakech and the plan was to drop the rental car at the airport there and take a taxi into town, where I seemed to have found an accommodation bargain. I'd read about a nascent travel trend which was taking off in Morocco, and particularly Marrakech, in the form of riad rentals. Usually situated in the medina, or old town, these traditional walled compound houses, built around a central courtyard were now being refurbished to attract European visitors. Riad actually means garden in Arabic, and strictly speaking, a riad should boast flower beds around a central fountain, without which it is merely a 'dar' or house, but 'Marrakech Riad' was becoming a popular Google search, and no one seemed to care too much about the detail.

Nowadays, it's possible to find reviews and price comparisons for just about any business in the world selling accommodation to tourists, but back in late 2002 when we'd arranged the Morocco trip, things were very different. TripAdvisor existed in an early form, but you'd have been very lucky to find a review of anything other than a large hotel in a tourism hotspot. In places like Marrakech, large hotels had websites, but few of the smaller ones did, and riads which boasted an online presence reflected their tech sophistication in their price tag. It was therefore something of a surprise when I spotted a 'Traditional Riad, in the real heart of Marrakech Medina' for around half the price quoted by its competitors. The website blurb mentioned a ten minute walk through atmospheric streets and local souks to reach Djemaa-el-Fnaa square, and the grainy pictures of a three storey construction around an elaborately tiled courtyard looked too good to be true. I emailed and booked three nights.

The airport taxi dropped us just inside the old city walls at the Bab Doukkala gate, where we were to be met by Rafik, the Riad caretaker, who, in keeping with the obvious local fashion, was dressed in an oversized brown djellaba robe with a pointed hood which hung down over his eyes. Identifying us was easy, as we were the only rucksack-bearing Westerners in the square, and Rafik briefly emerged from beneath his cloak to greet us with an enigmatic smile and a waved hand signal indicating that we should follow him.

It almost felt like we were in a fantasy movie as we struggled to keep pace with the slight, hunched, hooded figure who skipped ahead of us, as we stumbled over straw-strewn cobbles, dodged mule carts and bell ringing water vendors, and lugged our bags through tannery yards, quiet alleyways and crowded souks. The dusty air was filled with the aromas of turmeric, ginger, cinnamon, outside lavatories and farmyards, and every step we took was accompanied by a soundtrack of shouted sales pitches from stall holders and market traders.

Rafik darted ahead, occasionally turning to peer from under his hood to check that we were still trailing in his wake, until he stopped at a non-descript wooden door, below a three storey ochre-coloured building, and produced a large, dungeon style iron key, which required both hands to insert it into the lock. The door creaked open, and we stepped from the hubbub of the narrow alleyway into a different world. The buzz of passing scooters, cries of hawkers and clip-clop of hooves was instantly replaced by the cooing of perching white doves, and the gentle splash of water from an ornamental fountain. An old lady, Rafik's wife, appeared bearing a silver tray of mint tea and gestured for us to sit, and we were able to take in our surroundings. The guest house followed the classic riad design of an inwardly focused dwelling space, in keeping with the Islamic culture, where unveiled women could live and work without being observed by non-family members. Indigo patterned ceramic tiles covered every surface, and wooden balconies on each of the three floors shrank the blue square of sky above us, and provided welcome shade from the glare of the African sun.

Rafik showed us to our second floor room and it became clear that we were the only guests in the eight-room establishment. We were impressed by the almost palatial surroundings, which were topped off by a nice roof garden complete with sun loungers, from where it was possible to watch the comings and goings in the streets surrounding the riad. I congratulated myself on finding a bargain, and we speculated on why we were the only travellers to have found the place.

That question was partially answered when we made our way into the streets to try and find the centre of the medina and the famed Djemaa-el-Fnaa, or assembly of the dead, which was supposedly a ten minute walk away. We had a local street map, but asking Rafik to point out where our riad was located, prompted a scowl and much scratching of his wrinkled, shaven head. It quickly became clear that either our location was well off the page, or Rafik had never seen a map of his hometown before. We set off with vaguely pointed directions, and were soon lost in a labyrinth of backstreets. As we wandered the larger alleyways, with electronics shops selling early second-hand mobile phones alongside gore-filled butcheries and local fruit and veg stalls, we attracted the usual response to tourists in Arabic cities. Vendors were attracted to us like flies to a boiled sheep's head, and before long we had a trail of persistent hawkers offering carpets, magic lamps and herbs and spices all for 'cheap, cheap, Asda price!'

Moving deeper into the backstreets resulted in less high pressure sales tactics, but a greater level of culture shock. Two hundred yards from a shop advertising Nokias and computer repairs, a twisting, narrow, cobbled alleyway transported us back a couple of centuries. Long eared sheep peeped from ground floor doorways, while toddlers stared, wide eyed from the rooms above. Packs of donkeys and mules bearing bulky loads, driven by hooded figures who hissed as they passed, had obvious right-of-way and forced us to retreat on a number of occasions. The reaction of the people told us that foreigners never came to these streets. Old people stopped and glared from a foot away as we passed, children ran howling in terror and teenagers demonstrated their bravado by following at a distance while shouting 'You! What is your country?' and occasionally half heartedly throwing stones at us.

For me, one of travel's greatest pleasures is exploring non-touristed streets, chatting to locals, taking photos and generally soaking up the atmosphere. To do that though, you need to blend in. Once you become the attraction yourself, all hope of an enjoyable immersion in a foreign culture is lost. It was therefore something of a relief when we reached the Djemaa-el-Fnaa in the early afternoon. The square is famous for its nightly 'hoopla' of acrobats, magicians, fire eaters, dancing monkeys, pickpockets and arse-gropers, but is a more sedate affair in the afternoon. We wandered between food and spice stalls and watched snake charmers with whining 'pungi' flutes lure swaying, hypnotised cobras from wicker baskets. Elderly storytellers held court in Berber and Arabic, to assemblies of cross-legged youths and men. I stopped to watch, expecting a risqué comedy-club routine with Moroccan mother-in-law jokes, but the crowds were solemn faced, hanging on every word in rapt silence, and I wondered what sort of a story would have to be told to hold the attention of a crowd of European men in the same way.

We headed to the new part of town in the evening, where, unlike in the medina, alcohol was on offer, and a taxi back to Bab Doukkala would be more readily available. The police and army presence was high in the city, and there was a palpable air of tension in the bars and cafes, not helped when a group of young, bearded men of South Asian appearance appeared outside a pavement café carrying large backpacks, causing a rapid evacuation indoors!

The streets leading from the city walls to the riad were quieter after dark, so we persuaded the taxi driver to take us closer, and he crawled along the cobbles until the route ahead was so narrow, we were almost unable to open the doors to get out of the car. A rap on the large wooden door alerted Mrs Rafik, who announced her presence with a dramatic clanking of keys and loud sliding of bolts to admit us.

Rose petals had been scattered on our bed which is always a nice touch, but has a tendency to cause my hay fever to flare up, so these were swiftly consigned to the bin, and we lay, enjoying the silence, broken only by the distant braying of an ass, or buzz of a passing scooter. I wasn't aware that I'd even been asleep when the earthquake struck. I sat bolt upright, eyes blinking in terror as Kirsty yelped breathlessly beside me. The whole room was shaking, and my head was pulsating, filled with a deafening buzz which made my teeth ache and my nose run.

"Jesus...What is that? What's happening??" Kirsty pulled the covers over her head as I swung my legs over the side of the bed to investigate. As I did so, the ear splitting buzz was momentarily paused, before being replaced by piercing electrical feedback, then silence. I stood, shaking and taking deep breaths in the darkness. The room had stopped reverberating, but I was disorientated and tried to locate the light switch.

I was fumbling near the door jamb when I was hit by a discordant and deafening blast.

"Allllllllllllllllahuuuuuuakkkkk-bar!" The shutters on the room window rattled, as I flicked on the light and a pulse of feedback preceded the next onslaught.

"Alllllllllllllllllahuuuuuuakkkkkkkkkk-bar!" The muezzin sounded like he was trying to cough up a furball, before knocking over his evening cuppa, as the disembodied chant was now followed by the sounds of clattering and scraping.

Kirsty emerged from under the covers and asked me what time it was. Before I could tell her it was just after midnight, I was interrupted by another explosion of noise.

"Allllllllllllllahuuuuuuakkkkkkkkkk-bar!" The good news was that it wasn't an earthquake, but the Adhan, or call to prayer, being blasted from a minaret speaker which seemed to be attached to our riad. The bad news was that after four Allahu Akbars, there would be two recitals of the next five verses, than a single 'La ilah ill Allah'/ There is no God but Allah.

Then four hours later, in the 'Fajr' dawn call to prayer, we would have to suffer a repeat of the whole Adhan, plus an additional line, 'Assalatu khairum-minan-naum,' which translates as 'Prayer is better than sleep.' This wasn't a philosophy I shared at that point in time.

"Allllllllllllllahuuuuuuakkkkkkkkkk-bar! Ashhadu anna la ila ill Allah!" The noise was so deafeningly loud it felt like we were standing next to a speaker at a rock concert and made my ears hum. I turned off the light and got back into bed. I actually like to hear the distant call to prayer when travelling in Islamic countries, and usually find it to be quite hypnotic and relaxing. The key word in that sentence is 'distant'. Sleeping beneath the speaker of a mosque isn't conducive to a restful night, and after lying awake, awaiting the inevitable dawn chorus, Kirsty and I climbed up to the roof terrace to listen to the unavoidable Fajr call at 4.20am.

Next morning we emerged red-eyed for breakfast, and as the stooped, shuffling figure of Mrs Rafik appeared with our mint tea, I wondered aloud how old the couple were. I'd have guessed at late sixties but after the previous night's disturbed sleep I suggested they might actually only be in their forties, as I certainly felt that I'd aged significantly after spending one night in their home.

After the apparent suspicion and borderline hostility we'd experienced in the backstreets the previous day, I couldn't help wonder whether antipathy towards the West was a factor. The US, backed by the UK, had launched their 'shock and awe' bombing campaign of Iraq just two months earlier, which was widely viewed as the catalyst for the Casablanca attacks. As English speaking Europeans, we were clearly a target for any would-be Jihadists lurking in the alleyways of Marrakech. Luckily, I had the perfect solution in a t-shirt manufactured by the Napapijiri company, who confusingly have a Finnish name (meaning Arctic Circle) but a Norwegian flag logo. Norway was so far uninvolved in the Iraq campaign, so I felt the shirt would give me a convenient air of neutrality. Today, I would be Mats, the Norwegian, wearing a flag of convenience.

We set off towards the main square again, but decided to brave the hard-sell tactics of the street rather than risk getting lost in the labyrinth of back alleys, and soon attracted that most annoying of tourist-spot lurkers, the Self-Appointed Guide. Difficult to spot initially for the untrained eye, the S.A.G obtains their employment by stealth, walking in step with their quarry, but seemingly uninterested by their presence. An initial approach is likely to involve pointing out a hazard to the unwary visitor – a pavement pot hole, or dollop of horse shit. Thanks are met with a shy smile. Next, the S.A.G will draw their target's attention to something of interest on the route ahead. This could be anything from an elaborate palace or mosque, to a tethered cow or a street stall full of tomatoes. Not wishing to be impolite, the tourist will stop and allow the S.A.G to provide more details on the attraction. Ice broken, the conversation progresses to your name...your country...how many children you have. Your guide will share details of their own life, generally impoverished but striving to better themselves, spending their spare time learning your language. Of course you don't mind if they practice their English with you. GOTCHA! Congratulations traveller, you just employed a Self Appointed Guide.

Fortunately, I have a well attuned S.A.G. radar. I'm as alert to their presence as I am to nimble fingered child pickpockets, lumbering teen muggers, mouth foaming dogs and staggering, red eyed policemen brandishing rusty firearms. I therefore quickly noticed the small, swaying presence at my left shoulder. In fact, I smelt him before I saw him. A vaguely chemical smell, like paint thinner or car de-icer was noticeable amongst the normal greengrocery/gents toilets/spicy takeaway/farmyard aromas of the street. Five feet tall, early teens, with curly dark hair and a stained tracksuit top, shorts and flip-flops, he flashed a shy smile, then looked away, disinterested. Hmmm, straight to stage 2, I thought, and quickened my pace.

I spotted a metal pipe protruding from a wall ahead, which clearly served as a watering point for beasts of burden, and wasn't surprised to feel a tug on my sleeve, as our would-be guide pointed enthusiastically towards it. I kept walking as he stuck his head beneath it and gulped down a mouthful of suspiciously coloured water. Having failed to attract my attention, he plunged his head beneath the flow and soaked his hair, then ran in front of us, shaking it like an annoying labrador. It was at this point that I worked out the source of the chemical smell. The kid's chin and philtrum were a mass of scabs and sores, and were liberally caked in a dried yellow substance, which also appeared on his tracksuit, hands and bare legs. His eyes were glazed, his breath smelt toxic and it was clear this lad had foregone his Weetabix in favour of an inhaled solvent breakfast.

Having a fake guide in-tow is annoying enough, but having a glue sniffer careering along beside you, pointing out every object he knew the English word for, stretched our patience to its limits.

"Horse. Fruit. Dog. Shop. Door." A slurred running commentary and an arm tug accompanied us on every step of the way, until I'd had enough and moved into finger wagging mode.

"Look, we don't need a guide. Okay?" I turned and faced the urchin, who met my glare with defiance.

"I help you mister, you give me money." His breath nearly stuck my eyelids together.

"But I didn't ask you to help, did I? I didn't ask for a guide, did I?" I raised my voice and Kirsty began to encourage me to walk on, as passers-by were stopping to observe the altercation. Norwegian Mats seemed to speak very good English.

"Don't make me crazy, mister," the kid lowered his voice and narrowed his eyes in an attempt to look threatening. I laughed and turned to follow Kirsty who had set off walking,

"I'll kill you..." I'd taken two paces when I heard the threat, and turned and smiled at the boy, who was about a foot smaller than me and five stones lighter.

"Really? You're going to kill me? Come on then..." I beckoned him forward, as he stood scowling and repeating his threat "Don't make me crazy mister..."

I caught the eye of a barber who'd emerged from his shop to watch the exchange, and I shrugged and smiled. I imagined he'd reciprocate with a 'kids today eh?' response, but he just stared at me, then flicked his head in a gesture I struggled to interpret.

I quickened my pace to leave my young tormentor behind and caught Kirsty up. She was clearly agitated.

"I don't like the atmosphere. Everyone seems to be looking at us."

"No, I don't think so." I tried to reassure her, but found my usual smiles and nodded 'hellos' were being met by blank stares. I noticed people staring at the flag on my t-shirt and wondered if I'd made a mistake. Who would recognise the flag of Norway? They most likely knew though that the Stars and Stripes and Union Jack were red, white and blue, the same colours I had emblazoned on my chest. It suddenly felt like we were in the wrong place at the wrong time. There were no other foreigners here. If we were bundled into a sidestreet by kidnappers or attackers, would anyone see, or object?

We hurried on with our heads down, reaching a busier section of the narrow pedestrianised street. Souk porters in ragged djellabas staggered under the weight of head-borne baskets, and old ladies with inverted 'V' tattoos on their foreheads jockeyed for position with men in suits getting to grips with their first mobile phone. I was about to say it was starting to feel safer when I spotted a group of men staring at us. Five of them, mid-twenties to early thirties, gathered outside a rug shop ahead, engaged in an impromptu business meeting. Their clothing was a mixture of traditional and Western, with one man sat side-saddle on a parked motorbike, facing away from us. I looked away, hoping I was imagining the attention we were attracting, but when I looked again there was no denying it, as the motorbike man now turned to face us, and I felt Kirsty's pace slow beside me.

Things seemed to move in slow motion as the nearest of the group, a man taller than me, with a moustache and a sizeable paunch visible beneath his djellaba, seemed about to speak, but instead moved quickly and decisively towards us. One of his friends seemed to try to grab his arm to restrain him, but he pulled away and rushed towards us. I instinctively swerved to the right, almost knocking Kirsty over as the assailant brushed past me. Two other members of the group were rushing forward and drew my attention, just as the unmistakable sound of fist meeting skull filled the street. I jumped aside as they passed, and turned to see the man with the paunch stooping over a prone figure lying on the cobbles. I couldn't see his face but recognised the glue-stained shorts and legs immediately.

I stood open mouthed and uncomprehending as the men began shouting angrily, and manhandled the semi-conscious youth to the side of the street. It was only when one of the men turned towards me, brandishing a kitchen knife with a rusty six-inch blade that I realised I'd had my second lucky escape of the trip.

After thanking the vigilantes for potentially saving my life, or at least preventing the embarrassment of being carved up by a glue sniffing child, we headed to the relative calm of Djemaa-el-Fnaa square where I stopped to peruse the wares of the Tuareg medicine man. He spoke good English, having spent time in the Tunisian resort towns of Hammamet and Sousse, which were popular with Brits, and was able to provide a guided tour of his wares. Leaves, roots, barks and plant-derived perfumes seemed to make up most of his inventory, and he claimed his powders, potions and pot-pourri could cure ailments ranging from dysentery to cancer and mental illness to 'feeling cold', when accompanied by a laying-on of hands and some chanted incantations. I was well aware of the 'ju-ju' spells cast by the fetisheurs of West Africa, and asked if animal parts were used in Tuareg medicine.

"No animals, monsieur," he whispered unconvincingly while casting a wary glance over his shoulder. "Maybe only some birds...and perhaps lizards."

Rapidly changing the subject, he offered me an ostrich egg. "Very good egg monsieur, take for your friends in England," but I doubted it would survive the attentions of the Air France baggage handlers or a night at the pub when presented to my confused pals back home. Instead, we posed together for the photo which Kirsty took - My Tuareg friend displaying his very good egg, face mysteriously half concealed beneath his turban, and me with an expression befitting a man who has nearly been chopped up by a murderous street urchin, then had his leg gripped by a nomadic shaman.

Before we left, he furtively delved deep into his robes and produced a blue, palm-shaped amulet with a centrepiece fake sapphire, fashioned into the shape of an eye. I recognised this as a Hamsa, or 'Hand of Fatima', which supposedly offers protection for the wearer against the dreaded evil eye.

"For you, monsieur, special price. It will bring you good luck and protect you from evil."

I smiled. "To be honest mate, judging by my luck in the last few days, I really don't think I need one!"

Hostel Life

Day 104 -Samaipata, Bolivia

"What did you say?" I'd just climbed out of a cold shower and was drying myself as quickly as possible, to minimise time spent naked in the chill mountain air of our hostel room in Samaipata.

"It wasn't me, it was them," whispered Kirsty.

"Who?"

"The Belgians...or French, or whatever they are." She jerked a thumb towards the shuttered window of our tiny cell. We'd drawn a definite short straw in our room allocation, which was probably to be expected, as we were only staying for three nights, while most of the guests were long-termers, an eclectic mix of nationalities, all displaying a roadwise traveller vibe, and all at least twenty years younger than us.

The hostel had been easy to spot as we hiked the last half mile into the village from the bus stop, a bright yellow building with tiny windows, clinging to a hillside on a quiet cobbled lane. Finding who was in charge, or someone who actually worked there was more challenging. A wooden external door led to a courtyard garden area with multi-coloured picnic benches occupied by lounging travellers perusing maps and guidebooks or tapping away on laptops. No one looked up as we entered and removed our backpacks. There was an open-plan kitchen area to the left, where two girls in fluorescent, hiking technical gear and Andean woolly hats with ear flaps were chopping salad.

"Hola, hablan Ingles?" Their clothing told me they weren't locals, but opening a conversation in English would have been an unforgiveable faux-pas in South American backpacker circles.

"Sure," replied one of the girls with a slight Northern European inflection that I couldn't place.

"Do you work here?"

"No, we live here, you need Pachama. I don't know where she is right now. Just hang out, maybe she'll be back soon." The laidback approach to check-in at South American hostels was something we'd have to adjust to, and for a couple whose previous two week trip schedules generally utilised hotels with efficient 24 hour check in desks, 'hanging out' for an hour or two was a different experience which we'd need to get used to.

We dumped our backpacks next to two others beneath a tree in the garden, and went for a wander in the village, which bills itself as Bolivia's 'Little Switzerland'. With a population of around 4000 and located at an altitude of 1600 metres, Samaipata was a popular staging post on the Bolivian traveller circuit. Pastel coloured, single storey houses with terracotta roofs lined the narrow, cobbled lanes and the lower altitude was better suited to hiking in the surrounding hills than in most of the country's lung-busting destinations. The majority of travellers passing through the village were moving between the frenetic cities of Cochabamba, Sucre and Santa Cruz and the slow pace of life was immediately appealing after a few days of travelling on long-distance buses. Samaipata was renowned as a place where people arrived to stay for a couple of days, and ended up being there for a few months.

That certainly seemed to be the case at our hostel and when we returned, a dreadlocked Israeli youth was settling a bill which must have covered multiple weeks, judging by the number of crusty Boliviano notes being handed over to a dumpy local woman. She introduced herself as Pachama, and after flicking through the pages of a tatty, handwritten pad, handed us the key to Room 2. Looking on the bright side, Room 2 was only about ten feet away from the desk used for bookings, bill payment, trip organisation, kitten petting, salad eating and guitar strumming. The downside was that it had a communal picnic bench directly under the window. If I'd opened the shutters to let in some much needed light, I'd have knocked the iPad from the hands of a bespectacled Swede, who was prodding at a bowl of congealed noodles while Facetiming some friends who were surfing at Huanchaco in Peru. I established their location and plans while sat on our bed, as I could hear every detail of the conversation taking place an arm's length away through a flimsy glass pane.

We found ourselves involuntarily whispering, while plunged into a darkness caused by having to keep the shutters closed. The fact that the room was about 8'x 8' with a small double bed and nowhere to store our bags except the floor, meant that two people were unable to move around freely at the same time. One of us was forced to seek refuge in the wardrobe-sized bathroom or to interact with the rest of the commune in the garden.

I decided to take the latter option, and went outside to make some friends. I was well aware that I was old enough to have fathered the next oldest guest, Basil, a shaven headed Swiss who sported a t-shirt showing he'd volunteered at a Toucan sanctuary in Panama. I was therefore keen not to appear a middle-aged square, and as Kirsty showered, I wandered barefoot into the garden, prepared to play giant jenga or learn the Andean pan-pipes or maybe graze on some high grade coca leaves.

I nodded to a lentil munching blonde with pigtails who raised her iPad protectively, as I pulled a wobbly stool up to her picnic bench. I whipped out my Kindle and, fearful of being labelled a capitalist pig, furtively downloaded The Times, then read it while casting nervous glances over my shoulder like an 80's commuter looking at a porn mag on a train. It was clear that everyone knew each other and multiple games of 'Travel Top Trumps' were breaking out, with alpha males from opposing benches trying to outdo each other with their 'awesome' experiences.

"Did you do Tulum at sunrise? That was so cool..." The fact that Tulum was pronounced Tooo-Looom made me roll my eyes, even thought that might be the correct way to say it. Not in Yorkshire it isn't.

"Of course, the bus to Iguacu took thirty hours but it was cool. I just learnt Mandarin and meditated."

"Sure, in Guatemala we used the chicken buses the whole time. So authentic, I even caught scabies!"

I read the same paragraph five times while trying unsuccessfully to block out the travel-bants flying back and forth. I bit my tongue and reminded myself that most of my fellow guests were half my age. I was working before any of them were born, but thus far had limited my travels to two week journeys. It was unsurprising that they were approaching their first forays into the world like excited puppies, or that deep-down, I was jealous of them for managing to travel long-term at an age where I'd been stuck behind a desk. I resolved to be more open minded and to go with the flow. Maybe by the time we left Quito I'd be wearing calico harem pants and carrying a llama wool satchel.

The main agenda item for late afternoon at the hostel was planning the following day's activities. A hike to the waterfalls at Las Cuevas was being discussed, and Pachama was taking names to work out how many colectivo taxis would be required to transport everyone to the trailhead, 20km from town. There was much excited chattering and even some low level whooping, as secret swimming holes were mentioned. I kept my head down, having never been keen on arranged group excursions, especially ones where I would probably be viewed like an unpopular teacher on a school trip.

"Matthew!" I looked up. Pachama was waving her pen in my direction. "Are you and your wife coming to Las Cuevas tomorrow? It will be fun!"

"Ah no...erm...we're..." In reality we hadn't decided what to do, but faced with fifteen young travellers looking on expectantly I had to come up with something.

"We're going on a hike..."

"Oh cool! Where are you hiking to?" Shit. I wished now that I'd read the Lonely Planet section on local walks, rather than catching up on the UK news. With the entire Manson family still looking on, I had to come up with something impressive.

"El Fuerte." I blurted out. I knew the Mayan ruins were in the area but had no idea how far they were or how to get to them. My answer had the desired effect though, and the assembled travellers nodded their approval. Pachama raised her eyebrows.

"Do you need a taxi one way? It's going to be hot tomorrow." Her expression concerned me, but I couldn't back down.

"No it's fine thanks, we'll walk." I thought I heard someone say 'hardcore', and Pachama said something about hoping we liked hills, so I smiled and nodded.

After showering we set off for a night on the town in Samaipata, and as we left Pacahama shouted 'Don't be late, you need your energy for tomorrow!" Kirsty gave me a confused look and I told her I'd explain later.

The village nightlife was surprisingly lively, with a handful of bars and cantinas clustered around a corner of the tree-lined central square. Although first impressions were that Samaipata was Gringo-Central, with multitudes of foreign visitors, we soon realised that we were seeing the same people in different bars, and that there were probably less than fifty travellers in town in total. We were soon engaged in an entertaining people-spotting exercise, as we identified 'Arguing Americans', 'Limping Sex Tourist', 'Moustache Twister', and 'Idiots-with-four-kids'.

At the end of the night, we found that the hostel's laidback approach extended to after-hours support. We arrived back to find a distraught Austrian couple on the doorstep.

"The door is locked. We haff been here for more than twenty minutes," moaned the lanky youth as his girlfriend bobbed about beside him in an agitated manner.

"No one is coming." He prodded at a button on the door causing a distant bell to tinkle.

"And I need the toilet soooo badly." The girl's hands were between her legs and she danced a doubled-up jig.

At that point I noticed a tell-tale splash on the hostel wall, and the young man reddened visibly under the yellow streetlight.

"Ja, I too needed the toilet. But..." his girlfriend snorted in the manner of women the world over, who are forced to suffer while their partner is able to covertly relieve himself on a wall.

It was clear there were no staff members on duty, and I correctly guessed that the door should have been left on the latch, but had been locked by someone arriving back before us.

"Only one thing for it," I announced looking at a head height fence leading to the garden, "you'll have to get over there," I nodded at the Austrian.

"Me? No, I don't think...I heard a dog in there," he didn't seem keen, so I explained that he was a few inches taller and a lot of years younger than me, so was the obvious candidate to go over the top. A couple of minutes later, predictably, I was face down in a muddy cabbage patch on the other side of the fence, having succeeded only in getting the cowardly Austrian to give me a leg-up.

I hauled myself upright and began blundering through the undergrowth to a soundtrack of German-accented pleading 'Please hurry, I really need to pee now...' Needless to say, I took my time, then gave her boyfriend my best death stare as I opened the front door to let them in.

The Belgians were up early the next morning, which meant we were too. It was quite disconcerting to wake in the darkness of a strange room to the sound of a heated Flemish debate taking place just feet away. I vacated the room to give Kirsty room to move about, and spotted the bearded hipster who'd seen the sunrise at 'Tooo-looom' was checking out. That meant there was a room spare, so I set off to investigate. Most of the private rooms were set around the garden but there was a two-storey building on the southern boundary which I thought was the location of the dormitory. I climbed a creaking wooden staircase to arrive at the first floor landing, where a wooden door was slightly ajar. I poked my head round the doorframe to see four bunkbeds squeezed haphazardly into the small space. It may have been a bargain at $6 a night but I'd rather have slept on one of the picnic benches. I followed the stairs to the next level and found a landing with two doors. One was closed, but the other opened onto a scene of devastation, clearly wrought by the sort of chap who pronounces his 'U's as 'ooos.' Amidst a confusion of blankets and dirty towels was a double bed. Beyond that was a small balcony overlooking some tin-roofed shacks and the distant hills. Most importantly, it was well away from the hubbub of the rest of the hostel, and I decided that this room would be ours for the remainder of our stay.

There was no sign of Pachama, so I made for the desk which served as a makeshift reception. Two girls were using a landline to try and negotiate in broken Spanish with some form of Bolivian officialdom, so I confidently reached across them to retrieve the tatty notepad which served as a booking system. Each page represented a calendar week with the names of the occupants scrawled in a range of handwriting, alongside the twelve rooms. Room 11 had no name beside it for the following two nights, so I carefully replicated the handwriting style of 'Matthew' which was written next to room 2, in the space alongside room 11, then scored out the original entry. Job done. I then sought out the cleaning lady, a sparrow framed woman who jumped when I caught her on the stairs near the dorm.

"Limpia habitación once?" I pointed towards our new room and the old lady nodded.

Back in Room 2, Kirsty emerged from the shower to find our bags packed, ready to move. "I've got us an upgrade," I explained. "Room with a view, and no Belgians!"

We had breakfast while I consulted the Lonely Planet and various websites, which provided conflicting information on the distance to El Fuerte, with general opinion ranging from five to eight miles. 'Easy if we get a taxi back,' was my opinion and we set out along the road as the Las Cuevas excursion taxis sped by, with one of the backpackers giving us a raised fist salute as they passed, which I interpreted as meaning 'Hardcore, old dude!' but may have meant something else completely.

The walk was hot and uphill with some steep sections, but the terrain wasn't excessively difficult, as we were walking along a quiet asphalt road for much of the way. We arrived at the car park and unsurprisingly upon checking our phone-app step-counters, found that the actual distance was at the top end of the estimates, at just over seven miles. Ominously, there were no taxis in the sun-baked car park. In fact, there were no cars at all.

Sometimes referred to as a poor-man's Machu Picchu, El Fuerte, or the Fort, is a huge, saddle shaped rock, 700 feet in length and 200 feet wide, which straddles the summit of a flat hillside, providing an unrivalled vantage point to view the surrounding hills and valleys. The rock is covered with Incan carvings of animal shapes and geometric designs. Eighteen carved niches known as 'El Coro de los Sacerdotes' or 'Choir of the Priests', are located at the highest point of the rock, serving as grandstand seats for senior shamans at ceremonies and rituals. In the late 1960's, Swiss author Erich von Däniken identified a landing strip on the rock and interpreted some of the carvings as detailed maps of the world and modern inventions such as telescopes. His theory was that 15th century Incans were visited by UFO's piloted by time travelling humans, who were able to share secrets from the future. Though the idea was unsurprisingly scorned by scientists and archaeologists, it spawned a local cottage industry in genuine Incan, future-predicting rock artefacts such as cars, planes and even the Eifel Tower, which were eagerly flogged to tourists well into the 1980's.

It came as no surprise when we arrived back in the car park to find that there were no taxis cruising for customers. We hadn't seen anyone else on the walk from Samaipata, so it was obviously an unlikely spot to tout for custom. We set off walking with the intention of hitch hiking, and I tempted fate by repeating the mantra that you always get a ride on a quiet road. Three hours later we limped back into Samaipata, having only been passed by one already full car and thankfully not the taxis of our fellow hostel dwellers. I emptied my pocket of stones used to repel the dogs which appeared barking and snarling from every farm along the road, and we sneaked back into the hostel to patch up blistered feet in our newly upgraded room.

With a small balcony overlooking the outskirts of the village and the surrounding hills, and being tucked away from the

Kumbaya-singalong atmosphere of the garden, our accommodation now represented an absolute bargain. We benefitted from the laissez-faire management style too, with the only comment from Pachama on our room change coming the day before we checked out, in the form of a cheery 'Oh, you moved rooms? That's cool!'

Samaipata itself was similarly chilled and was perfect for wandering aimlessly. The locals were as photogenic as the village streets, with ancient crones in flowing skirts and wide brimmed straw hats, and improbably dark hair plaits which fell to below their waists. We hiked in the surrounding hills during the day and every evening at sunset I positioned myself on the edge of the market to take some candid people shots with my long lens. At night we ate and drank cheaply in the local bars, and even entered into a hostel-wide discussion on the best way to reach our next destination, Cochabamba.

We were woken by the sound of a distant brass band early on a Sunday morning, and I immediately grabbed my camera and set off to investigate. A slow-moving congregation of locals lurched and swayed through the streets of the village, each carrying a palm frond, as they filed in procession behind a gruesome effigy of Christ on the cross. I'd forgotten that Easter was approaching, and though we'd fallen prey to that familiar urge to stay longer in Samaipata, I wanted to reach La Paz in time for the parade of hooded penitents on Good Friday. The capital was another fifteen hours of tough bus travel away, on some of the world's highest altitude roads. It was time to move on.

Mean Streets

""Which dodgy place are you going to this year?" was a question I grew accustomed to being asked by friends and family in advance of one of my bi-annual fortnightly holidays. I'm sure some people were convinced that I deliberately sought out the world's most notorious locations to visit. The truth was that in most places, the reputation was generally worse than the reality. Every big city has its no-go zones, which even locals know to avoid, and there's no good reason for visitors to find themselves there. Even cities which are viewed as inherently dangerous, such as Bogota and Johannesburg, generally have a tourist friendly area where it's safe to walk during the day, and a designated nightlife zone which is heavily policed after dark.

I'm on the email update list for the UK Foreign Office travel advisories, so at any time, I can quote all the 'red zone' countries, and therefore avoid the disappointment of booking a camel trek in Chad or a cycling adventure in Niger, only to discover that I might end up using all my holiday allowance chained to a tree in a Boko Haram encampment.

More dangerous than the renowned high risk zones are cities where dodgy areas exist close to those frequented by tourists. Pre-Katrina New Orleans was one such place, and in the early 90's, a single wrong turn in the French Quarter would often deposit a careless reveller straight into the hands of the heavily armed muggers skulking in the side streets between Bourbon and Dauphine. Rio is another city where glitzy hotels and high-rise condos look out onto favelas which are lit up by tracer rounds from automatic weapons on most nights. Our hotel there was one block back from Copacabana beach, but the road leading to it passed the entrance to a notorious hillside shanty town. We became a couple of travelling Cinderellas on that occasion, as hotel management informed us that walking past there after midnight would most certainly result in a violent robbery or worse.

However, the biggest risk to personal safety when travelling, has to come from those places which sound benign, or at least, you've never heard of any crime occurring there. But then you realise you don't actually know anyone who's ever been to the country, and have never even seen the place mentioned in European newspapers. Guyana for instance.

Ask ten people where Guyana is, and nine will tell you it's in Africa. It's actually in South America, sandwiched between Venezuela, Brazil and Suriname in the north west. Guyana is the only English speaking nation in South America, and the only nation on the continent with an international cricket team. Culturally, it's a Caribbean island transplanted onto the South American land mass. It sounded an intriguing place, and when I realised it was only an hour's hop on a plane from Trinidad, and that my original two centre choice, Venezuela, was going up in economic meltdown flames, I booked the flight.

The photo which appeared on my laptop to remind me of Guyana was strangely appropriate. At the time, we were bumping along a rough Andean road, during a ten hour bus journey between the Bolivian cities of Cochabamba and La Paz, when the laptop screen was filled with a blurry image of my distorted, enlarged head, and Kirsty, sporting shades and looking faintly seasick, sitting behind me. The photo was taken on a bouncing speedboat traversing the Essequibo River between the towns of Parika and our destination, Bartica. The blurring was due to me trying to hold my phone to snap a photo, while being bounced two feet into the air every time we hit a wave, in a bone-jarring, maritime bucking bronco ride.

Guyana is a nation of rivers and jungle, with few navigable roads. Boats are the main form of transport within the country, so experiencing a river journey away from the capital, Georgetown, was an obvious attraction. Bartica was a mining town with a population of around 8000, set amidst dense, undulating jungle, 35 miles from Georgetown. It was described as a friendly place with abundant birdlife and canoeable mangrove swamps close by, and it boasted a highly rated hotel set on an island in the river. Unfortunately, after booking a room, my research had also unearthed the fact that a few years earlier the town had been the scene of the 'Bartica Massacre', when infamous gangster Rondell 'Fineman' Rawlins and his thirty strong pirate gang had attacked the town. After arriving by speedboat, the group first targeted the police station, killing three officers. They then stole ammo and vehicles and marauded through the town, strafing buildings and passers-by with machine gun fire, killing another nine people.

As 'Fineman' had later been shot dead by police, I'd decided it probably wasn't worth sharing this information with Kirsty, and we'd taken an hour-long taxi journey from Georgetown to Parika, where we thought we'd got lucky in bagging the last two places on one of the cramped wooden boats. The apparent benefit of this was that we didn't have to wait for the vessel to fill up before departing, and also, it meant that we were located at the front of the enclosed cabin, next to the entrance hatch. If the boat were to spring a leak or capsize after hitting a log, both of which had occurred in preceding years, we would be first in line to try to escape. What I hadn't realised was that being at the front meant being subjected to an hour-long spinal pounding, as the two large outboard motors powering us through the choppy waters, caused the bow to rise several feet in the air, before smashing back down every three seconds. The wooden bench seats, with an awkwardly positioned backrest, exacerbated the problem and I could almost hear my vertebrae cracking with every crashing descent. To make matters worse, I was sharing the front bench with a taciturn twenty-something, who objected to the spray coming through the open hatch and splashing his expensive sneakers. He let me know this by sucking his teeth, hissing and slamming the door shut every time I slid it open.

That meant there was no chance to take in the jungle scenery as we zipped past at fifty knots. A greater concern though, was that in the event of an emergency, our chances of survival were reduced considerably with the hatch closed. I therefore began to gag and retch theatrically, which caused him to look terror stricken and fling open the door, while instructing me in the entertaining local Creole dialect 'If you a gon get sick, be mek sure yu hang you mout tru de window!' Clearly, he felt that projectile vomit would be a greater risk to his trainers than river water.

The speedboat journeys to and from Bartica proved equally hair-raising and uncomfortable, and after a few days spent downriver, we were glad to sink into the fake leather seats of a taxi back to Georgetown from Parika boat dock. However, the journey to town provided another reminder that danger is never far away in countries like Guyana. The route into town took us along Carifesta Avenue, which ran parallel to the Atlantic Ocean, and our driver told us that recent storms, coupled with an expected high tide, were threatening to breach the 280 mile long sea-wall which runs the entire length of Guyana's coast. We hadn't realised that Georgetown is actually situated below sea level, and the wall is the only defence against the sea swamping the city entirely.

Our driver pulled off the main road and we trundled along a dirt track where, he told us, his brother used to own a house. There were scattered shacks surrounded by scrubby plots of land, grazed by an occasional dejected mule, but the wooden stoops of the houses were strangely devoid of human life. Turning a corner at the end of the track told us why. All the residents were assembled in chattering, pointing crowds, observing a truly terrifying sight. The settlement was bordered by the sea wall, fifteen feet high and adorned with ancient adverts for local businesses, which had peeled and blistered, as if the concrete had been afflicted by a bad case of eczema. Beyond the wall, and seeming to rise several metres above it, was a broiling, frothing, black mass of ocean. Clearly an optical illusion, I couldn't work out how the sea seemed to be so much higher than the wall, or how that immense volume of water could be repelled only by a crumbling concrete barrier. And as we watched, it looked as though that point was about to be tested, as a large crack appeared at the top of one of the adverts and water began to pour through the gap. Teenagers ran forward and began to jostle and shove each other under the flow, as the concrete started to bulge alarmingly in several places.

"Man, I never see it like this before." Our driver took out his phone and began to video the scene, as older residents shook their heads and cast nervous glances towards their homes. At that point it seemed certain that the wall would be breached in the next few minutes and the whole area inundated by a tsunami. The taxi driver seemed oblivious to this, and stood smiling contentedly as he captured the once-in-a-lifetime scene. I was now getting worried so decided to employ the likeliest tactic to spook him.

"How fast can your car accelerate?"

"What...? How fast?"

"Do you think you could outrun a tidal wave?" He glanced at his pride and joy, parked twenty feet away, then back to the water flooding through and over the wall, and quickly got the message.

"Guys, I think we better get out of here now."

As we bumped along the track at speed, I turned to look at the crowd of locals watching, waiting, totally powerless before the awesome force of nature, which could wipe out their very existence in minutes. What a place to live, I thought, and wondered how anyone slept at night knowing the weight of the Atlantic Ocean was constantly bearing down on their garden wall.

For our return to Georgetown, we'd opted for a homestay on the edge of the city centre, and first impressions were of a large single storey house in tree-shaded gardens, on a quiet road of colonial-style wooden dwellings. The eight-foot-high spiked fence and pack of four large guard dogs should perhaps have given us a clue as to the nature of the area, but as we sat in the spacious open-plan lounge with our hostess, Sally, everything seemed perfect, and I congratulated myself on picking a bargain. I'd studied the small Guyana section of the Lonely Planet's South America guide and had spotted a restaurant serving intriguing local dishes such as cow heel soup, cook-up rice and metamgee dumplings. The map suggested it to be about a kilometre away, and with my spine in need of a stretch after the punishing boat journey, I announced our intention to walk.

"Is it safe at night?" I enquired of Sally, who seemed somewhat conflicted in her answer.

"Yes, it's fine," she replied hesitantly, "but don't wear any jewellery."

"Makes sense," I agreed.

"And maybe don't take a phone or a camera...or any credit cards," she smiled unconvincingly, "you'll be fine, I'm sure."

I nodded and we headed back to the room to ditch anything of value. To unnerve us further, as we left, Sally appeared.

"Where did you say you were walking to again?"

I named the restaurant and asked if she knew it. She confirmed she did, but I was left with the impression that she probably didn't, and wondered why, as it was so close.

"So, it's definitely safe to walk there?" I decided to give her a chance to backtrack.

"Yes of course, you'll be fine. Have a great night guys!" She waved us off at the gate and I was tempted to ask if we could borrow one of her bull mastiffs for the evening.

The first block we walked, was like a reconstructed street in a plantation era theme park, with fine old wooden mansions set back from the road in extensive grounds, shaded by star apple and calabash trees. Streetlamps flickered and glowed orange, cicadas trilled electronically, and the only traffic was an occasional cycle, with its rider slowing to observe the obviously unfamiliar sight of white pedestrians. What should have been a pleasant stroll was made slightly unnerving by the amount of razor wire adorning the high, spiked fences and signs announcing 24-hour armed response security.

By the time we were halfway along the next block, the large wooden houses began to slowly give way to concrete apartment blocks, and cheap motels with prison style bars on the windows. Any colonial era architecture which remained, looked dark and abandoned, with haphazard wooden stoops and rusting corrugated roofs collapsing into weed-strewn yards. It was surprising how quickly the neighbourhood was going downhill before our eyes, and I realised it was time to move into urban-survival mode.

"Big antelopes Kirsty!" I announced, and we employed the survival-of-the-fittest tactic which says that predators always attack the weakest of the herd. Lions will go for the oldest, youngest or sickest antelope, not the big, aggressive buck at the front with the huge antlers, so that's what we had to become. I pushed out my chest, clenched my fists and snarled at a passing youth on a scooter. As usual, Kirsty followed behind me, trying unsuccessfully to look menacing, and I just hoped my act was more convincing than hers.

By the third block, we were firmly in the territory of inner-city urban decay. Houses were either small, ramshackle concrete squares or large ugly apartment buildings. Walls were decorated with gang graffiti and razor wire, and through every padlocked iron gate, protruded the slavering muzzle of a large dog. The lack of activity on the street had added to the tension, and the welcome sound of distant music had me wondering if we'd reached the restaurant. Unfortunately, the lights we could see were from a heavily fortified liquor store, outside of which a thumping bass was booming from a parked car. Shadows moved in the car's headlights and as we drew level, I was able to see the sources were straight out of a 'Grime' video shoot. Vests, bandanas, tight corn-braids, baggy jeans hanging below skinny arses, swigging from 40 ounce beer bottles, every gangster rap cliché was satisfied. I doubted a big antelope would deter these predators if they were in the mood to hunt, so we slunk past unseen, concealed in the shadows on the far side of the street.

After walking the length of another never-ending block, where our progress was closely monitored by the impassive stares of a group of youths on a first floor balcony, we spotted the flashing neon of a corner bar, located on the ground floor of an impressive old building with a colonnaded balcony. It wasn't the restaurant we were aiming for, but it would at least get us off the street.

We crossed the road towards the open fronted establishment, which was busy with drinkers congregating at the bar and on pavement tables underneath a striped awning. A Guyanese dancehall track, with shouted patois lyrics, electronic interjections and gunshot blasts exploded from a speaker, and the whole bar jerked and bobbed their heads to the rhythm. I'd have preferred the sounds of local legend Eddie Grant, but this place certainly looked lively. The worst thing you can do when entering a locals' bar is to appear uncertain, so I sped up as we approached, mounted the high kerb and bounced confidently through the door and towards the bar. The effect of my entrance was nothing short of sensational. Every single person I made eye contact with ceased their conversation in mid-flow and their mouth fell open. They then turned and followed my progress to the bar, where a tall man with a face of polished leather and teeth like a Tongan Queen was polishing glasses. His eyes widened when he saw me approaching, but then the novelty of welcoming two obvious tourists to his bar seemed to amuse him and he broke into a beaming grin.

"Ha Ha! Missa, wha' you go waan?"

I was still struggling to adapt to Creole, which is derived from 19th-century English and Dutch, with some African, Indian and indigenous Arawakan thrown in for good measure. I correctly guessed he wanted to know what we were drinking, so I settled on the local brew of choice, and ordered two bottles of Stag beer. It was only when I turned to hand Kirsty her bottle, that I realised that, to a man and woman, everyone in the bar had called a halt to their socialising and was staring at us. It was as if two Kayan long-neck tribeswomen had teetered on stage for Karaoke in a British council estate pub. Or a couple of West Papuan Kombay elders had turned up at a Wetherspoons curry night asking whether 'long pig' was on the menu.

A barstool drinker got up and tapped his seat, indicating we should sit, so Kirsty perched on the buffet while I stood and took in our surroundings. Two thirds of the drinkers were men, with an average age of around forty and a waist size to match. It seemed that body parts were viewed as optional accessories here, and a quick scan of the room revealed a missing leg, a half- arm and an eye socket which appeared to have been melted shut. The dress code was mid 80's sports tropical, with loud shirts unbuttoned to waist level, and baseball caps the compulsory headwear. The most prevalent female occupation could probably have been described as 'nightworker', and a coven of heavily made-up women with dress sizes ranging from skeleton to circus big-top, held court at the back of the room. Two were twins and judging by their physique and facial features, it was clear they took after their father, who was most probably a famous wrestler.

Strangers in a locals' bar are like catnip to drunks, and before long we'd attracted two red eyed staggerers, who looned about and tried unsuccessfully to entice Kirsty to dance, before being shooed away by the barman. I was monitoring the movements of two tracksuit clad youths, who seemed to be keeping us under close scrutiny from an outside table, when an old man in an outsized suit jacket, shorts, black socks and flip flops sidled up alongside me. He had a grey beard the texture of a tennis ball, which matched his thinning frizzy hair, and smelt of a heady cocktail of rum and mothballs. Gripping my arm, he drew me towards him, so that he could be heard above the pounding music.

"All cassava get same skin, but all nah taste same way. Yu knaa dis?"

Assuming he was a madman, I smiled and nodded, which caused him to clink his bottle on mine and wag his finger at me. Confused, I smiled at him again, before being distracted by a couple in matching tropical print shirts who wanted a selfie with Kirsty. One of the lads outside was on his phone, while his friend continued to cast furtive glances in our direction, and I wondered if they could be arranging an ambush. The old man tracked my gaze and nodded knowingly.

"Fish ah play a sea, he nah know watah ah boil fuh am." He prodded at my arm while delivering his gnomic message.

"Of course." I agreed, wishing that Google Translate featured Creolese.

An enquiry to the barman regarding the location of the restaurant, resulted in an arm waved down the road running at a right angle to the one we'd arrived on. That meant we'd have to walk past the youths sitting outside, who'd now been joined by a barechested associate wearing a baseball cap and hand towel combo, in the style of a Foreign Legion kepi. I decided that another drink was our best option, so I ordered two more bottles of Stag and one for the old man. We were clearly the main attraction in town, with multiple punters lining up to take selfies with us, and a steady stream of newcomers arriving, who I suspected had been alerted to our presence by friends. Unfortunately, the number of youths drinking outside from liquor store bottles had increased. Their alcohol intake seemed to embolden them, as a couple positioned themselves in the doorway, and they made little attempt to hide their interest in us. Another round of drinks kept us safe, but did nothing to quell our hunger, and I was beginning to consider an exit strategy when a slightly built, smartly dressed and bespectacled Indian man appeared beside me at the bar, and offered me his hand in greeting.

"My name is Rhajesh, and I'm here to help you," he smiled, and I immediately sensed a scam, and tried to brush him off.

He asked if we were working in Georgetown and seemed shocked when I said we were on holiday, and even more surprised when I said we were staying just down the road.

"Oh sir, who made your reservation? This is a bad mistake. You must stay at the Marriott on the ocean front, or the Ramada, not here."

"It's actually very nice," I tried to convince him, but failed to shift the grimace from a face which resembled that of a school teacher marking a badly spelt essay.

"This area of town is not for visitors sir, it's highly dangerous for you to drive here." I could have guessed at his reaction when I uttered the words 'we walked'. He winced as if I'd kneed him in the groin, and threw his hands to his face in horror.

"Oh sir, no! Did your hotel allow you to walk here? That is too irresponsible, you were lucky not to be killed."

"It's a good job we found this place then," I was still looking on the bright side, but Rhajesh lowered his voice and leant towards me.

"Sir, this bar is not safe. I would never come here myself. My colleague called me to say there were some foreign people here, so I came to help you. You can't trust the people in here."

I looked at the old man who took a sip of his drink and muttered "Cat foot soft, but he ah scratch real bad."

"He's right." Rhajesh nodded and I looked puzzled.

"That means that dangerous people often appear friendly. It's a well known proverb. The Guyanese love their proverbs."

The old chap smiled, and I asked Rhajesh for a translation of his earlier utterances, which after a brief consultation, were explained.

"All cassava get same skin, but all nah taste same way, means that even though people might look the same as in your country, it doesn't mean they'll act the same." I watched a boob-tubed hooker jiggling her hot-pants ass in front of a would-be punter, and reflected that I'd never seen anyone who looked quite like that in my local.

The second translation seemed more appropriate though. "Fish ah play a sea, he nah know watah ah boil fuh am? That means that when you're having fun, you may not notice that there is a threat close by." Rhajesh glanced towards the youths in the doorway and looked concerned.

I told him where we planned to eat, and he knew the place, saying it was at the end of the block, but that the road was dark, and he wouldn't dare walk there himself.

"I must call you a taxi sir," he insisted and produced a mobile from his jacket pocket and tapped in a number. "Promise me you will arrange for the driver to collect you?"

We bade farewell to Rhajesh and thanked him for his advice. We bought another drink for ourselves and proverb-man and handed him our half-full bottles when the cab arrived soon after.

"Rain ah fall ah roof, yuh put barrell fuh ketch am!" He grinned and raised his bottle.

The taxi journey was the shortest I've ever taken. The restaurant was around 200 metres from the bar and the journey took about 20 seconds. Even more disconcerting was the fact that the entire block we'd driven, housed a large police station. We couldn't believe it would have been unsafe to walk, but my mind drifted back to Fineman Rawlins and his gang, and I wondered how much control the police actually had on these mean streets.

We arrived at the 'restaurant' to discover that it barely merited that title, with a fast-food style counter greeting us on entry, and a handful of scarred formica-topped tables positioned at haphazard intervals in a bleak, strip-lit room. The local culinary delights were congealing in silver tureens beneath a glass fronted counter, where they'd clearly lain since the lunchtime rush. It was impossible to discern a cow heel soup from a mutton pepperpot, and the food looked as appetising as kebab meat on a Sunday morning pavement. We opted for chicken roti, and after spotting two tooled-up police officers snacking while lounging on concrete benches outside, decided that al-fresco dining should be safe in the presence of a couple of armed guards.

We ate our roti while listening to the sounds of the night. Dogs yapped, goats yodelled, a distant baby squawked and a passing scooter rasped out its need for a new exhaust. The distant crackle of fireworks caused us to pause, and I caught the eye of one of the officers. The unspoken question was obvious - firecrackers or gunfire? He looked away and carried on eating, seemingly unconcerned, and I wondered whether this was a good sign or not. Either it was fireworks, or machine gun fire was so common here it didn't merit interrupting supper for.

Heeding Rhajesh's advice, I'd asked the taxi driver if he could return for us in an hour, which now seemed about fifty minutes too late, especially when the policemen scooped their table waste into a bin, burped loudly and waddled back towards their barracks. We were now the only customers, and it was clear the café's owner intended to close shortly. My question to him about calling a taxi for us, was met with a non-committal shrug, and our own mobile phones were safely tucked in our bags back at the guest house. It wasn't long before the graffiti daubed shutters rattled down alongside us, and left us sitting in the dark street, contemplating the uncomfortable realisation that we'd have to walk home.

The first block which ran alongside the police station at least provided some level of safety, with an armed guard observing our stumbling progress along the darkened street. Beyond that, we had a ten minute walk through the murderous badlands of urban Georgetown to negotiate. The 'big antelope' technique has served me well around the world, but on this occasion, I felt that even our biggest, angriest antelope act may not be enough to deter a pack of hungry predators. On these streets, it seemed that a strategy of evasion was more likely to keep us alive, so instead of adopting the character of large, aggressive mammals, we needed to blend into the background like chameleons, or shuffle along in the nocturnal shadows, avoiding the light like a couple of moon-dodging kangaroo rats.

I thought that passing the bar would be inviting trouble from the youths gathered outside, so we ducked down a sidestreet to miss the corner. It was a difficult trade-off. The backstreets were quiet and unlit. It was much less likely that we'd bump into anyone here. If we did however, and they harboured any sort of malicious intent, there would be no one to hear our cries for help, and no passing cars to spook our attackers. Our pale faces were less visible in the darkness though, and we walked briskly along the alleyway, a block back from the main street, from where I could hear a car stereo's bass booming outside the liquor store. Disembodied voices, the sounds of TV conversations, children playing, and domestic arguments drifted from open windows in high rise blocks looming above us, and unseen creatures of the night scurried and scuffled in the shadows.

A streetlamp glowed orange at the end of the alley and I guessed that once we reached that, we'd be in the street directly opposite the guest house. We hurried on, not speaking, our senses in a heightened state of alert. Two hundred yards from the light, and with safety in sight, a lone figure appeared in silhouette at the end of the alley, closely followed by another, hunched and preoccupied by an object in his hands. They loped towards us with the unmistakably limber, athletic gait of young men.

"Shit." I looked, back in the direction we'd come from, and the street stretched away in darkness to a distant light at the far end. We paused, and had to make a decision quickly. Retreating would mean having to repeat the nerve jangling walk all over again. Carrying on would mean passing two youths skulking along a deserted back alley after dark. I decided to go for a middle ground option. It was pitch black where we stood, and every step forward took us closer to the streetlight and therefore increased our visibility.

"We need to time this right," I cautioned Kirsty and took hold of her hand while we maintained our position. We could hear the youths laughing and shouting in Creolese as they approached, still unaware of our presence. As their figures became clearer in the darkness, I waited until they were fifteen feet away.

"Look away," I whispered to Kirsty and we turned our heads to hide our white faces and stepped forward.

"Woooahh!" We clearly surprised the youths as we emerged from the gloom. "Me gon tink you a jumbee baiya..." which loosely translated as 'I thought you were a ghost, mate.' I was about to call out an apology as we walked on, but realised that would immediately blow our cover. No response at all would be similarly suspicious, so I resorted to a loudly cackled 'Haaa-Haaaar' which sounded like an amused pirate, and made Kirsty jump. It had the desired effect though, and clearly confused the two lads, as they paused momentarily in the darkness, then, obviously unsure how to respond, continued on their way.

We were met at the guest house gates by Sally, who rushed along the drive to greet us.

"Thank God! You're safe! I've been so worried. I thought something terrible had happened to you...I called the police station to see if they knew of any incident."

"No, it was fine. Why would anything happen?" I was a little annoyed that we'd been allowed to wander off into the night, when it was clear that most locals wouldn't consider being at large after dark.

"Oh no, of course it wouldn't... I just thought you might have got lost or something..." Sally avoided eye contact and turned away, clearly keen to avoid any mention of Georgetown's mean streets which could find its way onto Trip Advisor.

I made a thinly veiled reference to taking taxis at night and the 'colourful' local bar scene in my review of the guest house. My own research on Guyana had told me about jungles and rivers, a strange spoken version of English and being the only South American cricketing nation. It would have helped if I'd also known about back-breaking speedboats, crumbling dykes, the Rawlins gunslingers and some of the dodgiest streets I'd ever had to walk. I was glad we'd decided to visit though, after all, if yuh eye nah see, yuh mout nah muss tark!

The City in the Sky

Day 110- La Paz. Bolivia

There's something about certain cities that draws you to them from the moment you arrive, but it was perhaps surprising that I found La Paz immediately appealing. Kirsty and I emerged red-eyed from the Cochabamba night bus into the chill of a mountain dawn in the Bolivian Capital, known as the 'city in the sky'. We'd picked a bus company which advertised '160° Camas' referring to the angle the seats would recline to. 160° was as good as it got, and at that gradient you were more lying down than sitting. The drawback was that when one person decided to recline, the whole bus had to follow suit, to avoid having a fellow passenger staring up their nose. Our seats were more comfortable than some of the beds we'd been sleeping in, but unfortunately our $8 tickets were on the lower level of the surprisingly upmarket coach. This meant we were in close proximity to the air brakes, which were continually applied with a deafening hiss, as we sped through the Andes on the 380km journey. Coupled with the constant jolting and rocking as we tore around hairpin bends, it made for a restless night. The journey was scheduled to take eight hours and it was clear our driver was eager to reach La Paz in as little time as possible. For once, we were happy to remain oblivious to the Andean mountain scenery that we were speeding dangerously through in the dark!

We'd booked an Air B+B apartment in the city centre for the three nights we'd be spending in town, and I sent the caretaker, Alfonso, a message as we exited the bus station. Our maps app told us that it was only a kilometre away, but we were now at 3700 metres, a thousand higher than Cochabamba, and we knew we had to take it easy on the first day to avoid the dreaded 'soroche' sickness which could easily strike at these altitudes. We therefore jumped into a battered taxi, and were deposited beneath a grim looking high-rise block in a scruffy backstreet, where we shivered for twenty minutes, awaiting Alfonso's arrival. We knew the owner of the flat to be an elderly European who had been married to a Bolivian, and now spent most of her time in Belgium. Our contact duly arrived, huffing and puffing and offering apologies for his late arrival, and ushered us into the building, and a clanking lift which seemed steam powered as it laboriously hoisted us to the 9th floor.

Alfonso guided us to a dark wooden door, which he unlocked to reveal another world. It was like travelling back in time forty years, with décor and furnishings worthy of a 1970's pools winner. Parquet flooring in polished walnut set the tone, with an eight-piece dining table and chairs, and a large French dresser in similar dark wood adding to the sombre styling in the main room. A farmhouse style kitchen was replete with labour saving devices which would have been cutting edge in 1980. It was clear that the owner had spared no expense on kitting the place out when it was purchased, but it hadn't been updated since.

We'd now stayed in a number of Air B+Bs, and these were generally self-contained 'granny flats' within a larger property, or fully furnished apartments. As Alfonso bade us farewell and I began to take in our surroundings, I realised this was something entirely different. Silver framed, yellowing photos covered every horizontal surface and showed a handsome, moustachioed man in his thirties in a Panama hat; dark eyed children in sailor suits and short back and sides haircuts; a family group, women in mini-skirts with long straight hair and men sporting footwide lapels and flares; and in pride of place, a middle aged couple on a night out, champagne glasses clinking, big hair, shoulder pads and double breasted suits, suggesting peak eighties. Walls were adorned with diplomas and degrees earned by teenagers who would now be in their mid-sixties, and mementoes and curios from around the world were everywhere.

A bookcase bulged with non-fiction and medical journals, with one shelf devoted to a stack of board games. What made me feel most uncomfortable though, was opening a wardrobe to find it filled with the clothing of an elderly lady. I felt like a burglar prying into the most private elements of someone's life, and I hoped the owner knew about the Air B+B arrangement, and renting the flat out to strangers wasn't an opportunistic move on the part of her local caretaker.

Though the apartment was undoubtably strange, and chilly with no form of heating, it had one saving grace – the view. The main living room looked out across the city centre towards San Francisco church, Plaza Mayor and the one-million-population city of El Alto looming high on the mountain above us at an altitude of 4200 metres. Through the bedroom window we could see the cable cars of the Teleferico mass transit system disappearing into the cloud shrouded foothills of the Cordillera Real to the east. Though tired after a night's missed sleep, I couldn't wait to get out to explore.

Another benefit of our accommodation was the location, on the edge of the city centre and close to Calle Jaen which was billed as the 'old town' of La Paz. In reality, this was a single, narrow, cobbled street boasting colonial architecture, galleries and museums. It was there that we found an ideal base in the city, the Pacha café, which boasted a covered courtyard dining area, soroche-busting coca-leaf tea, good coffee, Western breakfasts, efficient WiFi and a travel agency which arranged long distance bus tickets. Basically, everything we needed! I also got a tip-off about the time and location of the penitents' parade which would be taking place the following day, Good Friday.

La Paz was a good location to explore on foot, and we crossed a flyover and headed to 'el Mercado de la Brujas' or The Witches Market. This was the source of animal parts and herbs used in spirit worshipping rituals by practitioners of the local Aymara religion. Dried Llama foetuses were clearly the desiccated ingredient of choice, and every stall displayed racks of long-necked ET lookalikes, in varying states of decay. Some were dried to dark, leather forms which more resembled birds than mammals, while others retained their fluffy white coat and could have served as a macabre cuddly toy for a particularly disturbed child. Llama corpses were by far the most popular product on offer, but dried frogs, snakes, turtles and armadillos were also all being sold by the 'yatiri', or witch doctors, who wandered the market in black bowler hats, offering services as diverse as medical consultations, fortune telling and curse casting.

Although interesting enough and fairly gruesome, the Witches Market was situated close to La Paz's main traveller enclave, and had a much more commercial and sanitised feel than the stinking hell-hole fetish markets of West Africa, which are guaranteed to put you off food for the rest of the day.

We decided to pass on a souvenir aborted llama, and headed downhill to one of the most infamous prisons in the world. San Pedro is unusual in that it's situated right in the centre of La Paz, but even more unorthodox in that the prisoners run it themselves. Guards patrol the perimeter, but that's the limit of their jurisdiction and they have no power within the prison itself. In fact, it would probably be fatal for them to enter the wings unless at battalion strength. 1500 inmates are housed in the jail, but the overall population is more than double that, due to the presence of the wives and children of inmates who also live within the walls, but are free to come and go as they please. San Pedro employs a system which might be seen as the way forward in privatised UK jails, with inmates having to purchase their own cell. Prices range form $250 to $10,000, and, as in the outside world, location is everything, with the top 'sections' boasting split-level duplex accommodation with en-suite bathrooms, heating, cable TV and city views. At the lower end of the property ladder, men are crammed ten-deep into tiny cells known as coffins, or live rough on the stairwells and in the exercise yards. The prison has a vibrant economy with barber's shops, cobblers, food outlets, and of course, this being Bolivia, an efficient cocaine production operation. Far from being lawless, many of the sections are ruled with an iron rod by elected councils, and rule-breakers can bizarrely be sentenced to solitary confinement in a jail-within-a-jail. More often than not though, they'll just be stabbed.

San Pedro was immortalised in the 2003 book 'Marching Powder', which details the experience of a British drug smuggler, Thomas Mcfadden, who was serving an eighteen year sentence. The story is definitely a case of fact being stranger than any fiction, as Mcfadden bribed guards in order to slip out of the prison for a night on the town. In a backpacker club he met an Israeli traveller and smuggled her back to his cell, where she ended up staying for a week. Upon leaving, she told her tale to friends, and others began to visit Mcfadden, with the guards happy to turn a blind eye in return for bribes which were way more than their salary. Lonely Planet picked up on the tale and featured it in the next Bolivia guidebook, and before long, you hadn't travelled in Bolivia unless you'd spent a night partying in San Pedro. Tours became big business, and at its peak in the late 90's it was estimated that up to a hundred thrill seeking tourists were visiting the jail daily, which wasn't surprising, with a night in a cell plus unlimited booze and cocaine costing less than an average hostel room.

Predictably things started to unravel, and TV documentaries highlighted the guards' corruption, with covert footage of scores of Westerners being admitted through the prison gates causing embarrassment to the government. Then in 2013 came news of a twelve-year-old girl becoming pregnant in the jail, accompanied by stories of her being abused by a group of prisoners from the age of eight. The authorities clamped down, and prohibited tourists from entering San Pedro.

We stood outside and got chatting with Luis, a tour guide who told us that he'd previously made good money by escorting travellers into the prison.

"Is it still possible?" I was wishing we'd visited ten years earlier.

"Anything is possible in Bolivia," he smiled, "If you have the right money. You need to be very, very well connected to guide tourists in there now though," Luis looked ruefully at the stream of uniformed junior school pupils heading home for lunch through the prison gates.

"You have to know the very top people, and I don't. I was offered a thousand dollars last week by two Canadian guys to get them in. I had to pass it on to someone else. Maybe they got in, I don't know."

That night we shivered on the unheated 9th floor of our tower block, and watched the lights of El Alto twinkling on the mountain top. I eventually went to sleep dreaming of being tucked up in a warm, centrally heated, ten grand cell in San Pedro Prison.

The following day was Good Friday, and I awoke and informed Kirsty that I'd had a premonition during the night. I'd been keeping a close eye on Leeds United's push for promotion to the Premier League while we were away, and was aware that in a couple of hours, they'd be taking on Wigan Athletic in a home game. The season was nearing its end, and things were going well with Leeds at the top of the division. Wigan were at the bottom, with the worst away record in England. Although I hadn't even thought about it the day before, the match somehow managed to invade my subconscious mind to appear in my dreams. I was in La Paz, in a small local shop we'd visited to buy bottled water. An old man wearing a brightly coloured poncho arrived on the back of a small pony, which he rode up to the counter. As I was browsing the shelves, I heard him greet the shopkeeper in Spanish. He then said 'Bloody hell, did you see Leeds lost 2-1 to Wigan?' At that point I woke up.

My first job of the day was therefore to access Pacha cafe's Wifi, to place a bet on the score using a betting app on my phone as we ate breakfast. 40/1 was probably fair odds, as Wigan hadn't managed to win away from home for about a year, but I trusted my poncho wearing dream-guide and wagered a fiver against my own team. That's something which many people refuse to do, but I view as the ultimate, financial/emotional hedging strategy – the pain of defeat is offset by monetary gain and vice versa!

With my bet placed and breakfast eaten, we set off to see the city in the most spectacular way possible. The La Paz - El Alto Teleferico is one of the highest and longest cable car mass transit systems in the world, covering a distance of 21 miles, and rising to altitudes of 4200 metres. Eleven lines with thirty six stations are used by almost 100,000 residents per day to negotiate the challenging geography of the two cities, which were previously separated by a steep ascent along winding mountain roads. The first phase of the cable car project was signed off in 2012 with a budget of $280m and three lines were fully operational within two years, having been constructed by an Austrian/Swiss conglomerate.

All the stations have two names, one in Spanish, one in the local Aymara language, and we paid our three Bolivianos, the equivalent of roughly 20p, at the shiny, tangerine coloured Armentia/Riosinho Pampa station, and were guided onto an Orange Line 'gondola' by two smiling, smartly uniformed teenage employees. It was clear that La Paz residents were justifiably proud of the Teleferico, and kept its bright, modern stations spotlessly clean, in stark contrast to many of the streets the cable cars passed over. We were the only ones boarding so had the gondola to ourselves, which was fortunate as we were soon giggling and whooping with delight as we soared high above a main road. We then swept directly over a black-clad funeral procession heading to the main cemetery, before finding ourselves looking down upon a Lego village of red brick, flat roofed blocks which stretched up the mountain ahead towards El Alto. Our passage in the glass capsule was smooth and silent, and it felt like we were in some futuristic science-fiction movie. I'm no engineering afficionado but this was seriously impressive, and Kirsty and I sat transfixed, with huge smiles on our faces, waving to passengers in oncoming cable cars who grinned and waved back. Clearly even the locals still got a thrill from riding their unique public transport system.

If the ascent to 16 de Julio station at El Alto was spectacular, the Teleferico's Silver Line running along the rim of the bowl-like canyon overlooking La Paz was even better. To our left was the city, stretching out towards the horizon, with the snow-capped, triple peak of Mount Illimani as a spectacular backdrop. Directly below us was a line of single room shacks, literally perched on the cliff edge, with a sheer drop of several hundred feet beyond their back windows. No sooner had I positioned my camera to capture these precarious dwellings, than we were passing above a teeming street market, with a bird's eye view of the vibrant colours of fruit, vegetables and flowers contrasting with the dark figures of traditionally dressed locals scurrying between the stalls. Then we were on the purple line, barely skimming the top of a huge white cross on the mountain top, to begin a steep descent over the rusting corrugated roofs of hillside shanty towns. La Paz spread out before us like an intricate model village created by a detail-obsessed genius, and again we found ourselves grinning like kids on a fairground ride. Back on the valley floor we rode the White Line, which was peak Sci-fi as it followed the long straight line of a dual carriageway through an affluent area of high-rise apartment blocks. We passed within feet of tenth floor apartments, and I wondered how the occupants had felt when their privacy was unexpectedly invaded by the construction of a mass transit system within metres of their balconies.

It was hard to imagine a project like the Teleferico getting past the planning stage in Europe, but I found it hugely impressive and wondered why cable cars aren't seen as a viable public transport option in more countries. If the poorest country in South America can build such an efficient system within two years, why can't we?

I could have happily ridden the Teleferico all day, but I had another appointment to keep. It was Good Friday and the scant information I'd managed to gather, suggested that the city's famous Easter parades would begin in the late afternoon. I'd initially assumed the main San Francisco Cathedral would be the location for the parade's departure, and we noticed other travellers congregating there as we passed, but word on the street amongst locals led me to a less well known spot, el Templo de la Merced, in the backstreets near our apartment.

As we crossed the fly-over heading away from the city centre, I couldn't help wondering whether I'd got it wrong, and we should stay with the other tourists at the more obvious cathedral location. After all, my previous track record of Easter rituals in devout Catholic countries wasn't something to be proud of. In the early 1990's, in a small town on the West Coast of Ireland, I'd called into a newsagents' shop to pick up a paper early one morning. The elderly female shopkeeper was still sorting the bundles of Irish Times and Racing Post, and as I paid for my own paper, I noticed a large smudge of newsprint on her forehead. Assuming she'd accidently daubed herself with her blackened fingers, I licked my thumb and reached towards her.

"You've just got a bit of ink...there you go, gone now!" I smiled as a quick swipe of my thumb removed the blemish.

The old lady looked as though she was about to speak, but didn't, and instead shook her head and blinked. I didn't give her a chance to thank me, as I cheerfully bade her farewell and headed for the door. As I left, I passed a smartly dressed, silver haired chap in his sixties, and as our eyes met, I noticed that he too had an ink smudge between his eyes. I assumed he must be the shopkeeper's husband, and that Irish newsprint was especially prone to being transferred to human skin. A few hundred yards down the road, I encountered a young woman hurrying to a bus stop, who was also bearing a large black mark on her forehead, which was clearly in the shape of a cross. It was only at this point that I realised it was Ash Wednesday, and that I'd inadvertently rubbed a morning-mass blessing from the head of the old newsagent!

Turning the corner into the small plaza in front of the small, honey coloured chapel confirmed that this time, I'd got it right. The square was full to bursting with sombrely attired locals, mostly wearing all black, with women in lace head squares holding umbrellas as protection against a persistent drizzle. There were a couple of TV crews and a dozen or so professional photographers wielding their obligatory long lenses, but I could only see a couple of other obvious tourists. My research had paid off and the expectant buzz told us we'd arrived just in time. The church doors had been opened and a disorderly congregation of clergymen were beginning to spill out into the square, to the accompaniment of the deep, steady beat of a drum, from somewhere within the bowels of the building.

An elongated trumpet blast segued into a mournful yet curiously unruly rendition of Handel's Dead March, as if played by a drunken jazz band, and the first of the hooded penitents exited the chapel in a swaying block of four. Their appearance, in long black cloaks and pointed white hoods with pin-prick eyeholes, prompted an audible gasp from the assembled onlookers. Closely following this advance guard, was a platform containing a lifesized effigy of Christ dragging his cross up the hill of Calvary, borne by twenty hooded penitents who swayed slowly in unison to the continued fanfare of the brass section. The appearance of Christ caused a flurry of sobs from the gathered crowd, and as flower petals were tossed towards the effigy, I was reminded of Princess Diana's funeral, though at close quarters I couldn't help thinking that Jesus had been modelled on Sly Stallone in Rambo.

The colour of the penitents' tunics and hoods, which are known as 'capirotes', denote which religious brotherhood they belong to, and the next group to emerge looked even more sinister than the first, with crimson robes topped with tall black hoods. The platform they strained to carry, held a blood-soaked Christ on the cross, attended by two weeping Mary's, and again the musical accompaniment was more New Orleans jazz funeral than church service. Next came sky blue hoods preceded by a penitent holding aloft a small glass coffin. Initially I thought it contained a llama foetus on a bed of purple silk, then the mummified corpse of a baby, but as it drew level with me, I saw that it was a tiny Jesus figurine, carved from wood and resembling a bearded action man toy.

The different brotherhoods continued to exit the chapel, as the procession began its slow progress through the streets of La Paz. Sometimes when travelling, you find yourself in a situation which feels totally foreign, and this was one such occasion. The hoods worn by the penitents were popularised in medieval times, when worshippers could demonstrate their penance while concealing their identity, but nowadays are synonymous with more sinister groups such as the Ku Klux Klan. The flowing robes and jerky, robotic motion of the penitents as they swayed in time to the mournful music, and the tear-streaked faces of the onlooking crowds added to the ominous atmosphere. It was clear that the parade merited the solemnity of a funeral, though photographers and film crews seemed to have no qualms about pushing their cameras into the hooded faces of the marchers, so I whipped out my Nikon and was able to capture some amazing still images, and some video footage on my iPhone.

Back at Pacha and reconnected to WiFi, I checked the football scores. Leeds had gone ahead early in their match, and Wigan then had a player sent off. Unbelievably, the visitors then hit back, with two goals to secure victory. The disappointment of a damaging defeat for my team was offset by a nice £200 windfall, which in South American terms represented around two weeks' worth of accommodation. If I saw the pony-riding tipster in the coloured Poncho in a dream again, I'd buy him a drink!

The following morning, we were sitting in Pacha having breakfast when I heard the distant beat of drums, and the familiar unruly brass section from the penitents' parade. I grabbed my camera and left Kirsty munching her omelette to investigate. I was stopped in my tracks at the top of the road by the sight which greeted me. Stretching away into the distance was a great tide of humanity. A cavalcade of thirty thousand people, all dressed from head to toe in white, were advancing in a jubilant, singing, chanting, horn-blowing mass of joyful delirium. Teenagers in white jumpsuits laughed and hugged; old ladies in bleached togas and bowler hats waved flags and jigged on shaky legs; toddlers in tiny white trilby hats were bounced on parents' shoulders, and dozens of marching bands blew bugles and beat drums to a triumphant rhythm. If the previous day was one of mourning for Christ's death, this was a feast of celebration at his rebirth. The sight of my camera drew the crowds towards me and before long I was enveloped in embraces from excited, muscular little men, and swept along in the procession, amidst the roar of thousands of voices joining in a football crowd chant of 'Olé, Olé, Olé, Jesu, Jesu!' The procession wound along the same streets as those which the mournful penitents had walked less than twenty four hours earlier, but the transformation was total. The sun shone, the black clothes were replaced by brilliant white, and the atmosphere was one of unbridled joy from all ages. It was clear that this was the highlight of the year for the people of La Paz, and that their faith is an integral element of their often uncertain lives.

I decided I liked La Paz. After the staid and safe feel of the cities we'd visited in New Zealand, the cosmopolitan frenzy of Bangkok and the bewildering vibe of Asuncion, the 'city in the sky' felt exciting and different, with a definite potential for danger, but without the feeling that you were going to get rolled at every turn. Before Venezuela began to implode in 2014, Bolivia was generally classed as the poorest nation in South America, with most families living on an income of around $6000 per year. Surrounded by high mountain ranges and with few navigable rivers, the loss of the country's coastline to Chile in the 1884 War of the Pacific dealt an irreparable blow to Bolivia's ability to trade internationally, and ensured the country would remain near the bottom of global GDP tables. However, the election of President Evo Morales in 2006 saw an increase in investment, a doubling of GDP and a halving in the proportion of people living in extreme poverty. Natural Gas was now officially the key economic driver, but coca farming remained big business, and Morales was accused of turning Bolivia into a Narco-State when he expelled the US Drug Enforcement Agency from the country in 2008.

As a visitor, it was clear that life was tough for most Bolivians, but we never felt threatened in La Paz, though the city had a sometimes sinister undercurrent. Masked faces appeared everywhere, from the hoods of the penitents to balaclavas worn by machine gun toting police and security guards. Then there were the 'Lustrabotas'. La Paz's army of shoeshiners, who squat on every pavement in the city centre, hoping to earn a few Bolivianos by polishing the shoes of passers-by, are viewed by society as undesirables, working in a shameful occupation. They therefore hide their faces behind bandanas and sunglasses, so even their own family may not realise what they do to earn a living.

Beneath the footbridge we crossed to the city centre from our apartment, the corpse of a man was suspended from a lamp post. Closer inspection revealed it to be a lifelike effigy, fully clothed in lurid sportswear, and wearing a pair of Adidas trainers. These homemade dummies adorn telegraph poles and lamp posts throughout the city, and serve as a warning to thieves, thugs and other lawbreakers. The police may not catch you, but the vigilantes will, and when they do, depending on your crime, you may be shot, stabbed, tortured or burnt alive, then suspended from gallows in a prominent position on the street.

La Paz was also a photographer's dream destination, with steep cobbled streets and mountain backdrops, or with a cable car suddenly looming into view where you least expected it. Even the most mundane streetscape was enlivened by the presence of the Aymara and Quechua people, particularly the female 'Cholitas'.

Derived from the word 'Cholo', which was a lower class person of mixed European/ Indigenous ancestry, the fashions of the Cholitas are as characteristic of the high Andes region as llamas and deadly roads. Women of all ages wear the same unique uniform - a heavy, multi-layered skirt with petticoats; a colourful knitted shawl with an often expensive jewellery clasp; small flat shoes, and long braided hair, usually extending to below waist level. The most recognisable symbol of the Cholita though, is their headwear. Unlike in the Andean lowlands, where a wide brimmed straw sombrero is favoured, the Alto-Plano Cholita is never seen without a bowler hat, perched precariously upon her thick dark tresses. As well as denoting social standing, with an expensive bowler costing up to $1000, the Cholita's headwear also indicates her marital status - A hat worn on the top of the head denotes a married woman, whereas an unmarried girl will wear her hat at a flirtatiously jaunty angle.

The hats always look a couple of sizes too small for the wearers head, which is a throwback to their introduction to Bolivia. In the 1920's, a Manchester company won a contract to supply bowler hats to British workers constructing Bolivia's railway system. Unfortunately, upon delivery, it was clear that an error had been made in quality control, and the hats were too far small for an adult's head. The unfortunate middleman left holding the unwanted consignment attempted to sell them to the locals. The male population were disinterested, but the local women snapped them up, and began a fashion sensation which has resulted in Bolivia being the biggest producer of bowler hats in the world today!

The presence of Cholitas added some unique local colour to any streetscape photo, and on our final day in La Paz I was surprised to discover a hidden benefit of their long flowing skirts. We were walking near the Witches Market and I glanced along a cobbled sidestreet of dilapidated three storey buildings, to see an elderly Cholita pushing a handcart, while framed by the faint afternoon sunlight. It was an obvious photo opportunity, so I reached for my camera and centred the old lady in the frame, while adjusting the focal length to get the correct depth of field. Suddenly, she disappeared from the viewfinder, and I lowered the camera to watch her bend her knees and lower her head. I wondered what she was up to, until I saw a fast-flowing stream pouring from beneath her skirts and along the cobbles. She hardly paused and was soon upright again and continuing on her way. With few public toilets in Bolivia, the Cholitas' flowing skirts were clearly a useful asset, and I suddenly realised why a gaggle of ladies had stood chatting in wide-legged circles behind the bus on our various journeys. I resolved to keep a close eye out for potential shoe splashing hazards the following day, when we left La Paz to head towards Lake Titicaca and the border with Peru.

About a Boy

D ominic had been late in collecting us from the ferry dock. I sat outside our hostel on Isla del Sol, and took in the 360° view of Lake Titicaca, while gasping to catch my breath after slogging up a dirt track, which began at 3800 and ended at a lung-busting 4100 metres above sea level. Dominic was loafing about next to reception, casting an occasional glance in my direction, seemingly unaffected by the rigours of carrying our two 15KG rucksacks all the way from the beach. I was glad I'd requested his assistance and wandered over to thank him. I scratched his ears and patted him on the nose. He snorted his appreciation and began munching on a trough of straw.

"Donde esta mi burro?" is not something I'd had to ask a hostel reception clerk before, nor am I likely to again, but the missing donkey was a problem. The ferry from the underwhelming town of Copacabana to the island, had left us on the beach at the foot of a staggered incline stretching to the top of a steep hill. At normal altitudes, lugging our backpacks up the slope would have been an inconvenience, but with the lack of oxygen at 4000 metres, we were struggling to make the ascent even without bags. Luckily my phone call soon prompted the appearance of an elderly cholita leading Dominic down the slope, and with our bags strapped to his fluffy back, they set off at an electric pace up the hill. We puffed and panted in their wake with the old lady, who must have been approaching eighty years old, occasionally looking back to ensure we were still following. In addition to her hill-climbing prowess, Kirsty looked enviously at her raven black, waist length plait, and wondered aloud whether Bolivian women are blessed with some genetic quality which prevents them from greying, or are just highly proficient with the hair dye!

Isla del Sol was a 5km long island with no cars or roads, and a population of a couple of thousand, split between three main villages. Yumani, in the south was the location of the ferry dock and most of the accommodation options, which were generally small hostels or homestays, and was where we'd be staying. Challa in the centre and Challapampa in the north were off limits to visitors, due to a dispute between the villagers of the three hamlets, which seemingly arose around distribution of revenue from the low-key tourist industry. The island's few minor Incan archaeological sites, including 'Titi Kharka' or The Rock of the Puma, from which the lake took its name, were in the north and therefore inaccessible due to the ongoing dispute.

Yumani was quiet and rustic, with mud brick shacks, and old ladies knitting in doorways. Rush hour was a herd of long eared sheep being driven along a rutted lane by a stick wielding shepherd, and the children's pet of choice was a fluffy baby llama, led on washing line reins. There were a handful of other travellers at our hostel but most of the visitors seemed to be day trippers from Copacabana, and I wondered whether the tourist trade was worth starting an island wide civil war over.

Lake Titicaca is the highest navigable body of water in the world and the largest lake in South America, straddling the border between Bolivia and our next destination, Peru. Our hostel stood on one of the highest points in Yumani village, so provided panoramic views of the surrounding islands and distant snow-capped peaks of the Cordillera Real. Our room was a small, spartan affair, looking onto a muddy plot inhabited by a family of snuffling pigs, and as usual, had no form of heating. With an average night time low of 3°, we would be thankful for the thick alpaca wool blankets piled on the bed. The hostel Wifi was strangely efficient though, and Kirsty took the opportunity to make a WhatsApp call to her parents, managing to get a clearer connection than she usually has at home, while stood in a field overlooking Lake Titicaca and stroking a donkey!

While she was chatting, I flipped open my laptop and inserted the Thai USB stick, for my regular photographic stroll down memory lane. The first image to appear on the screen was of three young men of African appearance, standing beside some small, colourful fishing cobbles on a sandy beach, backed by thin trees with sinuous roots. Two of the men are disinterested in the camera, with one looking away to the right and the other, a barechested youth, glancing to the left. The central subject is a small man in orange shorts and a 'Ronaldo' shirt, which is more likely to be the Brazilian original than the later Portuguese player. His face is partly obscured by a fish, possibly a Yellowtail Kingfish, measuring around four feet in length, which he is proudly holding aloft for the camera.

I recognise the photo immediately as having been taken in the coastal village of Tofo in Mozambique, Southern Africa, in 2007. 'Why Mozambique?' was a fairly obvious question that I was asked at the time. My boss was a keen wildlife photographer and excitedly enquired about the likelihood of snapping the 'Big 5'. I had to admit that was highly unlikely, with Gorongosa National Park having lost an estimated 90% of its large mammals during the civil war, which raged from the late 70's to the early 90's. A safari was therefore not a prime consideration when we'd booked our flights from South Africa to the capital, Maputo. The plan was to rent a car and drive north, with no real itinerary other than to experience a country which was being tipped as the 'next big thing' by a number of travel writers. The town of Inhambane, 300 miles north east of Maputo, and described as having a waterside setting, tree-lined avenues, faded colonial-style architecture and a mixture of Arabic, Indian and African influences, seemed a good point to head for.

As was usually the case on a two week trip, I undertook most of the research and accommodation bookings before travelling, in order to maximise use of our time in the country. Luckily, by that point, most hotels now had a functioning website and email, which eliminated the need for tortuous phone conversations with non-English speakers on crackly landlines. I'd spotted Tofo 20km along the coast from Inhambane town, and we decided that a few days in a seaside fishing village would be in order after a ten hour journey along the M1 'motorway', which looked like it had been used for target practice by a drunken tank battalion.

Tourism was just taking off in Tofo at the time, with sea fishing the main source of income, though a few enterprising individuals had seen an opportunity to offer accommodation on the wide sandy bay. Beach Cottages appeared at the top of my online search and seemed to be the only option which, as its name suggested, had direct access to the Indian Ocean. Six rustic, thatched wooden cottages stood on stilts on dunes at the southern end of the bay. All had a large balcony overlooking the sand and the two page website described them as being 'fully self contained.' I completed the online contact form and received a reply from the owner, Elizabeth, who, from her Afrikaans surname was easily identifiable as South African.

We agreed a price for a three night stay, and I began the laborious process of arranging a bank transfer to send a deposit, with online credit card payments still a few years away for African hotels. A week later, I received an email from Elizabeth confirming that the money had landed in her bank account. She also included a three page Word document providing information on Tofo, and a full inventory of the facilities we'd find in our cottage. 'Fridge, cooker, gas hob, sink with mixer tap, outdoor deck with barbecue area' all sounded fine, although cooking wasn't our idea of a holiday, so most were unlikely to be utilised. The document went on to describe in some detail the indoor dining area, sleeping arrangements and bathroom, and I skimmed through it quickly and almost missed a paragraph at the foot of the third page. 'All cottages come with use of a boy. Payment separate.'

I wondered whether 'boy' was a mis-spelling, or some South African slang I hadn't come across, and Elizabeth had invited any questions I had, so I replied and asked what a boy was. The reply was unexpected and a little disconcerting.

'Hi Matthew.

Yes, each cottage has a boy. For want of a better description, he's your servant while you're with us. He'll do whatever you ask. He is paid by tips only. We can provide guidance on the accepted rate.

Look forward to your visit.

Elizabeth'

I read the reply to Kirsty and predictably she screwed up her nose and shook her head.

"Why would we want some kid hanging around? Do we have to have him?"

I agreed. Self-appointed-guides are the bane of a travellers life in Africa and we do our best to shake them off whenever possible. Here, we were being designated an officially sanctioned tag-along, and would have to pay him, though we had no need for a glorified butler. I drafted a reply.

'Hi Elizabeth

I understand about the boy. Thanks for explaining. However, we don't intend to use the self catering facilities or spend much time in the cottage. Therefore, I don't think we really need him. Thanks anyway. Matthew'

My response clearly baffled Elizabeth and it took her a few days to reply.

'Matthew

Most of our guests comment on the excellent service they receive from their boy. Many come back every year and ask that they can have the same boy. It's not a problem if you don't want to eat in the cottage. The boy will tidy for you and wash your clothes if needed. He can buy fish on the beach and barbecue it for you. I'm sure you will be happy with the service your boy provides.'

Elizabeth'

I took that to mean the boy was compulsory.

"It will be okay," I tried to convince Kirsty, "I can play football on the beach with him. He can take you snorkelling, you know I don't like it if my feet can't touch the bottom."

"How much do we have to pay him for hanging around with us?" Kirsty remained unimpressed.

"I doubt it will be much, maybe a dollar a day or so. He might be happy if I just buy him an ice cream or something."

Three months later I was stood in Elizabeth's office on the beachfront in Tofo, while she talked me through the house rules, of which there were many. It was clear she ran a tight ship, and she jabbed a finger towards me with an orange faced scowl, as she let me know in no uncertain terms what was prohibited on the premises.

"Stray dogs and cats, trinket sellers, beach kids, beach bumsters... in fact any locals, smoking dagga, playing music after 10pm, lighting the barbecue after 11pm, drying towels on the balcony, guns....and knives, unless they're used for cutting fish..." I nodded.

"Bar girls...or bar boys," she regarded me suspiciously and I apologetically half-pointed towards Kirsty who was waiting by the car, to let her know that neither option was particularly likely.

"Did I say dogs and cats?" She spat out a heavily accented 'cets' with venom, and I pitied any stray feline that wandered onto the premises. A dishevelled local man in his late forties hovered in the corner of the reception area, nervously monitoring our exchange, and I assumed he was a gardener, about to be dismissed for some minor horticultural misdemeanour.

"Now, about your boy..." Elizabeth looked me up and down, correctly anticipating that I was going to try and wriggle out of that feature of the hotel's service.

"Well, I'm still not sure we'll really make use of a boy, so..."

"THE BOY...." Elizabeth increased the volume to silence my argument before it had begun "...comes with the cottage. It's non-negotiable Matthew. He will provide an excellent service and you WILL be very happy with him."

I decided to try a different approach. "Maybe we could just have him for one day, say at the weekend? I don't want to keep him from school."

This seemed to stop Elizabeth in her tracks and for once she paused. She then narrowed her mascara smeared eyes and pursed her thin lips, before raising a gnarled, perma-tanned hand in the direction of the gardener.

"This is Gilberto." I nodded and smiled at the man. He had a kindly, wise, nut-brown face and he removed a stained beany hat and dipped his head deferentially.

"So, how about that as a compromise? We just have the boy for a day at the weekend and he can go to..."

"GILBERTO...." Elizabeth's volume increased again, before subsiding as she delivered the punchline, "...is your boy."

Now it was my turn to pause, open mouthed, as Gilberto shuffled awkwardly while gazing at his patched-up sandals.

"Gilberto's place of work is your cottage." Elizabeth placed her hands on her hips and stared hard into my eyes. "Gilberto has a wife and three children. He receives no payment from the hotel. If you don't want to use his services while you are here, you are making him UNEMPLOYED. You are taking food from the mouths of his children. Do you understand?"

"Erm, well, yes." I whimpered.

"Gilberto will be available between 6am and midnight. If you need his services beyond those times, you must agree that with him. The going rate is 150 Rand per day. Obviously if you send him shopping you must give him money to cover the cost. Do you understand?"

I nodded, while shuffling my feet and looking at the floor, just like Gilberto.

"Now, do you want to utilise your boy, or do you want to make him UNEMPLOYED?"

I really wanted to point out that a middle aged man probably shouldn't be referred to as a boy, but Elizabeth had picked up a heavy desk stapler, and I had a feeling I'd exit the office wearing it on my face if I argued, so I nodded my agreement.

Kirsty was waiting as I emerged with the key to our cottage and with Gilberto plodding a few feet behind me.

"Did you tell her we don't want the boy?" she shouted, and I grimaced and rolled my eyes and surreptitiously flicked my head in Gilberto's direction.

"What? You didn't tell her did you?"

"It's him," I hissed as I drew level.

"Who's who?" Kirsty was unsurprisingly confused, so I decided an introduction was in order.

"Kirsty, meet Gilberto. Gilberto is...our..."

"Our....our what?" She whispered under her breath while smiling at the stumbling figure approaching her.

"He's our boy. Gilberto is our boy!" Saying it out loud didn't make it sound any better, but Gilberto seemed unconcerned and paused by the car, waiting to have our rucksacks loaded onto his back.

He was six inches smaller than me, a few stone lighter and nearly ten years older, and although he appeared wiry and muscular, there was no way I was going to let him carry my heavy bag. I opened the car boot and helped him retrieve Kirsty's rucksack, but made clear I would be responsible for my own. We set off to the room, but I'd only gone a few steps before I was halted by a loud 'Ahem!'

We all turned to see Elizabeth approaching at speed, wagging a finger in my direction.

"No, no, no Matthew! You must not carry your own suitcase. That's what Gilberto is here for."

I tried to explain that I was perfectly capable of carrying my own bag, but Elizabeth was already tugging it from my shoulder while glaring at our hapless servant, to let him know in no uncertain terms that the customer isn't always right. Straining under the weight of both bags and with our room key clenched in his teeth, Gilberto wobbled up the wooden steps which led to our cottage.

He unlocked the door, heaved our bags onto the bed and stood unspeaking in the doorway, as usual with his gaze directed downwards. I wasn't sure whether he was mute or shy, or perhaps didn't speak English, but I'd yet to hear him utter a word. A 'thanks Gilberto!' and a glance towards the door was required to dismiss him, and he shuffled away with an enigmatic half smile.

The cottage was huge, with a large wooden decked area overlooking the beach and, after unpacking our bags we stood outside and admired the view.

My muttered question, pondering where Gilberto stationed himself, was answered almost immediately as a head emerged from beneath the stilted cottage, smiling through the wooden balustrade.

"Sir?" was the first word I'd heard him speak, and made me jump as I stammered an excuse for my early false alarm.

Gilberto's ears were clearly attuned to detect his name being mentioned, and other sounds which he interpreted as requiring his presence. We learnt this at sunset, while sampling a couple of cans of Castle Lager we'd found in the fridge. No sooner had the welcome crack-hiss of the tins opening broken the silence, than Gilberto popped up from beneath the decking. I gave him a cheery wave, hoping that would indicate that all was well, but his eyes fixed on the cans and he ducked out of sight, only to emerge from within our cottage moments later, clutching two glasses. Before I could say that I was quite happy to drink from the tin, my beer was held aloft and tipped unceremoniously into the glass, leaving me with a 75:25 froth/beer ratio. I smiled and thanked our new waiter and he bowed and returned to his post beneath the cottage.

We learnt to adapt quickly, and took to opening our drinks inside, where Gilberto couldn't hear us. When we set off out for an evening meal, Gilberto followed in our wake like a lovesick cat, twenty feet behind us clearly being the required 'guest to boy' distance mandated by Elizabeth. We ate at a small beachside bar and Gilberto patrolled the pot-holed pavement, casting a wary glance as he passed, lest we escape through a toilet window.

We were woken early in the morning by the crowing of a resident cockerel, and I threw back the curtains to take in the sunrise. The beach was deserted, and I stood naked, watching a small pirogue canoe struggle to clear the waves breaking on the shoreline. I placed my hands behind my head and stretched, enjoying the stillness of a tropical morning, but was distracted by a slight movement to my left.

I glanced down to see a small dark face gazing up at me from beneath the cottage. It seemed futile to cover myself after a couple of minutes of exposure, so I nodded and gave Gilberto a thumbs up. I couldn't decide whether his expression was one of sadness or amusement as I re-closed the curtains and went back to bed.

Later, I spotted Gilberto sweeping leaves behind the cottage so sneaked down the steps to try and locate his lair. Directly beneath our bedroom was a makeshift bed and a small camp stove and rucksack of provisions. It was clear that Gilberto took his job seriously, and didn't want to miss any opportunity to please his guests. This was further demonstrated when we returned from an afternoon on the beach to find our room swept spotlessly clean, and our scattered clothes and belongings neatly folded and stacked on shelves. Kirsty immediately began to worry about the state we'd left the room in, and resolved to start tidying up before we went out in future. Our first venture into the village made it clear that everyone knew whose 'masters' we were, and we heard the muttered word 'Gilberto' a number of times as we passed through the market area. It was slightly disconcerting to think that we might be identified by gossip passed on by our boy. 'That's the tourist who sings Duran Duran songs in the shower and reads Barbara Cartland novels. Only changes his underwear every three days.'

Whilst we were struggling to adapt to having a servant, our fellow guests seemed to be having no such problems. The next cottage was occupied by a South African family who were fully utilising their boy, Carlos. Indeed, he seemed to have become such an integral part of the family that I wondered if they'd take him home with them. Sitting on our balcony it was impossible to miss hearing the shouted instructions, which ranged from running a bath to grilling some shrimps, and from ironing some shorts to becoming a horsey for the kids to ride along the beach. Carlos dashed back and forth like the proverbial blue-arsed fly, while Gilberto looked on enviously.

By the time we reached our final day at the cottages, we had a well honed routine. We'd slide silently from our bed and tiptoe around the room, to avoid alerting Gilberto that we were awake. Then we'd creep onto the balcony and eat breakfast in silence, dreading the sudden appearance of his face from beneath the cottage, which preceded him coming inside to try and chop bananas or make us more coffee. Kirsty would clean the cottage and we'd carefully tidy our possessions into neat piles. Then we'd wait until we saw Gilberto working in the garden, and would slip out of the back door and walk the long way to the beach, to avoid him tailing us. On an evening we'd open our beer inside and pour it into glasses, to avoid Gilberto feeling the need to do it. We'd then slip out silently through the back gate, and down a dark track into the village, where we could eat an evening meal without worrying that we were keeping Gilberto from his wife and kids.

We were exhausted when we left the cottages. In fact, I felt I needed another chill-out week on a beach, but this time without a servant. It's probably one of the top five things people say they'd do if they won the lottery, but my time in Tofo told me it's not something I'd ever really feel comfortable with. I happily paid Gilberto his daily allowance and would love to have told him to take the three days off, as his first ever paid holiday, if I didn't think Elizabeth would have killed him, and then me.

✳✳✳

Back on Isla del Sol, I watched Kirsty happily chatting to her parents 6000 miles away, while she scratched the ears of one servant we were truly thankful for. Dominic ignored her and carried on munching his straw, probably after realising he still had to carry our bags back down the hill.

The Curse of the Inca Kebab

Day 122 -Cusco, Peru

Located at 3400 metres above sea level, Cusco is one of the world's ten highest cities, but after travelling for two weeks across the Bolivian and Peruvian 'Alto Plano', we actually found ourselves descending in altitude to reach it. We'd spent the previous night in the Peruvian border town of Puno, at 3900 metres, after crossing the border from Bolivia. The former capital of the Incan empire, Cusco sits at the head of the Sacred Valley and is the principal location to arrange onward transport for the 75 km journey to the jewel in Peru's tourism crown.

The hillside citadel of Machu Picchu is widely viewed as one of South America's 'must-see' sights, but represented something of a logistical challenge for us. We'd been told that only a limited number of entrance tickets were available each day, but as we were largely making up our route as we went, had no idea when we'd be arriving in the area, so couldn't make arrangements before travelling. Our most important task upon arriving in Cusco was therefore arranging transport to the gateway town of Aguas Caliente, and admission tickets to the site. Luckily, we had a guaranteed early start as the Puno nightbus arrived at 6am after a ten-hour journey, and with our Air B+B apartment costing the grand total of $11 per night, it had made sense to reserve it for the evening before we arrived, allowing us to dump our bags and head straight into town to sort our Machu Picchu trip.

As one of the world's premier tourist destinations, it's no surprise that a myriad of companies offer every Machu Picchu experience you could possibly imagine. Single day, two and five days tours; Inca trail mountain hikes; alternative Inca trail jungle hikes; adventure journeys incorporating hiking, rafting and ziplining; Machu Picchu and salt mine combo tours; luxury tours; budget tours. The list was endless, and all options were heavily advertised by Cusco's thousands of travel agents.

We'd decided we'd done enough hiking in recent weeks and an Inca trail tour would take up at least four days from the ever decreasing number we had left in South America. A two day tour with guaranteed entrance tickets therefore seemed to be the best option, and we wandered between a multitude of tiny backstreet travel agencies, before we located one who spoke English. For $200 each, Ramon, a confident millennial in too-tight trousers, assured us he could guarantee entrance tickets to Machu Picchu, return train travel from Cusco to Aguas Caliente, bus transfers from the town to the mountaintop site, and a night in a hotel. My online research had indicated that if we booked everything separately, it would cost around that amount excluding accommodation, so we handed over our cash feeling that we had a bargain.

Aguas Caliente had the feel of a scruffy frontier town which had been thrown together in a single weekend by celebrities in a bizarre reality TV show. Bare brick, and cement applied using a water cannon was the prevailing architectural style. Restaurants offered homogenous tourist menus, cheap souvenir shops lined every pavement and accommodation ranged from budget flop houses to gaudy, wannabe mid-range hotels. Unfortunately, ours fell firmly into the former category, and helped explain how Ramon was able to turn a profit from his bargain basement price. If he was paying more than $5 a night for our room, he was being robbed. A large single bed with sheets like the Turin Shroud was the lone item of furniture, and the door lock looked like it had been booted in by the local drug squad, then refitted by a monkey. A two-fingered flick would have popped it open, and we were glad we'd paid the $11 to retain our Cusco apartment for an extra night and stored our bags there. I opened the curtains and came face to face with a scar-faced plasterer working five feet away on the building across the alley. He gave me a sullen nod which said 'rather you than me'. I closed the curtains and we headed out to pick up our Machu Picchu tickets.

A multi-national, passport clutching queue stretched around the block from the ticket office. Security was tight and you needed a passport to claim your tickets, to avoid black market touts getting in on the act and spoiling what is a highly lucrative revenue stream for the Peruvian government. Tourism accounts for 10% of the country's GDP, bringing in more than $20bn per year. The government's own figures show that over 1.5 million people visited Machu Picchu in 2018, which makes a mockery of the supposed 2,500 daily limit imposed to limit damage to the site. We'd been concerned about the possibility of not being able to obtain tickets, but were told by a number of locals that, providing you can pay the $50 entrance fee, you'll never be turned away.

Tickets collected, we set out to experience the culinary delights of Aguas Caliente. Roasted guinea pig, known locally as 'cuy' is a well-known delicacy in Peru, and as I'm always eager to sample the local fare, I was hopeful of being able to enjoy one of the cuddly childhood pets as a main course. Unfortunately, it was evident that cuy was a rite of passage for the many tour groups, especially those from the far east, and the price of a guinea pig supper was ten times that of a piece of beef steak. At the prices being quoted, I could have bought a whole family of fresh ones from a pet shop in England to cook myself, and have change left over for a gerbil starter.

A five minute stroll from the concrete explosion of the town centre led us to a quieter side street, away from the main tourist strip. Here we spotted a brightly lit establishment with a contradictory neon sign, displaying the unmissable silhouette of the Athens acropolis alongside the name Istanbul Grill. Food in Bolivia and Peru had been surprisingly bland, and the sight of an 'elephant's foot' of kebab meat rotating on a spit had me salivating.

The possibility of something different to the usual grilled chicken and meat stews sold in local restaurants was an obvious draw, and the place was buzzing with a mix of tourists and locals. We were shown to a table by an oilslick-haired, middle aged waiter in a white jacket, and two power-dressed Peruvian businesswomen, engaged in a heated discussion on the next table smiled a greeting. We were still taking our 'Soroche' tablets which made beer drinking a pretty unpleasant experience, so we ordered a bottle of the very drinkable Peruvian Malbec, and Kirsty chose a chicken shwarma, while I opted for the traditional comfort food which is a lamb doner kebab.

After enjoying the lively ambience of the restaurant for around fifteen minutes, the greasy haired waiter appeared with two plates which he dispensed with a theatrical 'Bon Appetit'. The meat was plentiful, the salad fresh and varied, and the dishes were each accompanied by a gravy boat full of bright red chilli sauce, which I dispensed liberally, to try and cajole my out-of-practice taste buds into action.

We'd only been eating for a couple of minutes when I heard a crunch and saw Kirsty raise a hand to her face. Our eyes met and hers rolled with an unmistakable 'something not right in the mouth department' expression. Her cheeks bulged, her lips flexed and it was clear that her tongue was engaged in a forensic examination of the foreign object that had unexpectedly appeared in her mouth. A dip of her head preceded a raised napkin, and the surreptitious evacuation of a chicken covered projectile, which was deposited on a side plate with a metallic clink.

We both stared at the object, which was cream coloured, square in shape and a half inch wide.

"I could have broken my tooth on that," Kirsty was probing her mouth with her tongue to establish if she had sustained any dental damage.

"Is it a piece of bone?" I jabbed at the object with my fork.

"Not sure, it's hard though. It hurt when I bit it." Kirsty seemed satisfied that her teeth were intact, and retrieved the mysterious object in her napkin, rubbed it clean, and dropped it back on the plate, where it suddenly became all too clear what it was.

"That's a tooth!" I picked it up between thumb and forefinger and looked at Kirsty accusingly. "Is it yours?"

Kirsty looked incredulous. "Don't you think I'd know if it was?! I've checked. It's definitely not mine."

We both stared at the offending molar, as the sickening realisation dawned that it had fallen out of someone else's mouth and ended up in Kirsty's meal, and then in her mouth. She pushed her plate away and put her hand to her mouth.

"That's disgusting. Oh my God, imagine the diseases I could have caught from that!"

I'd been enjoying my meal, but had suddenly lost my appetite, so I caught the eye of the shiny haired waiter and summoned him over. I hadn't even had time to consult Google translate, so didn't know the Spanish for tooth. I was therefore reduced to thrusting the wayward gnasher towards him, causing him to reach in his jacket pocket to retrieve a pair of wire framed spectacles, which he balanced on the edge of his nose. He gingerly took hold of the object and raised it slowly for examination beneath a ceiling light, which caught the attention of the businesswomen on the neighbouring table.

He screwed up his nose and shook his head whilst muttering some unintelligible questions to himself, then resorted to squeezing the tooth, seemingly in the hope that it may disintegrate or turn out to be a renegade ingredient from another dish. Unfortunately, it remained stubbornly intact, so he summoned a portly man, with beige slacks hoisted to nipple level, from behind the bar for a muttered conference. Heads were scratched and worried glances cast from the tooth towards Kirsty's plate. Other diners were now monitoring the situation, and the power-dressed women had paused their meeting and were visibly straining to hear what the waiters were discussing.

As the white-jacketed employees scurried away, holding the tooth at arm's length as if it was a ticking bomb, one of the women turned to us with a horrified expression to check what she'd overhead.

"Es un diente?" I was still unaware of the Spanish word for tooth so shrugged in reply.

"Pardon me. You speak English? Was that a TOOTH?" The woman's English was US accented, and the final word was accompanied by a curled lip and arched eyebrows. Her dining companion lowered her knife and fork and evacuated a mouthful of food into a napkin.

"Erm....we're not sure. It certainly looked like a tooth." I answered, trying unsuccessfully to diffuse the situation, with the whole restaurant now lowering their eating utensils and looking in our direction.

"Oh my God! That is truly disgusting! Perhaps you've caught HIV." The woman looked sadly at Kirsty as she delivered her downbeat prediction. Other diners began to enquire what the mysterious object was, and our two neighbours were only too happy to furnish them with the full shocking details, as they stood and delivered a rapid-fire indictment of the restaurant's hygiene failings, accompanied by flailing arms, tapping of teeth and mock retching.

Knives and forks were being loudly discarded across the room as the waiters returned and headed to our table, only to be accosted by the two agitated businesswomen, who were clearly demanding an explanation. A heated debate followed, which was monitored by the whole room, and translated for us by the woman whose eyebrows were still dancing around the middle of her forehead like angry black caterpillars.

"He says they've checked all the chefs' mouths and none of them are missing a tooth." It took a moment for me to digest this, as I conjured up images of cooks in white hats being restrained by colleagues so their boss could count their teeth.

"I don't believe him though. I've told him he must bring them here so we can look in their mouths."

"I don't think that's necessary..." The last thing I felt like doing was conducting a mid-meal dental examination of a Peruvian kitchenhand, but the woman seemed insistent and was loudly berating the distressed waiters, while her friend updated the rest of the diners on the ongoing situation.

The tooth was placed on a napkin on the businesswomen's table where it was prodded by the shrugging waiters and peered at from a distance by a growing crowd of grumbling customers. A young man of Chinese appearance approached and began to photograph the mysterious object on his mobile phone, before it was snatched away by the greasy haired waiter, who was obviously nervous about it re-appearing on Trip Advisor. Plates of half-eaten food were being brandished towards the staff and newly arrived diners were being appraised of the evening's unfortunate events, before grimacing and shuffling back out onto the street.

The restaurant was in uproar, and I noticed Kirsty fidgeting beside me.

"Let's pay and leave," she whispered furtively. I looked towards her and her eyes flicked nervously between the waiters and the crowd of irate customers, who were clearly using the incident as an opportunity to avoid paying for their meals. I could tell something was amiss.

"I think...erm...it might be mine after all." Kirsty's tongue was probing the inner recesses of her mouth in a hurried tooth counting exercise.

"You said it wasn't yours!"

"I know I did...I'm not sure. I just think the back of my mouth feels...different."

"How can you not know how many teeth you had before?" We were both whispering through the corners of our mouths, as the waiters were casting worried glances in our direction. It was too late now to admit that the tooth may actually have been homegrown.

"I haven't got a gap, but I think one might have snapped off."

"Stop poking it, you look suspicious!" I began to peck at my meal to demonstrate to the other customers that the experience hadn't put us off. I handed Kirsty a fork and we shared my kebab while doing our best to look like we were enjoying it. The businesswomen looked at us with disgust, and I could only imagine that those present thought that finding teeth in a meal must be a common occurrence in England. The waiters seemed pleasantly surprised at our laidback reaction and gave us a couple of free Pisco Sours, and even had to argue with us to waive the charge for Kirsty's meal.

Once back in our cell, Kirsty undertook an investigation of her mouth using the cracked bathroom mirror and confirmed that she seemed to be missing half of one of her back teeth. Luckily, the break didn't seem to have exposed a nerve and she wasn't in any pain. We pulled the bed across the door to prevent nocturnal intruders and fell into a fitful sleep, to the sound of a Peruvian hairless dog howling in the alley below.

We'd set our alarm for 7am to make sure we were at the Machu Picchu bus stop before 8, but in the event didn't need it as we awoke to the sound of the plasterer outside our window hawking up phlegm and gobbing it at the whining dog in the street below.

Ramon's tour included a 'picnic breakfast' and as we left the hotel, we collected two brown paper bags from reception, each containing a boiled egg, a banana and two cream crackers. The bald dog seemed happy enough with his two eggs, but less so with the crackers which he sniffed at, then urinated on, delivering what I felt was a pretty accurate assessment of both the breakfast and the hotel.

The scale of the Machu Picchu operation was apparent as soon as we turned into the road leading to the shuttle bus terminal. A five-deep line of gore-tex and hiking-shoe clad humanity snaked along the road, awaiting collection by one of a non-stop stream of coaches, which ferried tourists up and down the mountain throughout the day. Admission was split into hourly time segments from 6am to 2pm, and our ticket allowed entry after 8am, with a maximum of four hours spent at the site. Again, the 2500 person daily limit seemed highly improbable, as the number of people in the queue looked to be approaching a thousand, and there was an air of general excitement and anticipation amidst the buzz of conversations conducted in a hundred different languages.

The queue moved quickly enough and as we boarded, I felt something brush my legs and caught sight of a small black pig sneaking onto the coach ahead of us. It appeared again, from beneath my seat as we sat down, but a long, pointed nose rather than a snout identified it to be another Chimú hairless dog. Unique to Peru and a popular pet, the so called 'Inca Orchid' resembles a bald whippet, with a wiry plume on the crown of its head, looking like a 70's style 'comb-over' in a strong wind. The animals are a strange sight, and feel even stranger to stroke. Although they look reptilian, the dogs radiate heat, so are warm to the touch. In fact, they're popular in mountain areas such as the Sacred Valley for use as bed-warmers!

After a slow haul up a muddy mountain track, our bus pulled into a large car park filled with tour groups being herded by guides, each wielding a unique standard which would help locate them amongst the citadel's throngs. Patterned golf umbrellas were popular, as were small, coloured pennants attached to selfie sticks. Chinese guides went for a reverse identification strategy and handed out coloured baseball caps to their group, and shuffling gaggles of red, yellow or green topped heads could be seen bobbing along the ancient terraces above us.

The hiss of the bus doors opening prompted a swift evacuation from the dog beneath my seat, and I was left wondering what caused him to commute to the top of the mountain, what he did when he got there and how he knew what time the last bus back to town was?

Thankfully, our tour guide, Hugo, didn't go in for coloured hats, and adopted the low-tech strategy of waving a red ring-binder above his head and whistling loudly when he felt members of his group were straying. I generally avoid guided tours, but at sites such as Machu Picchu, an oral commentary helps transform an admittedly impressive collection of skeletal stone structures into homes and businesses, civic buildings, temples and streets. Hugo's red binder also contained colourised artists impressions of what the structures we were observing would have looked like in the 15th century. It was drizzly and overcast, with thick swirling cloud as we began the tour, and Hugo waved a hand towards the mist and told us that somewhere in the grey abyss was the peak of Huayna Picchu, the cone-shaped peak which is the backdrop to the archetypal Machu Picchu postcard shot.

"Thick cloud today. I don't think it will clear until late afternoon," was Hugo's gloomy forecast and, given our general bad luck with weather conditions and natural phenomena, this came as little surprise to Kirsty and I. We scrambled onwards in Hugo's wake at the rear of our group, as he explained that no one is sure why the Inca abandoned the city in the 1500's, and that it was lost to the world before being rediscovered by American explorer Hiram Bingham in 1911. As I paused to catch my breath and turned to look back down the valley, a shaft of sunlight cut through the mist. The cloud was clearing, and I called for Kirsty to wait. The blanket of dense, grey fog was dissipating and tantalising patches of green and grey were becoming visible. As we watched, the cloud-shrouded peak of Huayna Picchu slowly appeared, with the stepped terraces and ruins of the citadel in the foreground, to present us with the famous image reflected in a million tourist photos.

It was amazing to think we were witnessing the exact same scene that an Incan Emperor may have surveyed some five hundred years earlier, and, unbelievably, the only other person around to see it was a grey-bearded tourist with a long lens, and a khaki bush hat bearing the Canadian maple leaf logo. We quickly exchanged cameras, and each took turns at capturing each other in the classic Machu Picchu 'money shot.'

We caught up with Hugo and the group and couldn't resist showing off the photos we'd managed to take in the couple of minutes before the cloud cover returned.

"You were very lucky," was Hugo's snapped assessment as the rest of the group grumbled at missing out on a prime Instagram moment, and he realised I'd probably just blown his tip-earning potential.

One of the great mysteries of the Incan civilisation is how they constructed cities, temples and great walls, using huge slabs of rock, slotted together so precisely in the style of a jigsaw puzzle, that no mortar or cement was required. It would be impossible for us to replicate these feats of engineering and architecture today, and modern scientists and archaeologists have long speculated on how they achieved such accuracy in carving and shaping the rock.

Hugo told us that he'd once met an explorer who had spent time with a rarely visited jungle tribe, and had witnessed a shaman 'melting' stone using an ancient potion of springwater and herbs. The theory therefore, was that the Inca didn't have to carve the stone into such precise angles and shapes, because they could turn it into a semi-liquid and mould it while in a malleable form. Running my finger along a joint between two huge slabs of rock, fused so tightly together that it was impossible to even insert a knife blade between them, the rock-melting theory seemed almost feasible. Implausible as it sounded, I'm a firm believer that ancient civilisations around the world may retain knowledge handed down via word of mouth through the centuries, that we've long since forgotten in the developed world.

Our four hours at Machu Picchu cost us roughly the same amount as we'd spent on a month's accommodation in South America, but we never doubted it was money well spent, not withstanding Ramon's dodgy hotel! We were well aware of the risk of losing sight of the real value of money when travelling for a long period, and missing out on once-in-a-lifetime opportunities as a consequence. Before setting off on our journey, we'd promised ourselves we wouldn't fall into that trap, quoting the Taj Mahal story as a reminder.

We knew a couple who spent six months travelling in Asia and became obsessed with keeping their average cost per day below a certain dollar value. Four months into their trip, they arrived at Agra and headed to the Taj Mahal, only to be horrified at the $25 per person admission charge. Instead of viewing the amount in terms of value in England, which was roughly a few drinks and a curry on a night out, they fell into the trap of equating it to average costs on their trip. A week's worth of accommodation or the cost of a month's meals was too high a price to pay, and they walked away without seeing one of the wonders of the world. They then told us about their error on a night out in London, having just spent more than the Taj admission fee on a single round of drinks!

The relative value of experiencing the wonders of Machu Picchu was further brought home to us when we'd returned to the UK, and Kirsty visited the dentist for an appraisal of the damage caused by the kebab incident. He confirmed that the 'tooth' was actually a crown which had become detached. The good news was that he could re-fit it easily enough. The bad news was that the waiters in Aquas Caliente had retained the evidence, so the crown was now 6000 miles away and Kirsty would have to pay for a brand new one. The £400 charge probably made it the most expensive kebab she'd ever ordered, and also ensured our Machu Picchu tour looked a bargain in comparison!

243

Barca Bandits

Another day, another night bus. Another ten hours on a '120° cama', being serenaded by the relentless hiss of airbreaks as we travelled along the Peruvian coastline, from the city of Trujillo to the surfer town of Mancora. At least now it was warm again. We'd descended from the chilly mountains of Cusco to Lima, where we'd stayed in an Air B+B in the seaside suburb of Miraflores, which felt more Mediterranean than South American. Our plan was to follow the Western Seaboard north into Ecuador, from where we'd fly home in around two weeks. Mancora was billed as a buzzing little town, popular with travellers and Peruvian sunseekers alike, with brightly painted tuk-tuks serving as the main form of transport and simple, beachside driftwood bars and smoothie shacks conjuring up a Thai island vibe.

We arrived at our funky, luminous green hostel and were assigned a room on the ground floor, next to a communal area with hammocks occupied by somnolent backpackers reading paperbacks or tapping on iPads. As usual, we were old enough to be the parents of all the other guests, but weeks of travel had normalised a disturbed night's sleep, and I found myself less concerned about loud discussions in foreign tongues, and second hand music than I had been back in Samaipata. I hauled myself into a hammock, opened my laptop and inserted the Thai USB stick.

My iPhone is set up to automatically download from the camera roll to my photos file, and the image which appeared was clearly a phone snap. Five men in early middle age, drunkenly looning around in front of a sign saying 'Manchester'. Two are gesticulating offensively towards the sign while two are holding half eaten bananas. The facial expressions indicate that all are well in drink.

Stag parties or lads' trips are often described in tabloid-speak as 'riotous', and I've been on a few over the years which have met the literal definition of that word. If an overseas trip is involved, there's a tendency for the invite list to rapidly spiral out of control, with friends of friends, their friends, and friends three or four times removed 'booking on'. I've been on trips where the 'stag' has never even met half the people on 'his' trip. The calibre of attendee can then easily nosedive, resulting in an inoffensive weekend away descending into an international incident, with mass arrests and hospitalisations, and with the innocent 'stag' being held responsible.

John 'Ibby' Ibison made it clear that couldn't happen on his leaving 'do'. He and his wife had secured enough immigration points to emigrate to Australia with their family. They were leaving at the end of October, and deportation or a spell in a foreign jail would be particularly badly timed. He was therefore reluctant to have any sort of leaving trip at all, but eventually relented on condition that the guest list would be limited. The attendees would be the small group of us who still persevered in a Saturday lunchtime drinking session, to diminish the pain of watching Leeds United in the third tier of English football. Me, Iain, Ibby, Cuz, Little Gav and Posh Andy. We sounded like Top Cat and his gang, and we'd be going to Barcelona.

A two day, three night trip is the optimum length of a lads' trip in my experience. In recent times, week long excursions to Las Vegas or a Balearic Island seem to have become fashionable, but aside from using up valuable work holiday allowance, to me, that's just too long for concentrated drinking. Rather than a trip which incorporates a couple of days 'taking it easy' or even 'nights off', it's far better to approach the job like a military exercise. Go in quick and hard, take no prisoners, get the job done and get out. Then spend the next few weeks suffering from PTSD.

This would be no cakewalk. Everyone knew Barcelona's reputation as the international home of petty street theft. Anyone who'd been to the city a number of times, as we all had, had tales to tell of the almost magical deftness of the professional pickpockets, and the synchronised teamwork of the African prostitutes. It was almost a badge of honour to be robbed in Barca, but we all resolved not to be caught out.

Our trip followed the standard Friday to Monday format. A few drinks and a late, overpriced breakfast to line our stomachs at Leeds-Bradford airport on Friday lunchtime. A couple of cans on the plane, then a couple more on the train from El Prat airport into the city centre. We dumped our bags in the hotel, and headed straight out, grabbing a handful of cards with the hotel's address as we passed through reception. This is very important as, at some point during the night, it's highly likely you'll lose your friends and resort to thrusting one of these cards into the hands of a taxi driver to request that he transports you home.

Failing to carry a hotel card will result in you ending your night lost and alone, as happened to me in Madrid, at the end of a two-day, cross country drinking spree. Luckily, I'd remembered the name of our hotel - Los Americanos. I spent two hours in various taxis and even at one point, a police van, searching in vain for the elusive Los Americanos. It was only when my cab drove, by chance, past the hotel that I realised it wasn't actually called Los Americanos at all. That had been our accommodation on the previous night in Barcelona!

I was determined that wouldn't happen again, so took a handful of cards and placed one in every pocket, along with one in each sock, both of which also concealed a fifty Euro note. Another fifty note and some change were thrust deep into my jeans pocket. Only a madman would carry a wallet on a night out in Barcelona.

The first night of a stag trip is very much the calm before the storm. You're essentially already 'out' after drinking during the journey, so it's a case of identifying the first bar close to the hotel with outside seating, and arranging to meet there once the bags have been dropped off. My designated roommate was Posh Andy, who was travelling ultra-light with 'luggage' consisting of a carrier bag containing a clean shirt and pair of underpants, a toothbrush and some anti-perspirant. It wasn't long before we were enjoying our first double-pint glasses of Estrella Damm, while savouring the experience of drinking outside in short sleeves in mid October.

It's important to remember that a lads' weekend is a marathon not a sprint, and you don't want to over-do things and peak too early. The first night is therefore one of serious drinking, but is tempered by the knowledge that in a few hours you have to be ready to get up, and go again. We slowly headed towards the bars of Plaza Real, just off Las Ramblas, but I'm unsure whether we actually ever reached there. True to form, at some point we managed to split up, and in the early hours, Iain and Cuz found themselves wandering the streets, trying to locate our hotel. Barcelona had won a home game that evening and the bars were full of celebrating fans wearing the club's famous claret and blue shirts. As they stood on a street corner, trying to identify a landmark, two youths reeled along the pavement towards them, chanting Barcelona songs. Strangely for Spanish football fans, they seemed well inebriated and one of them threw his arms around Iain and danced a celebratory jig, before peeling away and staggering towards his waiting friend.

Remember I said that only a madman would take their wallet out on a night in Barcelona? Well, Iain was that madman carrying a wallet. Only, now he wasn't. The now suddenly sober 'fan' was, and he stood twenty feet away, grinning and waving it in his right hand. In his befuddled state, Iain's first thought was that the friendly Spaniard had a wallet just like his, until a quick check of his pocket revealed the truth. He charged towards the pickpocket who nonchalantly tossed the wallet towards him and took off running. The wallet sailing over his head stopped Iain's charge and he bent to retrieve it, only to find it had already been emptied of cash.

Next morning we shook our heads in admiration, as Iain recounted the tale over breakfast in Plaza Real. Not only had the pickpocket got close enough to extract the wallet from his jeans pocket without being detected, but he'd also somehow managed to remove the cash before displaying the wallet as 'bait'. We were less surprised by the skill of the Catalan criminals than the fact that we'd got through a night with only one of us being robbed, and we all vowed to be extra vigilant with Day 2 upon us.

Day 2 is the main event of the three-night stag party. You're still feeling the effects of the previous night's alcohol as you tuck into a hearty, cooked breakfast, outside the Irish bar which is a feature of every major city in the world. You'd still blow double on a roadside breath test though, and the danger now is falling victim to a hangover. The only way to prevent that, is to start reducing the percentage of blood in your alcohol as soon as is practical. Personally, I draw the line at beer as a breakfast accompaniment, so rehydrate with a pint of water and a couple of cups of strong coffee. Then, I'm ready to go again, before my egg and bean smeared plate has even been cleared away. The first couple of alcoholic mouthfuls must be viewed as medicinal rather than enjoyment, and are best dispensed as quickly as possible. Dallying with your first pint is a sure-fire way to prolong the agony- get it down as quickly as possible, then on to the next.

By the time you're halfway through your second pint, this new infusion of intoxicant will have started to nudge the percentage of alcohol in your blood back towards where it was the previous night. You'll start to experience a magical endorphin surge, which will feel like a home visit from the Devil's doctor, as it sets about curing your self-induced ailments. Your stomach will begin to settle, and your pounding headache will subside. The dryness in your mouth will dissipate and you'll no longer feel like retching with every sip of beer. The conversation of your fellow sufferers, too loud and frankly annoying half an hour ago, will start to become enjoyable and amusing. You'll throw down that second drink triumphantly and signal to the waiter, 'Same again!' It's 11am and Day 2 is underway.

And that was how Barcelona Day 2 began. We had a prime position in Plaza Real, with its million-euro apartments and Gaudi designed streetlamps. It was a mild October Saturday, and now the midsummer rush of stags and hens had subsided, Barcelona was a pleasant place to be. We drank and chewed the fat, reminiscing over similar weekend excursions we'd enjoyed over the past twenty five or so years. We'd all been to Barcelona a few times before and had no desire to seek out any sights, so the 'Same again!' signal continued well into the afternoon, until the surface of our table was no longer visible beneath a crop of outsized Estrella glasses.

At some point we decided to move on, but by now we'd entered the ethereal netherworld of the contented drunk, where memories come in flashes rather than cohesive sequences. My recollections would undoubtedly be totally different to those of my drinking companions, which in itself forms the basis of Day 3's discussions and analysis. A heavy handed, sharp knuckled beach massage administered by an elderly Thai woman as I lay face down in the sand; Posh Andy stealing a bicycle and gliding along the Malecon like a vicar on a Sunday outing; all of us buying a pair of luminous mirrored shades; cans of San Miguel bought from a backstreet store to ensure no drinking time was wasted when walking; occasional pitstops at bars, where we sat in the sun, spilt beer and talked loudly, while other patrons tutted and shook their heads. At some point we came upon a shuttered bar, bearing the 'Manchester' sign, and took the opportunity to pose while flicking obscene gestures towards the name of our city's footballing, commercial and cultural rival.

At some point, the faint Autumn sunlight on the cobbles of the alleyways around Las Ramblas was replaced by the orange glow of streetlights, as late afternoon turned to evening. Eating is cheating, as the old saying goes, but solid nourishment of some form is required to soak up the beer and prevent hitting 'the wall' in the alcoholic marathon. We somehow ended up in a tapas restaurant, and I returned from the toilet to see my friends recoiling from a blast of flame rising from the table. It was clear that someone had inadvertently ignited the tablecloth, so I picked up the closest pint and doused the flames. It was only as we surveyed the sorry scene of sausage pieces floating in a slick of oily liquid, that I remembered we'd ordered chorizo in brandy served flambeed, and I'd just drowned it.

An assortment of other dishes duly arrived, and we found that the brandy-soaked sausage chunks were actually quiet edible when accompanied by dry bread. The fact that the alcohol had only remained alight for a couple of seconds, meant each mouthful was akin to a meat morsel washed down with a shot of cheap spirit, and there was a lot of chorizo. Obviously, we'd stopped drinking Estrella while we ate, and had replaced the beer with a couple of bottles of red wine. It was therefore unsurprising that our 'soaking up' exercise was less than successful, and we staggered out of the restaurant in a worse state than when we'd entered.

The rest of the night passed as a timeless, out-of-focus, out of body experience which can only be achieved by drinking almost non-stop for more than 24 hours, with memories appearing as random, snatched clips, like alcohol induced GIF's. At some point, in a bar with flashing lights and a live band, which may actually have been a loud juke box and a couple of sing-a-long drinkers with big hair, Little Gav developed a severe squint and told us his wallet had been stolen. Once outside the bar, he scratched his head and admitted to a vague recollection that he'd left it on the bar while he went to the toilet, or maybe given it to a stranger to hold.

Once in an advanced state of inebriation, you'll remain in that happy, semi-insensible condition until you either fall asleep or experience an incident which shocks your system back into life, like being run over, falling off a high building or getting gored by a bull. Or in my case, being robbed.

I was roused from my alcoholic catatonia by a young man in a flat cap, while standing in a crowded, narrow street after leaving a late night bar. I was trying to locate my friends in the milling crowd. I spotted Iain, doing what he does best, holding court and annoying a group of locals, while entertaining himself with some provocative banter. Cuz was leaning on a litter bin, swaying, and grinning like a tranquilised chimpanzee. Little Gav, Posh Andy and Ibby were nowhere to be seen, missing in action.

I was obviously an easy mark. Unsteady on my feet, eyes glazed and half closed, probably mumbling complaints to myself about my mates' inability to leave anywhere quickly. The young man was of Eastern European appearance, but without Slavic features. His clothes gave him away. Marble-wash skinny jeans, a denim jacket with square shoulders and a pair of white platform soul trainers, the horrific outfit was topped off with an oversized flat cap. He approached at speed from the midst of the throng vacating the bar and avoided eye contact before brushing up a little too close as he passed. The contact wasn't enough to be classed as a collision but even in my befuddled state, something didn't feel right. I turned and watched him join two friends at the top of the road, and they set off walking at pace, as I patted the left front pocket of my jeans where I kept my phone. Empty. The jeans were standard 501's, not low-slung arse-barers, and I struggled to believe that someone had got their hand in my front pocket and lifted the contents without me realising. I turned again just in time to see the lad raise his right hand to examine his haul - my iPhone 7.

It was a company mobile so represented no financial loss to me, but it would cause a whole heap of inconvenience. Before they turned the corner, the pickpocket gang glanced back to check they weren't being followed. Happy that the drunk hadn't even noticed that he'd been dipped, they felt confident enough to pause and light cigarettes, while laughing and smiling. It wasn't the theft that enraged me, it was the smug, laughing faces. And that stupid bastard cap.

"Iain! Cuz! Iain!" I was calling the posse to arms. These clowns had bitten off more than they could chew this time. Within minutes they were going to be hunted down by three of Leeds finest.

"Cuz! Iain!" Couples leaving the bar swerved to avoid me, and I realised I was acting out the famous Alan Partridge 'Dan' sketch. Iain was shaking hands with a crowd of young Spaniards and Cuz was bent double over the litter bin, preparing for a nap and going nowhere. I was on my own.

I jogged to the top of the road, and had it not been for the flat cap, the three robbers would have disappeared into the night. As it was, there was only one hat-wearer on the street, and he was ambling along with his two friends, scanning the crowds, looking for his next victim.

I once witnessed a street robbery in Stone Town in Zanzibar. It was early evening, and as Kirsty and I strolled along a quiet street in the old town, a youth emerged from a sidestreet, and executed a slick bag-snatch from a middle-aged German who was walking with her husband. What happened next had long stuck in my mind. The woman's husband's 'fight or flight' mode kicked in suddenly, with the former instinct taking precedence. He emitted a terrifying, animalistic roar and hared after the thief, bellowing like an enraged beast as he closed in on the teenage miscreant. Not surprisingly, the bag was quickly ditched with the culprit happy to escape without physical harm.

I'd actually laughed at the German's reaction at the time, but to my surprise, I now involuntarily copied him. Seeing the three thieves nonchalantly going about their business with impunity, looking for other innocent victims, laughing and joking, with my phone in their grasp, wearing their stupid Tirana-chic clobber, tipped me over the edge as I stagger-jogged along the road towards them.

"Yoooooofuuuuuurkkkkiiiiiinbastaaaaaaards" I announced my presence when I was about thirty feet away from them. Three startled faces turned towards me, and surprisingly, given that they could have stood their ground and beaten the shit out of me, they turned and set off running. Adrenaline had now begun to counter my drunken state, but as I pursued the youths, I quickly assessed the likely scenario, was I to actually apprehend three criminals who were all twenty years younger than me. Common sense kicked in and I picked up a half brick, then resumed the pursuit, while continuing to loudly inform my quarry what I was going to do when I caught them.

I'm unsure how long the unsuccessful chase lasted, but unsurprisingly, it ended with me sat on a kerb, breathless, phoneless and lost. I flagged down a taxi and handed the driver my hotel card. After a twenty minute drive, I was despatched at our multi-storey hotel, where I found Posh Andy fully clothed and sprawled face down on the bed. The room looked like the Manson family had paid a visit, but I knew my room mate hadn't been murdered as he was loudly snoring, in a honking crescendo sounding like a trapped goose. I stripped off and climbed into my bed. Day 2 was over, and I hadn't emerged unscathed.

No matter how many times you visit the toilet during a prolonged drinking session, your bladder will always retain some hidden reservoirs of fluid to surprise you during your deepest hours of sleep. Generally, you can attend to the function of urination without really waking. If in your own home, you can negotiate a route to the toilet, evacuate your bladder and go back to bed with your eyes still closed. In an unfamiliar room, that becomes more difficult.

That was the reason I found myself prising open my eyelids and blinking in the harsh light of a strange bathroom in Barcelona. A very strange bathroom...eighty feet long, carpeted, decorated with pot plants and with multiple doors, each displaying a double digit number. It took me a few seconds to realise that the door to our bathroom was on the right and the room to the corridor was on the left, and I'd clearly chosen the wrong one. Then the door had slammed shut behind me and the lock had clicked into place. This wasn't good – luckily I'd only stripped to my underpants so wasn't completely naked, however I was in very urgent need of the toilet which was at the other side of the door. I hammered on the thick dark wood with my fists, then took a run up and launched an unsuccessful barefoot drop kick. I even picked up a fire extinguisher and began smashing at the door, beyond which I could still hear Posh Andy's rasping, comatose snoring. Not surprisingly, my attempts at getting back in the room attracted the attention of our neighbours. The door opposite opened to reveal the oversized, woollen-haired head of a man of Samoan appearance, who peered round the doorframe to see me hopping from toe-to-toe, close to tears and clutching my crotch while wailing like a scalded cat.

Appearing in public in the small hours in my underpants would be embarrassing, but appearing in obviously soiled underwear would be the stuff of nightmares. Andy was in a drink induced, unwakeable stupor, and there was only one thing for it. Clutching my pulsating genitalia, I shook my head sadly at the Samoan and set off running down the corridor. I'd recalled two ornamental pot plants placed next to the twin lifts, and these represented my likeliest salvation. Reaching the elevator, I homed in on the nearest Yucca, sitting stylishly in a minimalist steel cube container, embedded in silver pea gravel. Thankfully, it offered little resistance as I hoisted it from its container, which I then gratefully filled with recycled Estrella Damm, while nervously monitoring the location of each of the lifts on the floor indicator above my head.

With the pressure on my bladder relieved, I now only had the problem of accessing our room to address. After another failed attempt at rousing Andy, I considered asking the Samoan if I could use his phone to call our room. My knuckles hovered inches from knocking on his door, but I was perturbed by the memory of his half smile and a glance he'd cast towards my Y-Fronts, and was worried he may misinterpret the reason for my late night visit. He looked like a big bloke and I didn't want to risk becoming his in-room entertainment for the rest of the night.

I walked back past the overflowing yucca pot and summoned the lift. The interior was mirrored, and I spat on my hand and flattened my dishevelled hair as I descended towards the lobby, then looked at my lower half and realised it was unlikely anyone would be looking at my hair. I was busy 'positioning' myself as modestly as possible, as a loud ping preceded the doors sliding open.

I had no idea what time it was, but had hoped we were in the dead-zone between 4am and 6am, where the bright lights of the large lobby area had been dimmed to allow an elderly night porter to grab a couple of hours of shut eye. Unfortunately, and predictably, that wasn't the case.

We'd booked a well-reviewed, mid range, city centre hotel with a 24 hour reception which allowed check-in throughout the night, which was an obvious advantage for travellers arriving on late flights. Travellers like the twenty-member South African gospel choir and their entourage of musicians, publicists and management, who were massing around the fully manned reception desk as I exited the lift. My immediate reaction to the explosion of colourful Madiba shirts and patterned kaftans filling the lobby was to step back into the lift, but it was quickly occupied by a porter pushing a trolley containing the luggage of a smartly dressed couple who both regarded me with ill-disguised disgust. I smiled and tried to appear completely at ease in my underwear, as the lift doors slowly closed on their scowling faces.

Some of the South Africans had formed queues in front of each of the three check-in staff, while others monitored the porters as they loaded luggage onto trolleys. Others sat on leather sofas, tapping on their phones. There seemed little point in trying to maintain a low profile, so I strode confidently to the reception desk, feeling the eyes of everyone in the lobby fall upon me.

It was unsurprising that my arrival at the counter caught the attention of the closest desk clerk immediately. My nipples were immediately visible above the counter, but he had to stand on tip-toes to lean forward and confirm that I was also trouserless. The large South African lady he was checking-in was resplendent in matching multi-coloured tribal robes and turban, but it's fair to say I also instantly commanded her attention, as she looked me up and down before inhaling loudly and saying 'Oh my Lord.'

The receptionist unsurprisingly seemed lost for words and merely swallowed and shook his head slowly, so I responded with a friendly smile to let him know this wasn't some form of protest or mental breakdown.

"Would it be possible to make a phone call please?" I leant on the counter as if I always conducted business in the small hours in my underwear.

"Are you a guest here sir?" I was about to ask why he thought I'd be wandering the streets in my underwear, but assumed he thought I'd been fleeced by a particularly efficient gang of thieves, so bit my tongue. I explained my predicament and the clerk picked up a desk phone and tapped in three numbers without flinching. His laidback demeanour gave me hope that this sort of thing happened regularly, though when I turned round, all the South Africans were staring at me, and a couple of them seemed to be filming me on their phones.

It took a few minutes for the ringing phone to bring Andy out of his coma, and the receptionist summarised the situation quite well, while critically surveying my 'George at Asda' underpants.

"Mr. Watts, please open the door. Mr.Lightfoot is in the reception and he's causing a bit of a commotion. Okay? Thank you Mr.Watts. Don't go back to sleep Mr Watts…"

Unsurprisingly, Andy was asleep again by the time I reached the room, but he had propped the door open with a rubbish bin. I resisted the urge to fill it with his clothes and put it in the corridor.

Day 3 was a Sunday, and followed the standard stag party agenda. A very late breakfast, with a more gradual reintroduction of alcohol, as we undertook a forensic analysis of the previous day's events. Aided by phone photos and snatched memories, the timeline of hours lost to a fog of inebriation was slowly reconstructed. The good news was that apart from the loss of my phone, and Little Gav's wallet, we'd emerged unscathed in terms of further acts of robbery. It seemed that from a group of six, we'd suffered a 50% crime rate, which was pretty good for three nights in Barcelona.

Unfortunately, that percentage increased on Sunday evening and again, I was the victim. As we approached our hotel after another afternoon and evening's drinking, we were spotted by a group of African prostitutes loitering on a corner.

"Hey you!" one shouted and we all responded by thrusting our hands deep into our pockets to guard our remaining cash, wallets and phones.

"You! You! Crazy man!" they crossed the road, and it was clear I was the object of their catcalls.

"Did you catch those boys?" The girl was skinny, late teens and spoke with a West African accent and grinned a brilliant white smile.

"You saw me chasing them?"

"Oh mister, you were crazy, you were going to smash their heads with a rock!" her friends nodded and laughed and mocked my animal roar which amused my friends.

"Wow, that's so strange that I've seen you again so far from where it happened." The girls seemed puzzled at this.

"No, it's not so strange. We are here every night. This is our corner." She waved a dismissive hand towards her place of work.

"But I wasn't chasing the boys here. That was miles away."

"No, mister, it was here. I think you were too drunk!" They all giggled and chattered excitedly, and Cuz and Ibby recoiled as a couple began testing the defences of their pockets.

"No, that's not right. I came back in a taxi." I was beginning to suspect what the girl was about to confirm.

"You chased those boys, but they ran away. You sat on the pavement there. Then you got in a taxi and went away. Twenty minutes later you came back and got out there." The distance between the two points was around thirty feet, across a main road. I wasn't sure how much I'd paid the taxi driver, but it was clear he'd executed the second robbery that had befallen me that night.

"Crazy man! Go to bed!" the girls trilled as we crossed the road. It felt like good advice, especially in the days which followed. You know you're getting too old for three days of heavy drinking when it takes you twice that long to recover!

They Think It's All Over

Day 138 Quito -Ecuador

At the start of our South American journey, we'd viewed overnight bus journeys as a necessary evil. They allowed us to cover large distances utilising 'dead time' in which we'd have been asleep anyway, and also saved on the cost of a hostel room. It was true that we may have missed out on some spectacular Andean mountain scenery, but given the speed attained by most drivers along winding roads with hairpin bends, that was probably no bad thing. By the time we took our final, nine hour night-bus journey between Mancora in Peru and the Ecuadorean city of Guyaquil, we'd actually come to enjoy the overnight bus ritual. The initial confusion, arriving at a chaotic bus station and pushing through thronging crowds of traditionally dressed locals and bamboozled backpack carrying travellers; trying to locate the correct bus company and negotiate the usual knot of Spanish-language red-tape; nervously monitoring your bags as they disappeared into the luggage vault of the bus, overseen by skulking youths with sallow, diesel stained complexions; shifting an uncomprehending old cholita in a bowler hat from your seat (South Americans don't understand seat numbering systems); the hiss of the doors closing, then the crackle and boom of the speakers as the driver cranks up a trashy shoot-em-up or Kung Fu movie on the DVD player; the eventual dimming of the lights and reclining of seats as you get comfy for a night of road-sleeping.

The passenger list on our final journey had been far from typical though. Half the seats were occupied by hand-luggage only, nervous looking Africans, and I'd speculated that we'd stumbled upon a new people smuggling route heading towards North America. At the Ecuador border, the Africans were held and photographed by border control officers with barking Alsatians, as we'd queued to get our passports stamped. They seemed to be accompanied by a smartly dressed Hispanic couple, who engaged in intense negotiations with the senior customs officer, before the entire party was ushered back onto the bus without any form of passport check. The portly, uniformed official looked happy enough that all immigration requirements had been met as he

256

patted his breast pocket and waved our bus into Ecuador, whilst avoiding eye contact with his scowling subordinates.

In Guyaquil we'd stayed in the most depressing room of the whole trip. Located in a multi-storey city centre block with labyrinthine, dimly lit corridors populated mainly by doctors, dentists and psychiatrists, our Air B&B apartment was a square box with no furniture other than a bed, a shower cubicle and sink. Disconcertingly it had no windows and was located so deep in the bowels of the building that no sound penetrated its solid oak door. Given that our near neighbours seemed to be mostly mental health professionals, the feeling that our room was some kind of isolation cell was inescapable. We were glad we'd only booked for two nights and couldn't wait to escape to explore the Ruta del Sol which hugs the country's Pacific coast.

On our last night in town, in addition to the worst room of the trip, Guyaquil had also delivered the worst toilet. In fact, it was one of the worst pub toilets I've experienced anywhere in the world. We'd headed out of the city centre to the Cerro del Carmen barrio, with its pastel coloured block houses extending up a hillside like a model village made of painted cereal boxes. We seemed to be the only tourists in town, but the locals were friendly enough, and we'd settled outside a concrete shack splashed with electric blue gloss, which served 500ml bottles of Club Pilsener for the equivalent of about 30p. We were the only customers, and a bored looking barmaid with trowelled-on make-up was trying to read a magazine beneath flashing disco lights, when I entered and asked for the baños. The whole concrete structure was shaking to the pulsating beat of a Brazilian Techno track, as I was directed to a doorway behind a stack of plastic beer crates. I knew I was heading the right way when still around six feet from the battered wooden door, as my nostrils were assailed by the stench of ammonia. Opening the door literally took my breath away, and my eyes prickled as I entered a long room which was painted in the same garish blue as the bar's exterior. Two urinals were suspended unevenly on the right hand wall, but the first bore a deep crack which caused a thick, discoloured liquid to dribble into a two inch puddle covering the floor. The other seemed to have been used to store a pint of pea and ham soup, which was being tentatively investigated by a fat golden cockroach. Deep down I'd known I shouldn't, but it seemed to be my only other option, so I'd nudged open the barn-style door of the sole cubicle, and retreated quickly after a snatched glimpse of a conclusively pebble-dashed pot. I badly needed to go, so there was only one thing for it, and I stood on tip toes and relieved myself into a lychen coated sink, whilst being observed by another large roach, which twitched its antennae disapprovingly.

The following day we'd rented a car with a failing clutch, which finally gave up the ghost in the surfing enclave of Montanita. Changing gear had become progressively more difficult, until I was almost dislocating my shoulder crunching the gear stick into position as we stuttered and lurched along the thankfully quiet roads. Luckily, we'd had Carlos looking out for us. An octogenarian Brazilian, living in a rustic wooden guest house on Montanita's white sand beach, he'd demonstrated his need for stronger glasses when I walked in to ask about a room.

"You here for the big wave?" Apparently, a four metre swell was envisaged, and I'd been pleasantly surprised that Carlos mistook me for an expert surfer. We'd agreed a rate and checked in for a few days. Montanita had sounded pretty horrific in the Lonely Planet but was somewhere I grew to like. The main part of town was renowned as Ecuador's main seaside party town, and buff, bronzed young males showed off their 'keepie-uppie' skills in front of reclining, silicone enhanced girls with big hair and tiny bikinis. Night clubs with names like Space Beach Club and Club Lost advertised cut price drinks and foam parties, and bars in the sandy backstreets battled to outdo each other with get-pissed-quick promos.

Carlos's guest house was at the far end of the beach, less than a mile from the neon madness but seemingly in a parallel universe. Neighboured by a low-key resort and a chilled-out beach bar, our end of the beach was favoured by the surfing crowd and long term travellers. Carlos had snatched the phone from my hand as I struggled to explain our mechanical issues to the rental company, and let the call centre agent have both barrels in an arm waving crescendo of Portuguese and Spanish. A replacement vehicle duly arrived that afternoon!

Our night bus to Guayaquil turned out to be the last of our South American trip. The initial plan to stick to overland transport had been thwarted by a lack of time, and the fact that internal flights to the capital, Quito, were so cheap, it made taking the bus a false economy. After a couple of weeks of warm beach weather, it was a shock to be at high altitude again, with Quito located at 2850 metres above sea level in the Andean foothills. We were unsure whether the weeks we'd previously spent in the mountains now protected us against altitude sickness, but decided to give the

'Soroche' tablets a miss, as our final day in Ecuador coincided with an important date in my sporting calendar.

True to form, Leeds United had suffered an end of season collapse, and now faced a play off to gain promotion to the Premier League. The final was due to be played at Wembley Stadium one week after I returned from South America, but before then, the team had to beat Derby County in a two legged semi-final. The first leg, played away from home, had resulted in a 1-0 win for Leeds. The deciding match would take place the day before we flew home from Quito. I was hopeful of watching the game while enjoying a few beers which didn't taste like battery acid, so decided to dispense with the Acetazolamide tablets and rely on the natural remedy of coca tea.

We also promised ourselves we'd take it easy initially in Quito, but by the end of our first day in town we'd walked over seven miles of hilly, cobbled streets, as we explored the plazas of the colonial centre, and by evening were glad to be staying close to Plaza Foch, which was the city's main nightlife area. There were an abundance of bars and restaurants in the streets around the pedestrianised square, including an Irish bar called Finn McCool's. Signs outside the bar indicated that they showed European football, broadcast on the Fox Sports Channels, which was good news as I'd seen the Leeds game listed in a local newspaper to be shown on Fox Sports Plus.

Next day we were out early to take the cable car up the east side of Pichincha Volcano, to the Cruz Loma lookout point. Quito is located in the Guayllabamba River basin, and from the windswept peak, the scale of the city of two million inhabitants was immediately apparent, as it spread as far as the eye could see along the valley floor. The highlight of Cruz Loma is undoubtably the famous swing over the side of the mountain, which is a 'must-snap' photo opportunity for anyone who dares to propel themselves over the lip of a 4100 metre cliff face...only it's not. Clever positioning provides the optical illusion that you're taking your life in your hands, while in reality, the drop is only a few feet. Kirsty and I waited our turn and took the obligatory photos, before hurrying back down to ground level where we hailed a cab to Plaza Foch.

The Leeds game was due to kick off at 13.45 local time, and we were running late by the time we arrived back in the city centre. The driver dropped us in the square, a block away from Finn McCool's and I was soon jogging ahead of Kirsty, telling her I'd meet her there. By the time she arrived, I'd already befriended the tall, skinny barman, who'd either borrowed his clothes from a giant or suffered a recent alarming weight loss.

"El Loco Bielsa!" He grinned while flicking through the channels, confirming that Leeds' Argentinian coach was one of the most recognisable names in South America.

"Yes!" He beamed triumphantly as the Fox Sports Plus logo appeared on the screen over the bar, and two grimacing players tussled for a loose ball. I breathed a momentary sigh of relief at the sight of a white kit, but then spotted a worrying red flash across the shoulder. Closer inspection revealed an unfamiliar stadium, and a scoreline which read- FC Utrecht 2 Heerenveen 1.

"No, this isn't the right game, this is Dutch!" I wailed, and the lanky barman took the newspaper clipping I produced from my pocket and checked the channel.

"Fox Sports Plus. It's correct. They must have changed it..." That wasn't what I wanted to hear with ten minutes to kick off, and I sank onto a barstool with my head in my hands.

As the old advert goes - If Carlsberg did Ecuadorian bars...they'd be like Finn McCool's. Seeing my obvious distress, the barman took control.

"I have on my laptop...a software...I don't know the word?"

"Like an App?" I offered hopefully.

"Yeah, that's it. An App. I can get most Sports channels, maybe I can get UK. Sit down, what do you want to drink?"

Kirsty had barely had a sip of her bottle of Club beer, but I'd nearly demolished the pint I'd bought to calm my pre-match nerves, as the familiar Sky Sports logo appeared on the big screen, with the game just about to kick off.

"Is this the one?" My new friend's head popped up above the bar and he could tell from my expression that indeed it was. I ordered another drink and settled down to watch Leeds book their place in the final.

The bar had been empty, but began to fill up with a mix of suits holding business lunches and furtive, hand holding office-romance couples, who were just in time to see me rise from my seat and punch the air to celebrate Leeds opening goal after 25 minutes. At 2-0 up and coasting to victory, I launched into a WhatsApp frenzy, and began messaging friends to arrange purchase of match and train tickets for the final. It would be good to have something to look forward to on our return home, and in advance of our next trip, our campervan excursion to Europe.

I was still focusing on the logistics of a Wembley weekend, with the seconds ticking down to half time, when out of the corner of my eye, I saw the ball bounce off a couple of heads in midfield and roll towards the Leeds goal. Three Leeds defenders tracked its progress, and a lone Derby attacker trailed in their wake, more in hope than expectation. I was about to resume tapping on my phone, when I noticed the green shirted figure of the Leeds goalkeeper, Kiko Casilla, entering the frame at speed from the left. He was striding purposefully towards the edge of his penalty area, with the gait of a hiker on swampy moorland, and seemed oblivious to the presence of his advancing team mates. Unsurprisingly, they also seemed unaware of Casilla's impending arrival, nearly 60 feet from his goal line, and the Leeds captain, Liam Cooper, shaped up to clear the ball. As he drew back his leg, he seemed to suddenly notice the goalkeeper bearing down upon him with murderous intent, and went to ground to avoid being decapitated. Thankfully, Kiko's flailing boot missed Cooper's head by inches, but also failed to connect with the ball, which wobbled away slowly towards the unguarded goal. The astonished Derby attacker only had to tap it into an empty net.

There was an anguished howl of agonised frustration and strangely it didn't come from me. The bartender was stood beneath the screen with his head in hands.

"Why that guy do this?" he wailed. I stood open mouthed and shook my head. It was a question that would be asked for years to come in Leeds. A group of middle aged businessmen had left their seats and were pointing at the screen, shaking their heads.

"Who is this team?" A paunchy accountant in a cheap suit seemed amused at what he'd witnessed. The words Leeds United elicited an excited acknowledgement of recognition as he passed the news on to his group.

"Ha Ha! Bielsa is el Loco, the crazy one! Maybe this goalkeeper is his son!" They thought the joke was hilarious, but I struggled to join in with their laughter. There's an old adage that scoring a goal just before half time is psychologically the best time in a game to do so. Derby now set out to prove the theory correct, as they picked up the ball from the second half kick off, and scored again almost immediately. The businessmen hadn't even noticed that the second half had begun, and the barman was absent as the ball hit the net and I slumped with my head in my hands, with Kirsty grimacing beside me. By the time the barman returned fifteen minutes later, munching a sandwich, Derby had scored another. Three goals in little more than ten minutes either side of the half time break had put them ahead on aggregate.

The whole bar was now taking an interest in the game, and in the reactions of the distressed Englishman who was pacing beneath the big screen, gulping from a pint glass and muttering obscenities which they fortunately couldn't understand.

"Man, how can this be happening?" The barman had never seen a Leeds game in his life, but was being slowly drawn into the world of heartache I was born into. The Sky TV footage homed in on the faces of the Leeds fans in the packed crowd. The buoyant, celebratory atmosphere of just a few minutes before, had been sucked out of the stadium, and the pictures on the screen showed the drained, stunned expressions of people who knew the script, having seen this happen too many times before.

A well-dressed man in his early forties and a giggling younger woman, who I imagined might have been his secretary, had occupied the table next to ours and were canoodling over a plate of nachos. Their presence helped temper my reactions as the game roller-coastered through the second half. Leeds equalised and I leapt from my stool and high-fived the barman, causing the wide-eyed secretary to flick guacamole onto her boss's shirt. The momentum had swung in Leeds' direction again, and the stadium was rocking. The barman cranked up the speakers and everyone had now abandoned their meetings to watch the game. I paced beneath the screen like an agitated, caged bear, sloshing down Club Pilsener to calm my nerves. With twenty minutes remaining and the tie evenly poised, Leeds had a player sent off and the numerical superiority spurred Derby on. I could see what was coming, and it was no surprise when they scored the winning goal with five minutes remaining.

"Aaaaaargh! I can't believe this has happened. I'm so sad!" the barman's head was resting on the table beside me, his long, stringy arms extending limply towards the floor. I felt empty. Drained of emotion and energy, as I watched the Derby players and fans celebrating 6000 miles away, in a place I knew so well. Sky TV were revelling in the Leeds fans' misery and ran close-up shots of tear-stained faces and sobbing bodies slumped in their seats. I'd known many days and nights like it in the past, but this time it felt harder, being so far away. I spotted faces I recognised in the crowd and imagined my friends, standing shellshocked beside my empty seat, contemplating cancelling London trains and hotels and another year in the second division. For the first time on the whole trip, I suffered a pang of homesickness and felt I should be there, suffering with my own people, rather than sitting in an Irish bar in South America, shaking hands with commiserating strangers who'd had a lunchtime to remember.

It was time to go home.

Back to Reality

Day 218 – Villandry, France

It was just after 8.30am when I spotted the email on my phone. I stepped from the heat of our motorhome into a shaded woodland glade, and pulled a camping chair away from the rays of an already baking hot sun. It was late July, and Europe was experiencing one of the hottest summers on record, with temperatures soaring above 40°c on a daily basis. We were camping in a forest near the town of Villandry in France's central Loire region, after nearly two months of travelling through Spain and Portugal. We'd caught the ferry from Portsmouth to Santander at the beginning of June, a couple of weeks after returning from South America, and a week after my Wembley trip which never happened. We'd devised our route on a daily basis, and travelled along Spain's northern coast, through the Basque country, Cantabria, Asturias and Galicia, then down the Portuguese coast to Porto. Here we'd arrived in town during the Festa de São João and for the first time in a month, had to pay to stay on a campsite, having previously wild-camped every night. We'd found Spain to be perfectly set up for campervan travel, with phone apps showing locations to fill up water and empty toilet cassettes in even the smallest towns, making us totally self-sufficient. We'd stayed on beaches, in woods and forests, beneath the city walls of medieval villages and, acknowledging that you have to take the rough with the smooth, in a run-down tower block car park on an Oviedo housing estate. I carried a baseball bat in the van for protection in isolated locations, but we only had to move on one occasion, when the gravel car park we were staying in became an evening stock car racetrack for local joyriders.

From Porto we'd headed inland along the Douro River valley, then back into Spain and the white sandstone city of Salamanca, which felt like a stroll in a pizza oven as the streets cracked and shimmered in 45° heat. Then it was on through the little-visited regions of central Spain, where we camped beneath orange hills with floppy eared sheep grazing on dust, before driving towards the tourist hell of San Sebastian, where we crossed the border into France. Again, we had no firm plans in terms of our route, apart from one location that I'd earmarked before the trip. Situated near the city of Limoges in West-Central France, is a harrowing reminder of the Second World War's impact on the country.

On 10 June 1944, Oradour-sur-Glane was a quiet farming community of nearly 700 people, and had so far escaped the worst of the conflict. Although French resistance fighters harried the occupying German forces in the countryside around Limoges, it was said that prior to that fateful date, few Oradour villagers had even seen a German in the flesh. That all changed at 2pm on a sunny Saturday afternoon, when the battle-hardened troops of the 2nd SS Panzer Division 'Das Reich', appeared and surrounded the village. Theories vary on the cause of the events which followed, though it seems likely that the German commanders mistook the village for nearby Oradour-sur-Vayres, where it was rumoured an SS officer was being held by French partisans. What is beyond doubt is that the villagers were rounded up and divided by sex. The males were led into six barns where machine guns were already in place, and within minutes, the assembled men and boys had all been sprayed in the legs with bullets, before being burnt alive as the barns were set alight. The 247 women and 205 children, including babies in prams, were herded into the church, before grenades and incendiary bombs were tossed through the doors. Anyone who survived the blasts was finished off by machine gun fire. In total 642 villagers were murdered in one of the worst atrocities of the war, and the site became known to the French as the 'martyr village'. After the war, it was decided that it should be rebuilt on a new site a mile away, and the old village preserved exactly as it was on the day of the attack, as a memorial.

I've visited some disturbing sites around the world, such as the genocide museums of Cambodia and Rwanda, but Oradour-sur-Glane was particularly shocking, in that its state of preservation made it all too easy to imagine the horror of that day. The skeletons of the buildings remained, albeit without roofs and windows, lost to flames and bullets. Rusting street signs still adorned wall corners, and flaking paint above doorways announced the Post Office, bars and cafes, tradesmens' workshops and the village hotel. The railway station looked much as it did seventy years ago, and it was all too easy to imagine the shock and terror the local teenagers felt, as the evening train from Limoges brought them back from a Saturday afternoon in the city, to find their families massacred and their village destroyed. Scorched stonework and bullet riddled walls told of the events in the church and a rusty, machine-gun strafed pram lay at the foot of a soot-stained font, in a poignant reminder that no one was spared the massacre, no matter how young they were.

The atmosphere was understandably sombre, although there were many families exploring the mile-wide site. The dusty, traffic free lanes and broken buildings were a child's dream playground, but all present walked slowly, with heads bowed, in a shocked silence. It was another red hot afternoon and Kirsty slumped in the shade of a barber's shop shell, while I explored further, and it was peering into homes and businesses, and seeing the mundane artefacts of everyday life, that I found really shocking. I wondered who the child was who'd parked his little cycle in his backyard that morning, not knowing that he'd never ride it again. I looked at the baker's ovens, and wondered whether he'd just retrieved the final batch of pastries, and turned his attention to the next day's loaves as he heard the revving of engines and a strange language outside his window. I looked into the café and saw upturned chairs and tables and wondered who had been sat enjoying a coffee with friends that Saturday, speculating on the D-Day landings which had taken place a few days earlier. I didn't have to guess who the owner of the wheelless Peugeot 202 parked in the Champ de Foire was. As one of the village's most photographed relics, it's widely known that the vehicle was owned by Doctor Desourteaux, and he'd unfortunately returned from visiting a patient at an outlying farm as the villagers were being rounded up. His standing in the community and that of his father, the mayor, was of no consequence to the Germans, and they were herded into the barn to die alongside their neighbours.

That night we experienced an invasion force of our own in the crowded motorhome parking area near the school, in the new village centre. With all places taken, a late arriving French family abandoned the standard bumper-to-bumper configuration and manoeuvred to park with the rear of their motorhome at a 90° angle to our van's side, in an unorthodox T-formation. I gave them second prize for invasion of space on the trip, behind the Germans who had set up their picnic table so close to our bathroom window, that I nearly knocked Klaus's baseball cap off when I opened it!

Now we were on the home straight, heading north through France towards the channel ports, from where we could catch a ferry back to England in mid-August. My return to work a couple of weeks later was looming like a large black cloud, and seeing my manager's name in my email inbox caused a knot to form in my stomach. Birds twittered in the forest canopy, and a lazy bee buzzed around the dandelions beneath my feet. Two chestnut horses in an adjacent pasture swished their tails at the persistent flies, as I clicked into the email and was transported back to a world that I'd left behind seven months earlier.

It was the first contact I'd had with my manager since I'd started my career break back in January. An ever cheerful thirty-something, she launched into her missive with the usual pleasantries, hoping I'd had a great time on my travels and looking forward to hearing about my adventures. Then it was straight down to business, reminding me of the date I was due back at work, confirming that I'd be returning to my old role, and plunging into the operational detail of an important product launch which was scheduled a couple of weeks after my return. I felt vaguely sick and pulled myself from the chair with a heavy sigh, and ambled over to stroke the horses.

The truth was, I'd had enough, physically and mentally. Thirty five years of desk work had left me with chronic back pain, and my chiropractor, who I saw more than my friends, had told me that I needed a lifestyle change to stop my condition deteriorating further. 'You need to keep moving. Get out from behind the desk. Stretch and walk more, or things will just get worse.' That was easier said than done with a demanding job which meant tapping at a keyboard and staring at a screen for ten hours a day. I'd also become disillusioned with my role, the company, and the corporate world in general.

Company wide 'right sizing' programmes with mysterious project names had become an annual occurrence. Half the year was spent speculating on which department would be affected in the next wave of cuts, and half on then trying to cover the gaps caused by the latest redundancies. This climate of fear resulted in a culture where everyone, from the lowest intern to senior management, became fixated on demonstrating to their bosses how busy, and therefore valuable, they were. Instead of delivering what customers wanted, everyone's focus was on being seen to just deliver something, whether it was of any use or not.

Being away from work had made me see things in a new light. I saw the whole organisation as a huge ant hill. The worker ants toiled all day carrying huge leaves from one side of the mound to the other, from where other ants would carry the same leaf back. It was back-breaking work, and totally devoid of any useful purpose, with the ultimate aim being that the Queen Ant saw her subjects working hard. Anyone not looking busy and constantly engaged in carrying leaves would be earmarked to be eaten, or 'right-sized'.

I'd worked in the Marketing department for twenty years, and had come to understand the cyclical nature of the business. Ideas and initiatives which had been tried unsuccessfully, five, ten, fifteen years previously were resurrected as new, by a conveyor belt of senior managers. I was in an invidious position. Pointing out that something had been tried before and had failed, was seen as being negative, by those who just needed to be seen delivering something, whether it worked or not. Staying silent saw me working long hours on the same initiatives I'd undertaken years earlier and knew were doomed to fail again.

Office space had been squeezed, and working from home became the norm. That at least gave me more freedom to 'stretch and walk' but it also put an end to the banter we'd enjoyed in the Leeds office, where many of us had worked together since the 1980's. We'd grown up together through a period of workplace change not seen since the industrial revolution, and could always laugh at the mergers and takeovers, management doublespeak and corporate bullshit we experienced. Then, over time, as people reached their fifties, like me, they began to see that they no longer fitted in. Old, negative, and cynical, we'd become like the grey-haired dinosaurs in cheap suits we'd once laughed at back in our twenties. The tap on the shoulder in the annual 'right sizing' exercise was seen by most as a welcome get-out-of-jail card.

Some hadn't made it though, and as happens when you reach middle-age, I'd seen friends and colleagues die suddenly. My father had died at sixty, without reaching retirement, and I'd promised myself that would never happen to me. Now, thirty years later, I was fifty two years old and wondering where the time had gone.

"I don't want to go back." The horse shook his head in agreement and looked at me with big brown eyes. I once read that a tripping Ozzy Osbourne spent two days in a field talking to a horse, but there was no point with this one. It was unlikely he'd speak English.

The Dharma of Mr.Zin

I went back into the motorhome where Kirsty was boiling the kettle for our morning coffee and retrieved my laptop. Back outside in the sun, I held down the power button and inserted the now well-scuffed USB stick, which had accompanied me from Thailand to New Zealand and back, to Fiji, then to South America, and now on a tour of Europe. This time I wasn't hoping for a random snapshot memory, I knew the photo I was looking for. I clicked on Windows Explorer and selected the option for 'Extra Large Icons'. My screen, which had previously shown around 100 thumbnail images, now changed to show eight clearly defined photos. I clicked on the slider on the right hand side of the page and began scrolling down through the thousands of images, searching for the one I had etched in my memory.

***

In 2009, we visited Burma and the country had made a big impression on me. At the time, Aung San Suu Kyi was still in jail and the nation was the subject of an international travel boycott – it was essentially a closed country, with few tourists and even less travelling independently, as Kirsty and I did. We therefore found ourselves very much in demand wherever we went, especially in the cities of Yangon and Mandalay, where we were rarely unaccompanied by at least one young person, eager to practice their English, and in Burma, a young person is very often a monk. Collectively known as the Sangha, there are over half a million Buddhist monks in the country, evenly split between fully-ordained monks, known as bhikku, and novice monks, the samanera. Shaven headed and clad in saffron robes, monks are everywhere in Burma and to a Westerner, often seem otherworldly, aloof and occupying a higher spiritual plane than other mere mortals. That was certainly our opinion after travelling extensively in South East Asia, but that view changed in Burma, especially after we met Dave.

It was early evening and we'd walked into the centre of Yangon to see the Shwedagon Pagoda lit up like a golden beacon against the night sky. After dodging the annoying little women with Thanaka-paste-smeared faces selling baby owls from baskets at the entrance, we climbed the stairs to enter a white tiled courtyard, and blinked at the glare from the hundred metre tall, gilded stupa. We were immediately approached by a couple of teenage monks who tried out their rudimentary English skills on us, before grinning proudly and returning to their mates, who were loafing on the marble steps like teenage lads anywhere in the world. A couple more tried their luck and we indulged them with some limited 'what is your name-how old are-you-David Beckham' type conversation, before sitting on a wooden bench to consult our Lonely Planet for a likely destination to eat. We were soon joined by a spikey haired monk in his late teens who extended a hand in greeting, and broke protocol by also offering it to Kirsty - women are strictly forbidden from touching monks. He introduced himself as David, though also admitted to a quad-barrelled name that I couldn't attempt to repeat. I called him Dave.

He wasn't a typical monk, or rather, he wasn't what we'd expect of a typical monk. He spoke excellent English and explained why many monks fall short of the saintly standards we associate with a holy order. All Burmese men must spend two periods of their life in a monastery, one as an adult ordained monk and one as a novice. Most boys become a novice monk between the ages of five and fifteen, though in rural areas it's not unusual for toddlers of 18 months old to take part in the Shin Pyu ceremony, which sees them become a novice before they can even talk. Therefore, in Burma, for young men, entering a monastery is something akin to military service and doesn't necessarily mean they are a particularly devout Buddhist.

That was certainly the case with Dave, who was cheeky and made us laugh, and we agreed to meet him the next day. He took us to his monastery and showed us his tiny windowless cell, which he'd decorated with English and Italian football team photos and fixture lists. He also seemed to be a big fan of ladies tennis and had an impressive collection of Anna Kournikova pictures. I gave him a knowing look and a wink, and he grinned and then blushed when Kirsty caught his eye. We arranged to meet up again with Dave after our travels around Burma, as he told me he had someone he wanted us to meet.

"Mr. Zin is my Lama, my teacher," he explained proudly. "He taught me to speak English and is a very special monk called a weikza. He is very wise and meditates for many hours every day."

Our nodded agreement must have seemed a little half hearted, which prompted Dave to toss in a couple of additional details to seal the deal.

"He killed many men and spent half his life in prison, he was like the mafia. And he can fly." We agreed to meet up again in ten days.

Mr. Zin was expecting us, as we clambered from the tuk-tuk outside his monastery on the outskirts of Yangon. Dave had made a call on his Nokia en-route, which I'd assumed was to tell the old monk to get the kettle on. Like most Burmese, he was short in stature, but still had to stoop to exit the tiny doorway in his wooden monastery.

He was dark skinned, and wore a loose saffron robe and blue flip-flops. His head was shaved to a sheen which glistened in the bright sunlight, but his most striking feature was the extensive tattooing covering most of his body. Burmese lettering stretched along the length of his right bicep, and what looked like an elaborate armoured pattern covered his thighs and extended to cover both knee-caps. Most of the designs were unmistakably homemade though, and had been etched into his skin by an obviously unskilled hand. Swirls and shapes, a badly drawn dagger and a couple of squares filled with symbols, which looked like never-to-be-forgotten noughts and crosses games, filled the remaining canvas of leathery skin. I was immediately reminded of kids at my school who had mysteriously disappeared for a term, then returned bearing similar doodles on their arms, or tell-tale 'borstal spots' beneath their eyes. Mr. Zin's tattoos bore no resemblance to the well considered and skillfully executed designs that are popular today. They were a permanent reminder of long hours of extreme boredom and incarceration, in a room filled with similarly confined men, one of whom had obviously smuggled in a needle and a bottle of ink.

Mr. Zin bowed to us, and in perfect English invited us to take a seat. Dave had told us he was very old, but his face was unlined, and I'd have accepted his age at being anywhere between fifty and eighty. He had a kindly face and smiling eyes which he closed as we told him about our travels. Ordinarily I would have assumed that my stories had sent him to sleep, but he nodded as I spoke, and occasionally made a satisfied 'ah' sound as I mentioned a place he recognised.

I was eager to know his story and the tattoos were an obvious conversation starter.

"Are these religious tattoos? I haven't noticed them on any other monks."

Mr. Zin smiled and cast a glance towards Dave, which I guessed meant 'I bet you've told them I can bloody fly as well haven't you?'

"My tattoos are a reminder. A lesson," he closed his eyes again as he spoke in a soft voice which caused Kirsty and I to lean in, in order to catch all the words. "They are a reminder of the man I once was. A very bad man who was following the wrong path."

Born in 1940, Mr Zin was jailed for petty theft as a teenager. In prison he made connections, and upon being released, began working for a Yangon crime syndicate. He rose through the ranks to become a feared enforcer in the 1970's and 80's.

"It was like a mafia. I lived a bad life. Taking from poor people, torturing, killing..." his voice trailed off as Dave caught my eye, and nodded and grinned with a proud 'told-you-so' expression.

"How old are you?" Mr Zin looked deep into my eyes and I told him my age.

"I was nearly fifty years old before I understood life. I thought that a happy life required money and possessions, until I had those things, but I still wasn't happy. I always wanted more. Do you understand?" It was clear that this was a lesson rather than a Burmese mafia war stories session, and I nodded.

"Every person must reach a place where they are happy. A certain amount of money, and possessions. It's different for everyone." Mr. Zin lifted a tattooed arm horizontally, and raised and lowered it in front of my face to demonstrate the varying level of needs.

"Once you reach that place, there is no point in gaining any more. It won't make you more happy. It will make you unhappy because you will always be chasing more. Many people don't understand this..." The old monk looked from me to Kirsty and smiled serenely. I guessed he suspected we were those people.

"I changed my life and left my old world behind. I gave away my house and my motorbike and my money and joined the Sangha. My possessions now are my robe, my bowl and my razor....and a water filter machine. Now I am happy." His eyes lit up at the mention of his only concession to the modern world. Mr. Zin then raised his hand to deliver the key point of the lesson.

"We must learn to recognise happiness and once we have it, don't chase more. If you are not happy with your life, then change it. You cannot change the world, but you can change yourself."

After the delivery of such a profound statement, it seemed inappropriate to ask Mr. Zin if he'd mind swooping around the stupa a couple of times, so I probed with a gentler question about the weikza cult, which is seen as a form of wizardry, achieved via long periods of a special discipline of meditation. Weikza monks are said to have a range of skills including powers of healing and alchemy, forseeing the future, the ability to walk on water, fly and become invisible. Burma's most famous weikza, Bo Bo Aung is said to have lived to over 200 years old.

Mr Zin again cast a disapproving glance towards Dave, who shuffled his feet and looked to the ground.

"In your religion, you have saints, I think?" I nodded in response.

"Well a weikza is the same as this. Do you think I am a saint?" His eyes took on a mischievous glint, and for a second I caught a glimpse of the old Mr Zin, challenging and combative. I shook my head and realised I wouldn't be seeing a human flying display that day.

∗∗∗

So our visit to the old monk had unfortunately not included our witnessing any miracles, but his words had stuck in my mind throughout the next decade, and now seemed especially appropriate. Kirsty and I ate breakfast in the sunlit forest glade, while I kept my finger on the scroll button and monitored the images rolling across my laptop screen. After about an hour, a flash of crimson caught my eye. I carefully clicked my mouse to move back up through the frames, and suddenly I was reacquainted with Mr Zin. Like most Buddhist monks, he'd been more than happy to pose for some photos with us, and I'd cheekily asked if I could capture the full extent of his tattoos, and he'd hitched up his robes to expose his thighs. I zoomed in on the old monk's face. He had an enigmatic 'Mona Lisa' expression, which could equally be a smile, smirk or sneer, but his eyes seemed friendly and wise, not the eyes of a murderer. I recalled Mr Zin's message and considered how it applied to my current situation, as I flicked a buzzing fly from my laptop screen.

'We must learn to recognise happiness, and when we have it, don't chase more.' I'd learnt a lot in the previous 8 months, not least that we could happily travel for long periods at relatively low cost, and that there was so much of the world left to see. Returning to a job I had no interest in, filled me with dread. Of course, I'd be continuing to earn good money but what was it for? Was I just chasing more, that I didn't really need, while making myself unhappy in doing so?

'If you are not happy with your life, then change it.' I pictured Mr. Zin and recalled the old monk staring deep into my eyes as he'd delivered his message, and it suddenly felt very relevant and personal. Maybe he had been able to foresee the future after all?

The feeling of dread at returning to work began to lift. I couldn't change the world, but I could change myself. I knew I had to get out, to change my life. I just needed to work out how.

Epilogue

Returning to work was tough, and I was thrown straight in at the deep end, with a new product launch requiring an 18 hour, through-the-night shift, within two weeks of my return. If I had to give anyone advice on taking a sabbatical, it would be to consider the return. If you hated your job before you took time off, you'll hate it even more on the day you walk back into the office, with a head full of memories and a mindset that's been changed forever.

Maybe, as Mr Zin had pointed out, I couldn't change the world or the culture at work, but I could change myself. I began to point out the awkward facts of life in the 'ant hill' to my managers, and resolved to only spend my time on activities which I felt were actually worth working on. I only attended meetings and conference calls where I knew my input was specifically required, and found that I suddenly freed up around 80% of my day. Tellingly, no one ever commented on my absence, and many colleagues were probably unaware that I'd even returned from my career break. I became the invisible man.

In a company with a prevailing show-and-tell culture, an employee who no longer wants to show, and is highly likely to tell the wrong story, is a dangerous element. When I attended conferences with board members present, I sensed a nervousness from senior managers that I may ask an awkward question or highlight an inconvenient truth which would reflect badly on them.

After eight months of waking up in a different location every day, immersed in a challenging and foreign environment with no set plans or agenda, it was a shock to the system to be suddenly tied to a desk again for ten hours a day. Watching the birds on the feeders outside my window while working, I came up with an analogy to explain why I was finding it so tough. I felt like a bird which had spent its whole life in a cage. I was fed regularly and a couple of times a year I was allowed to fly around the room, occasionally crashing into the window, before being returned to captivity. I whistled now and again and admired myself in my cage mirror. I was a happy bird. Then one day someone left the window open and I was allowed to fly free, to explore the whole forest. I knew for the first time what a bird's life should be, and what it really meant to be happy. Then I was captured again and returned to my cage. It was the same cage as before, and my owner still fed me and occasionally let me out to fly round the room, but I wasn't happy anymore. I'd seen life beyond the cage, and I could never forget it.

I continued my 'invisible man' existence as 2019 became 2020. Everyone in the company was required to have a 'Personal Development Plan' for the year. Except me. I said I didn't want to be developed. I actually felt sorry for my manager – I certainly wouldn't have wanted to supervise me, though I delivered everything that was asked of me, and was never anything less than professional with colleagues. I just refused to play 'the game' anymore.

I'd clearly become something of an inconvenient anomaly, and seven months after returning from my sabbatical, I came to an agreement with the company that I would leave, after thirty five and a half years of service. I had no set plans for the future beyond a notepad full of ideas, and no income beyond a small amount of advertising revenue from some websites I owned. I'd done my sums though, and in the spirit of Mr. Zin, I knew how much I needed to live without constantly chasing more.

Kirsty had taken a short term contract when we returned from our travels, and this was due to end in the Summer, at which point we planned to set off to Europe again in our motorhome, before spending the winter travelling in some warm, low-cost lands. I'd managed to follow Mr. Zin's advice and changed my life. It had never been so easy to travel anywhere in the world, and we now knew we could do it for less than it cost us to live at home. I'd escaped from my cage again, and this time I wasn't going back.

It was March 2020, and the future was bright. What could possibly go wrong?

The Two Week Traveller by Matthew Lightfoot is available in all Amazon stores.

What elevates this book beyond a collection of water-cooler anecdotes is richly detailed storytelling and the author's deep interest in the people and places he visits. Oh, and it's also frequently laugh-out-loud-on-the-bus funny. As well as great stories, his book brims with good, practical travel advice. It's easy for travellers to either shy away from local culture or over-romanticise it. Lightfoot treads beautifully between the two, engaging local people on their own terms. Frank, thoughtful and brimming with lust for life, this is one of the most downright enjoyable and, yes, interesting travel books I've read. Bill Bryson would approve. *Amazon Review*

***

This book is not just for travel enthusiasts, but for everyone who loves a great story. From start to finish it is filled with humour, suspense and beautiful descriptions of the landscapes the author has encountered. *Amazon Review*

***

Matthew Lightfoot communicates his travels from an early age all the way through to 2019 in an interesting, relatable, humorous and engaging way. I found myself laughing in some parts of the book and on the edge of my seat in others, with a whole mix of emotions thrown in. If you're looking for your next travel book, this is the one. *Amazon Review*

***

A great book, very entertaining, and hilarious in places, yet inspiring at the same time. You feel like you are sharing in the author's many adventures. Really makes you think about stepping outside your comfort zone! *Amazon Review*